EDUCATING FOR
A CULTURE OF
SOCIAL AND ECOLOGICAL PEACE

EDUCATING FOR
A CULTURE OF
SOCIAL AND ECOLOGICAL PEACE

Edited by
Anita L. Wenden

State University of New York Press

Published by
State University of New York Press, Albany

© 2004 State University of New York

For information, address State University of New York Press,
90 State Street, Suite 700, Albany, NY 12207

Production by Judy Block
Marketing by Susan Petrie

Library of Congress Cataloging-in-Publication Data

Educating for a culture of social and ecological peace / Anita L. Wenden, editor.
    p. cm.
Includes bibliographical references and index.
ISBN 0-7914-6173-4 — ISBN 0-7914-6174-2 (pbk.)
1. Human ecology—Study and teaching.   2. Peace—Study and teaching.
3. Peace-building—Study and teaching.   4. Environmental education.
5. Sustainable development.   6. Peaceful change (International relations)
7. Peace Education International.   I. Wenden, Anita.

GF26.E37 2004
304.2'071—dc22

                                                              2003190068
                    10 9 8 7 6 5 4 3 2 1

Contents

Figures

Introduction

Integrating Education for Social and Ecological Peace— The Educational Context

Anita L. Wenden

. . . I want to point out to you my personal view of this NATO war against my country. The Balkans, and especially Serbia, Montenegro and Kosovo have been known till now as a safe part of Europe, [free] from different kinds of ecological pollution, and their economical future has been designed as producers of healthy food and different kinds of tourism. The bombing of NATO has not only destroyed any possibility for such development in the future but has also endangered the survival of the whole population. The dangerous chemical reactions and explosions caused by the bombing of oil production installations has poured hundreds and thousands of tons of oil in the rivers and fields and completely destroyed some chemical factories which produced exclusively for civilian needs (e.g. "Azotara" Pancevo, producer of fertilizer for agriculture). This is only one example of the pollution the war has caused in the region. Here we also have to include the contamination of our fields and rivers and forest by the millions of tons of explosives of different kinds, mostly with dangerous radiation which bring a great risk for health not only for the present, but for many future generations. There is data from some obstetrical clinics that the number of premature births is six times the level of the pre-war state. . . .[1]

The above account details the environmental degradation caused by the NATO bombing of Serbia, a consequence of war. The bombing leaves in its wake not only human casualties, but also a degraded Earth. Moreover, the various kinds of pollution caused by the bombing will negatively affect the economy of the country, its food supply, the health and longevity of its citizens both in the present and in the future. This link between human actions that result not only

1

in social violence but also environmental degradation, which, in turn, leads to the further violation of human rights is dramatically illustrated in war if often ignored in the assessment of its impact.[2] It is also evident in nonmilitary activities, specifically unsustainable economic activities in the North, motivated by the needs of a mass consumer culture, and similarly unsustainable development projects and practices in the South, driven by a desire to emulate the lifestyle of the North and by the need to alleviate poverty created and exacerbated by a growing population and the inequitable distribution of resources. The examples that follow are representative of some of the varied dimensions of this reciprocity.

THE ESSEQUIBO RIVERIAN AREA OF GUYANA[3]

*Unsustainable mining practices result in a **sudden** environmental disaster which disrupts the sustainable lifestyle of the local inhabitants and exacerbates their poverty.*

On August 22, 1995, the Government of the Republic of Guyana (a country situated on the north coast of South America) declared the upper Essequibo region between the boundaries of the Omai River and the Atlantic coast an environmental disaster. The tailing dam of a gold mine had ruptured, releasing 3.2 billion liters of cyanide-injected water and wastes into a region containing immense biodiversity, including many rare and threatened species of wildlife and the site of one of the few pristine rainforests left on Earth. A number of wild animals, such as the jaguar, the agouti, and the caimana, all frequent this river to drink and bathe in it. After the incident, a number of dead animals were found washed up on the banks of the river, including domestic chickens which were fed with water from this river. While this sudden environmental disaster may have been considered an industrial accident by the mining company, in fact, it was the result of unregulated and unsustainable mining practices. Uncontrolled discharges were not always reported, nor was the company fined when an earlier "minor" incident of cyanide leaking into the river occurred. Moreover, criticisms made by nongovernmental environmental specialists about the design of the mine's tailing dam, and their warnings about an impending disaster were not heeded.

Because of the degradation of the river and surrounding land, the lives of the people living in the affected region were thrown into turmoil as they battled to cope with the problems that came in the wake of the accident. They all faced the lack of potable supplies of water for daily consumption and domestic use. The fisher folk, who relied on the river for income, were now without an adequate source of income to maintain their families. Amerindians, a river community, lost their main source of sustenance, that is, food, water, and means of travel and communication. Many residents were concerned about the long-term effects of cyanide given that it is a carcinogenic substance. In sum, contaminated as a result of human action, the river could no longer be depended upon to provide for the people's basic needs, and as a result, their basic rights to life, health, food, water, a source of income, and communication were violated.

THE ARAL SEA[4]

Unsustainable agricultural practices cause **cumulative** *environmental degradation, which, in turn, deprives local residents of the resources needed to provide for their basic human needs.*

In contrast to the sudden disaster in the Essequibo Riverian area, the degradation of the Aral Sea, the rivers, and agricultural land in its vicinity has been a cumulative process resulting from unsustainable agricultural development—an ill-planned and poorly monitored irrigation scheme and the extensive use of artificial fertilizers and pesticides. Located in a semi-arid region of south-central Asia, in the 1950s the Aral Sea covered an area of 66,000 square kilometers with a mean depth of 16 meters. Its waters were fresh with a mean salinity of 1% to 1.1%. The water from two large rivers, the Amu Darya and the Syr Darya, flowed into the sea and together with the annual rainfall, maintained the volume and level of water in the sea. However, since the early 1960s, a few years after the irrigation scheme was put into operation, the irrigated agricultural land expanded rapidly reducing the flow of the water into the Aral Sea to approximately 13% of its pre-1960 total. As a result, by 1990 the sea had shrunk to about 55% of its original area and had become two separate lakes. Its total water volume had dropped to less than one third of its 1950s volume, and the salinity of its waters had increased from a mean of 1/1.1% to about 3%.

The decrease in water flow and the increase in salinity led to a decrease in the size of the Aral Sea. It is gradually disappearing. While the Sea once contained more than 20 species of fish, now all but a few have died as shallow spawning grounds have dried up. Food reserves have disappeared, and commercial fishing, which used to be a productive economic activity when the sea produced over 40 million kilograms of fish a year, has practically stopped. Without the moderating influence of the vast expanse of the original sea, climate in the area has become more extreme. Rainfall has decreased, while summers have become shorter and warmer, and frosts are now more likely to occur later in spring and earlier in the fall. As a result, there are no longer enough frost-free days in the year for growing cotton, once the main crop of the Amu Darya Delta. Forests on either side of the sea have dried up; bird and mammal species have disappeared. The salinity of the agricultural land has increased and its fertility decreased as salt from the exposed sea bed is spread by storm and as water from the inefficient irrigation system evaporates causing crop-damaging salts to accumulate. The water used by farmers to wash these salts out of the soil enters the rivers and ultimately increases the salinization of the areas downstream and the Aral Sea itself. The extensive use of artificial fertilizers and chemical pesticides to support production of the two main crops, rice and cotton, has also polluted the water that drains back into the Amu Darya and the Syr Darya with high concentrations of phosphates and nitrates as well as chemical pesticides.

Thus, affected by a chain of events initiated by human decisions to implement unsustainable agricultural practices, the degraded sea and rivers, the changed climate, and the polluted land threaten the well-being of the population. They are deprived of the sources of their livelihood—fishing, cotton growing, and fertile land for agriculture—with the consequent incapacity to provide for the basic needs of their families. The accumulation of toxic chemicals in the river is now contaminating local supplies of drinking water, and since 1975, people living in the area have begun to suffer from a number of serious health problems. The incidence of typhoid fever, hepatitis, kidney disease, and others have increased. Babies are born weak and ailing. In the city of Karalpakia, for example, the 1989 mortality rate for children was among the highest in the world. Thus, the benefits people of the region should derive from their basic rights to a source of income, food and water, to good health, and even to life are denied.

WESTERN UNITED STATES: A GRASSHOPPER INVASION[5]

Unsustainable agricultural activities gradually result in the degradation of basic environmental processes which, in turn, pose a threat to farmers' source of income and a source of the country's food supply. This (threat) leads to human action that brings more harm to the environment and as a result, further threatens the farmers' livelihood and the quality of the food supply.

In the summer of 2002, states west of the Mississippi suffered from the largest grasshopper invasion since World War II. Grass, crops, and pastures were ravaged by the pests, with as many as two hundred grasshoppers per square yard ultimately reaching up to one million grasshoppers per acre, each one capable of eating more than half its body weight per day.

To deal with this threat to the farmers' source of income and one source of the country's food supply, large amounts of money were invested in pesticides though with limited effects as the grasshoppers adapt and resist. Besides, the pesticides pose long-term risks by disrupting Nature's balance. They kill many beneficial insects, including the natural predators that might destroy the grasshoppers, thus requiring the use of more or different pesticides when they (the grasshoppers) reappear, or when the next major pest appears from the shadows. Pesticides also pollute the land, water, and air. Eventually these toxins move up the food chain and, ultimately, threaten human health.

Global warming, brought about by the use of fossil fuels for human activities and by the consequent emission of CO_2 and other greenhouse gases, is primarily responsible for the northern migration of pests, the threat they pose to the country's right to food, and a farmer's right to a source of income. To cope with the threat, the government provides financial support for pesticides, which further degrade the environment by polluting the land, water, and air and so places at risk the population's right to an uncontaminated food supply and to good health. The pesticides also destroy natural predators leaving the crops vulnerable to future attacks by similar or different pests. Thus, the cycle of social and ecological violence is fueled and maintained.

DEFORESTATION IN NEPAL[6]

Unsustainable agricultural practices motivated by people's need to subsist result in a gradual process of environmental degradation which, by exacerbating poverty, leads to further environmental damage and the consequent threat to the source of livelihood of the local inhabitants.

In the hill regions of Nepal, where available agricultural technology to improve farming in the more fertile lowland soils is scarce, Nepalese farmers cannot maintain their incomes as the population increases and farms become smaller. To subsist, they are forced to clear and crop the hillsides, the less productive lands. This exacerbates soil erosion which causes flooding and the concomitant pollution of the more fertile lowlands, thus forcing people to destroy more of the forested areas in an effort to survive. In fact, between the late 1960s and early 1980s, the area under agricultural production expanded from between 15% and 35% while forested areas in Nepal's hills decreased from between 40% to 55%, and depending on the specific location, to 60% of the total area.

Because Nepal's forests have been pushed so far back from rural populations, it takes an average of 1.4 hours more each day for women to collect firewood and fodder than it did a decade ago. These extra hours spent collecting firewood are taken from women's work in agricultural production and reduces the total farm labor by as much as 24% per household and so, lowers overall household productivity. The decrease in agricultural productivity caused by deforestation has also reduced food consumption on average more than 100 calories per capita per day. Time for food preparation and child care has been lost, furthering the decline in nutrition, especially for children. Because expanded planting on hillsides shifts cropping patterns away from rice and other high quality calorie sources, the nutritional content of the family diets is reduced even more.

A result of the local people's efforts to subsist in the face of an increase in population and a decrease in agricultural land, deforestation exacerbates their poverty and further encroaches on their right to a basic livelihood. Thus frustrated, the farmers place added pressure on the forest, and, as in the case of the grasshopper plague, the cycle of ecological and social violence is intensified.

In sum, it appears that the underside of environmental degradation is the violation of human rights. Humans bring harm to the Earth by their economic activities thus limiting her ability to provide adequately for their basic needs. As a result, they are prevented from enjoying what their rights allow and are led to further damage Earth systems. This damage, in a cycle-like fashion, further encroaches on their quality of life and may even threaten their survival. In other words, it may be concluded that since the Earth is the primary context and essential foundation of all social activity, a comprehensive social peace can neither be achieved nor sustained if Earth rights are not respected. Conversely, a society which allows humans to benefit equitably from what their rights allow is essential if ecological sustainability is to be achieved.

By now there is an emerging agreement about the social causes of environmental degradation, and the impact of such human action on the environment has been documented and categorized, for example, reduction of biological diversity, deforestation, depletion of natural resources, climate change, desertification. Similarly, the causes of varied forms of social violence and the effects of this violence on human quality of life are recognized. However, the reciprocity between ecological violence and social violence is not frequently made explicit in assessments of their separate impacts and in policy statements that aim to deal with this harm. Nor is this link a topic of common concern. Yet it is this dynamic between the two which intensifies their impact and maintains their existence and as a consequence, inhibits the achievement of their converse, that is, ecological and social peace.

This reciprocity between the violation of Earth rights and human rights presents a challenge to educational institutions, whose task it is to inform students about and prepare them to cope with and even remedy social and environmental problems. Of special relevance is the response to this challenge of peace education and environmental education, two educational specializations whose task it is to respond, respectively, to social violence and ecological violence. To what extent is there a recognition within these two fields of the link between social and environmental crises? Has awareness of the social consequences of environmental degradation changed the manner in which peace educators understand their task? Has it influenced the development of their curricula? The same questions can be asked of environmental educators regarding the ecological consequences of physical and structural forms of violence. For insights into these questions, it is necessary to turn to the literature in both fields where selected writings, dating back to the early 1980s, do in fact reveal an emerging recognition of the link between environmental integrity and social peace among a critical core of peace and environmental educators.

PEACE EDUCATION

Early developments in peace education were shaped by the notion of peace as the absence of war and by the threat of nuclear war among superpowers. Nuclear education assumed that the arms race would lead to a nuclear war, and efforts were centered on informing the public about its possibilities and catastrophic effects. Disarmament education, a second earlier development, took a comprehensive view of the arms race and extended its educational efforts to the abolition of both nuclear and conventional weapons, thus questioning the viability of war as a social institution. The recognition that even when there is no war, if social institutions condone and encourage injustice, discrimination, violation of human rights of individuals or groups, then there can be no peace (Galtung, 1964) led to new developments in peace education in the 1980s. A distinction was made between education for negative peace, directed towards organized physical violence, and education for positive peace, directed towards structural violence and ecocide, which recognized the environment as a living ecological system that can be the victim or object of violence (Reardon, 1988).

Thus, starting in the early 1980s, literature in the field of peace education evidenced an awareness of the destructive impact of human activities on the Earth. This was reflected in theoretical discussions on the definition of peace and on the link between social and ecological peace/violence and in curricular writings, specifically conceptual models that are foundational to curriculum development and the learning goals and objectives proposed to shape the curriculum.

Definition of Peace

As the definition of peace began to be extended beyond the notion of negative peace, that is, the absence of war, the harm wrought upon earth systems by human activities was also recognized by peace educators as a form of violence impeding the achievement of a peaceful society. Writing in 1982, D. Sloan notes that a peace that ignores ecological destruction is unsustainable. B. Reardon and E. Nordland (1994) recommend that ecological violence be a part of the context and motivating force for peace education together with the violence of armed conflict and the structural violence of oppression and poverty. Similarly, S. Toh and V. Floresca-Cawagas (1987), A. Bjerdstedt (1990), L. Castro (2001) include violence towards the Earth in their analyses of the types of violence facing humans both on a planetary and interpersonal level.

Definitions of peace proposed in the writings of peace educators further included the notion of peace with Nature, for example, ecological balance as one of five values which should underpin any definition of peace (Hicks, 1988); the absence of the effect of damage on Nature by pollution and radiation as one of four dimensions of peace (Brock-Utne, 1989); ecological well-being as the foundation of a positive, or just and sustainable peace (Mische, 1991); and peace with our planetary ecosystem as superordinate to international peace in a schematic of cross-cultural definitions of peace (Hutchinson, 1992; Castro, 2001). Based on this expanded definition of peace, environmental themes and topics were included in conceptualizations of comprehensive or holistic peace education (cf. Toh & Floresca-Cawagas, 1987; Vriens, 1990; Bjerdstedt, 1990; Hutchinson, 1996; Reardon, 1999) although Reardon (1999) sets the following criteria that would determine when educating about the environment can be considered peace education, that is, when (1) environmental degradation is referred to as ecological violence, violence being a fundamental concern of traditional peace educators; (2) the fact that preserving the environment is a basic prerequisite to the achievement of peace is emphasized; and (3) the links between poverty and environmental degradation and between war and defense preparation and environmental well-being are recognized.

Link between Social and Ecological Peace/Violence

Implicit in a definition of peace that includes an environmental dimension is the link between social and ecological peace. This link is also referred to in the literature. "Peace with the planet is seen as inextricably interwoven with peace among and within nations" (Reardon, 1994a, p. 28). Similarly, both D. Hicks (2000) and G. Pike (2000, p. 221) see the welfare of people and planet as inextricably connected—interlocked. More specifically, according to S. H. Toh (1988, p. 132), the conditions for more environmentally sound development will improve when structural violence decreases and more justice prevails.

The relationship between social and ecological violence has also been pointed out. References have been made to the link between war and environmental degradation (Toh and Floresca-Cawagas, 1987; Vriens cited in Burns & Aspelagh, 1996; Zuber, 1994; Educators for Social Responsibility, 1998); global inequalities and ecological violence (Toh and Floresca-Cawagas, 1987); poverty and lack of ecological responsibility (Zuber, 1994); resource exploitation in the United States and poverty in the developing world (Reardon, 1994). In other words, it is acknowledged that social violence can lead to environmental degradation while exploitation of the environment results in social violence, or as Toh and Floresca-Cawagas (2000, p. 377) remind us, if we do not learn to live in peace with the Earth, it is not likely that humanity will survive.

The need for students to be made aware of and understand this inter-relatedness of social and environmental realities has also been recognized. When asked whether the risks of nuclear war and of far-reaching environmental damage through pollution and overuse of resources should be discussed together in school, 14 of 17 experts in peace education saw this twofold risk as interrelated and agreed that they needed to be treated together (See Bjerstedt, 1992a; 1992b; 1993a; 1993b; 1994a; 1994b; 1994c; Udayakumar, 1993). The need to consider the links between social and environmental peace in education is a basic purpose of the anthology, *Weaving connections: Educating for peace, social and environmental justice* (Goldstein & Selby, 2000). Representing educational philosophies that are collectively directed toward equity, justice, peacefulness, and Earth awareness, the contributors to the volume write about the need for young people to understand the roots of social and ecological violence and to learn to respect and reverence social differences and all life forms. And while the editors acknowledge that only a few of the individual chapters actually "weave the connections" explicitly, they encourage the readers to do so (Goldstein & Selby, 2000).

Conceptual Models

On a curricular level, *environment* is included in conceptual schemata intended to contribute to a clearer understanding of peace education and its implementation. Toh (1988) includes *environmentalism* as one of the concepts that constitutes his five point paradigm, that is, Participation, Equity, Appropriateness, Conscientization, Environmentalism, for assessing development projects and development education materials. Earth-consciousness and ecologically sustainable futures is one of the themes that constitutes the PEACE paradigm that F. Hutchinson (1992) has derived from the Gandhian tradition as a guide for developing peaceful pedagogies and the processes and conditions for making peace with people and planet. J. Synott (1994) lists eco-ethics as one of three global paradigms which determine how we understand and implement peace education, depending on the needs of the local context. Finally, R. Burns and R. Aspelagh (1996) include *environment* in their images of preferred worlds that underly those approaches to peace education which strive either for a nonviolent or unsustainable world.

Ecological Topics as Learning Objectives in Peace Education Curricula

Consistent with the theoretical writings, ecological topics have been advocated as learning objectives or goals in a holistic/comprehensive approach to peace education, for example, environmental literacy (Toh, 1988); issues related to ecology (Hicks, 1988); ecological balance, global environment, and world resources (Reardon, 1988a); respect for the integrity of the Earth (Global Campaign in Peace Education cited in Reardon, 2000), environmental destruction and environmental care (First Mindanao Congress for Peace Educators, 2000); ecological security and environmental sensitivity (Harris, 2002). The need to cultivate in students a sense of responsibility for both the local and global environment, sometimes referred to as planetary stewardship, is also cited as a goal for a curriculum in peace education, for example, Hicks, 1988; Reardon, 1988; 1988a; Wahlstrom, 1991; Nordland, 1994; Muller (cited in Reardon, 1988). Such responsibilities would include participating effectively in environmental politics (Hicks, 1988); working to build harmonious relationships between society and the environment (Toh & Floresca Cawagas, 1987; Reardon, 1994); and to resolve environmental problems (Wahlstrom, 1991); promoting sustainable development (Toh & Floresca-Cawagas, 2000; Werner & Case cited in Pike, 2000; Castro, 2001).

Fulfilling these responsibilities for planetary stewardship, students would need to learn to make rational judgments about environmental issues (Hicks, 1988) and to understand our planet and its place in the Universe (Mueller cited in Reardon, 1988), our planetary life systems, and our relationship to them (Reardon, 1988a). Additionally it is recommended that they learn an ethic of interdependence, seeing themselves not as masters of Nature but as part of Nature, that is, of the web of life (Hicks, 1988; Nordland, 1994; Reardon, 1999). Educational activities, therefore, should help them develop respect and concern for Nature (Maxwell, 2002; Castro, 2001; Toh & Floresca-Cawagas, 1987; Hicks, 1988) and a sense of place, that is, an appreciation of their bio region—the life forms in their environment (Reardon, 1994). Finally, ecological lifestyle training is advocated to highlight the link between social and ecological violence, that is, that what we consume and waste, how we spend our leisure time and set personal priorities "have profound significance both for human rights work and ecological healing" (Zuber, 1994, p. 202).

In a few cases, education for both social and ecological peace has been advocated as a two-dimensional goal in peace education curricula. Planetary stewardship, global citizenship, and humane relationships were shown to be superordinate value concepts central throughout the materials and to the curriculum content, design, and choice of which issues were to be studied, according to a mid-1980s survey of K–12 teacher-designed curricula for peace education in the United States (Reardon, 1988a). Entitled *Growth for peace and environmental responsibility*, R. Wahlstrom's report (1991) of a survey of peace education programs conducted in Finland between 1986 and 1991 maintains a twofold focus on both peace and environment in its discussion of the programs' objectives, that is, to promote the will to save the environment while at the same time helping to develop a sense of social responsibility and solidarity with less privileged members of society, and its basic purposes, that is, to shape human behavior towards nonviolence among humans and between humans and nature.

Participants in the Project on Ecological and Cooperative education, undertaken by a group of peace and environmental educators from Russia, the Ukraine, the United States, Canada, and Norway, sought not only how to understand the nature and consequences of the abuses of war, injustice, and environmental degradation and how they can be avoided, but also to consider positive alternatives, the advantages and social manifestations of peace, justice and ecological balance—how they are related and how they can be achieved and maintained (Reardon & Nordlund, 1994, p. 24). Educators who participated in this project agreed that ecology and cooperation must be at the center of all education (cf Nordlund, 1994; Zuber, 1994, Reardon, 1994, Mitina, 1994). They borrowed from ecological education and adapted for their purposes what B. Reardon (1999) refers to as ecological thinking, that is, an understanding of humans as part of the web of life and human social systems as one among several of those that constitute the larger planetary system. Such an approach they felt would more easily lead to the change in consciousness necessary to envisioning the change in the global social system that is the goal of transformative peace education.[7]

ENVIRONMENTAL EDUCATION

Nature study, outdoor education, and *conservation education* are generally acknowledged to be among the predecessors of contemporary environmental education (e.g. Wilke, 1993; Palmer, 1998).[8] All three appeared in school curricula during the nineteenth century and continue to exist today in multiple forms (Wilke, 1993). Nature study has emphasized the need to understand and appreciate Nature, while outdoor education has focused on the venue of such learning. The aims of conservation education, on the other hand, have been to help people understand the importance of conserving natural resources and related conservation issues, such as good agricultural practices. As a result of the 1968 UNESCO

Biosphere Conference, the aims of environmental education were expanded to include the promoting of a global awareness of environmental problems, and with the adoption of what J. Palmer (1998) refers to as the "classic definition of environmental education," social factors were recognized as essential to an understanding of environmental problems. This view is reflected in the aims of environmental education, which acknowledge the interdependence between social, political, economic, and ecological factors, and in theoretical and curricular writings, which list socially oriented topics and learning goals, similar to those typically included in peace education, as a part of environmental education.

Interdependence

The notion of the link between human activities and the quality of the environment, that is, "the inter-relatedness among man, his culture and his biophysical surroundings. . . ." (IUCN, cited in Palmer, 1998, p. 7), referred to as interdependence in the environmental literature, was included as one of the major objectives of environmental education by W. B. Stapp (1969) and introduced in the definition of environmental education formulated and adopted at the 1970 International Meeting on Environmental Education in the School Curriculum in Nevada. This was reiterated in the objectives for Environmental Education set by the UNESCO/UNEP conference in Belgrade (1975) and the UNESCO conference in Tbilisi (1977), that is, that environmental education should "foster clear awareness of and concern about economic, social, political and ecological interdependence in urban and rural areas" (Palmer, 1998, p. 7, 11). Explaining how education should take into account the conclusions of the 1992 United Nations Conference on Environment and Development (UNCED), D. Sitarz (1998) adds to this aim, stating that students and adults should acquire an *understanding* (author's italics) of the interdependence of economic, social, political, and ecological conditions—*locally*, *regionally*, and *internationally* (author's italics). Examining environmental issues from the perspective of the natural and human elements and systems involved, which had become a common, if not ubiquitous, practice in American K-12 science classes by the 1990s, is one approach to achieving this aim (Federico, Cloud, Byrne, & Wheeler, 2002).

Theoretical and curricular writings have elaborated on the nature of this interdependence between humans and the environment. Some have emphasized the interconnectedness of humans and all Earth systems (Byrne, 2000; Federico et al., 2001), acknowledging that "human well being and the health of the planet are inseparable (Agenda 21, cited in Federico et al., 2001, p. 610), or that we cannot have environmental quality without human equality (Fien & Tilbury, 2001). Others have referred in general terms to the impact of human activities on environmental quality (e.g. Huckle, 1991 cited in Palmer, 1998; Wilke, 1993) or the reverse, that is, the relationship between environmental quality and the continued satisfaction of human needs (Tbilisi Plus Ten Conference cited in Palmer, 1998). Others, yet, have been more specific, referring to the link between environmental degradation, militarism, and war making (Orr, 1992; O'Sullivan, 1999); human actions and soil erosion, species extinction (Orr, 1992); sustainability and peace, equity, cultural diversity and the structure of political institutions (Orr, 1992; Hopkins and McKeown, 2001); sustainability and poverty and inequality (Grundy & Simpkin, 1996); environmental issues and issues of development, peace and conflict, and human rights (Wals, 1999). Others, yet, have referred to a reciprocal relationship between the social and ecological, that is, that human actions that degrade the Earth will result ultimately in a decrease in quality of life in both the social and ecological sphere. This notion is reflected in curricular writings which:

- propose contextual sustainability, a concept that recognizes the reciprocal relationship between human-earth mediations, as an organizing principle for curriculum in secondary schools (Verhagen, 1999; 2001);

- include the development of an understanding that human lives and livelihoods are totally dependent on processes and resources that exist in the environment and of an awareness of the impact of human activities on the environment as educational aims in environmental education (National Curriculum Council of the United Kingdom cited in Palmer, 1998);

- offer the development of an ecologically sound way of thinking, feeling and acting toward the Earth as a condition for living harmoniously with each other and our environment as a theme for environmental education at elementary levels (Stapp & Cox cited in Braus & Wood, 1993).

Socially Oriented Topics as Learning Objectives in Environmental Education Curricula

While the notion of sustainable development had already appeared in 1980 as a part of the World Conservation Strategy and in *Our Common Future*, a report written for the World Commission on Environment and Development (1987), which linked ecological sustainability with economic development, it was the 1992 United Nations Conference on Environment and Development (UNCED) which placed education for sustainability as central to environmental education.[9] Conference documents, that is, Chapter 36 of Agenda 21, proposed that environmental education be positioned in the context of sustainable development (Orellana & Fauteux, 2000); that environment and development be integrated as a cross-cutting issue into education at all levels (Palmer, 1998); and in a multidisciplinary manner (Federico et al., 2001). The *Treaty on Environmental Education for Sustainable Societies and Global Responsibility* (NGO Working Group for the Treaty on Education, 1992) was also developed at the UNCED. However, unlike Agenda 21, which considered the role of education as supportive of efforts of political and business leaders to manage development better, it viewed education as an agent of change and pointed to the fundamental causes of environmental degradation, that is, the dominant socioeconomic system and the deep social injustices which characterize the contemporary situation, and to the links between population, peace, health, human rights, democracy, and the environment.

Thus, after the UNCED, education for sustainability was included as a part of environmental education and while views as to its ultimate goals or purposes varied, there appeared in the environmental literature concern about the social causes and consequences of environmental degradation as well as questions about how to resolve the problems it posed (Fedrico et al., 2001).[10] Thus, social issues, which typically have been the concern of comprehensive peace education, became key to education for sustainability. S. Ahearn (1994), for example, includes justice, dignity, and nonviolence as the basis for building security in an ecological society. The *Montreal Declaration* (Quebec Association for the Promotion of Environmental Education, 1997) calls for a commitment to position environmental education more comprehensively and globally, that is, linking environment and development and including the dimensions of education for peace, justice, and democracy (Orellana & Fauteux, 2000). E. Flogaitis (2000) suggests that the principle of social and ecological solidarity, of social justice and democracy be used to design future societies while according to J. Fien and D. Tilbury (2001), education for sustainability actually seeks to develop closer links among environmental quality, human equality, human rights and peace, and their underlying political threads.

Central to peace education curricula on structural violence, *social justice* is a value concept that is also often included in the curricular literature in environmental education. A precursor to views that would appear after the UNCED (1992), the sample scope and sequence for environmental education presented in J. Braus and D. Wood (1994) notes that a human ethic based on social justice for all is a necessary part of an environmental ethic. J. Huckle (cited in Palmer, 1998) refers to helping students develop an awareness of how the costs and benefits of using Nature are not shared equally in most societies as one of nine components of education for the environment. Curricular writings in environmental education appearing after the UNCED have proposed an integration of social justice and ecological sustainability as the basis of a transformed world view for all, including educators (Sterling, 1996); justice as one of the goals towards which education for sustainability strives (Fagan, 1996); social justice as one component of political education in youth work training (Grundy & Simpkin, 1996), and as one of the three value goals of the Earth Community School Model of Secondary Education (Verhagen, 1999). Students are also expected to develop a concern for injustice (Federico et al., 2001). Related topics, that is, *environmental racism* (Kaza, 1999; O'Sullivan, 1999), *equity* (Sitarz, 1998; Paden, 2000; Federico et al., 2001), *human rights* (Wals, 1999; Federico et al., 2001; Hopkins & McKeown, 2001) are also advocated as a part of the social dimension of environmental education.

Though referred to less frequently, *peace, conflict,* and *cultural diversity* are three other topics included in curricular writings for environmental education which recognize the social dimension of ecological sustainability. Peace is considered an issue that must be confronted in dealing with ecological sustainability (Orr, 1992; Wals, 1999) and in building an ecologically secure society (Ahearn, 1994). Moreover, an analysis of the causes of social violence, including environmental racism, on a regional, local and personal level is viewed as essential to planetary education that aims for personal and social transformation (O'Sullivan, 1999). Curricular objectives further include the need to transmit knowledge about conflicts that can arise about environmental issues (Palmer, 1998; Wals, 1999); to consider alternative ways to resolve these conflicts (Palmer, 1998); and to learn to resolve environmentally related conflicts peacefully (Sitarz, 1998). Cultural diversity is also an issue that must be considered in dealing with ecological sustainability (Orr, 1992). Respect for diverse points of view and values is part of the emerging understanding of environmental education for sustainability (Byrne, 2000; Federico et al., 2001; Hopkins & McKeown, 2001); it is included in standards for environmental education proposed by the North American Association for Environmental Education, the World Resources Institute, and members of President Clinton's Council on Sustainable Development (Sitarz, 1998), and by the National Association for Environmental Education in the United Kingdom (Palmer, 1998).

The Convergence of Peace Education and Environmental Education

The need for environmental education and specializations in education which focus on the causes and manifestations of social violence, for example, development, peace, human rights education, to come together and perhaps even to integrate is yet another theme that appears in the environmental literature. *Caring for the Earth*, a revised version of the World Conservation Strategy states that to appropriately prepare children and adults to live sustainably, environmental education should be *linked* (author's italics) to social education at all levels, the former helping people understand the natural world and the latter imparting an understanding of human behavior and an appreciation of cultural diversity (IUCN/UNEP/WWF, 1991, p.53). S. Sterling (cited in Palmer, 1998) also affirms the need to *integrate* (author's italics) the concepts of sustainability in environmental and development education with other related cross disciplinary educational approaches. D. Sitarz (1998) extends the fields that should work together beyond education to include related areas in the social sciences, noting that if they are brought together, they can "explore the potential synergy that can be unleashed by creative *interdisciplinary* (author's italics) thinking (p. 201). Moreover according to D. Selby (2000), each of these fields, for example, environmental, peace, human rights, development education, needs to recognize that their respective fields of interest are *mutually enfolded* (author's italics)—part of a larger web.

The literature in environmental education also includes frameworks which have been suggested as a means of effecting such integration on a conceptual level:

- *Education for Sustainability*—weaving together into a core framework educations oriented toward social change, for example, development, environment, peace, human rights, multicultural, futures . . . (Sterling, 1996)

- *Viability*—encompassing environmental issues and issues of poverty, population, health, food security, democracy, human rights, and peace with environmental education as the primary means for education for a viable future (Orellana & Fauteux, 2000)

- *Transformative Peace Education*—addressing the problems of conflict and violence, both social and ecological, on a planetary/global regional/local and personal level (O'Sullivan, 1999)

- *Global Environmental Education*—exploring the interface between environmental education and other progressive educations, for example, peace education, humane education, ecofeminist environmental education, education for human rights and social justice and others (Selby, 2000).

- *Education for the Development of Responsible Societies*—including dimensions of present day education which contribute to resolving the main social and ecological challenges of our world (Sauvé, 2000).

Arguments put forth for a "vigorous interdisciplinarity" (Selby, 2000), which would link fields of education that deal with the social and environmental challenges of our day, refer to the present confluence of environmental and social crises (Selby, 2000) and the increasing commonality of the aims and goals and of the vocabulary and educational approaches of these fields (Argyeman cited in Sterling, 1996). In fact, according to S. Sterling (1996) while a state of integration has not been reached, there has been an interesting and significant convergence among these areas in recent years.

Indeed, as this review of selected literature in peace education and environmental education has shown, such an overlap is evident in the theoretical and curricular developments in each field though it clearly does not yet reflect a majority view or common practice. Some educators in both fields recognize the link between social violence and environmental degradation and the converse, social peace, and ecological sustainability. For peace educators the well-being of people and planet is "interwoven," "inextricably connected," "interlocked"; for environmental educators it is interdependent. The definition of peace used by peace educators has been expanded to include peace with the planet while environmental educators who educate for sustainability view social justice as essential to achieving sustainability. Finally, these notions are reflected in the learning objectives and topics of both fields. Environmental concerns have been incorporated into the curricular writings in comprehensive peace education and social factors are now an essential part of environmental education for sustainability. Each field has incorporated values and concepts which traditionally form part of the conceptual core of its counterpart into its curricula. In the case of peace education, *education for positive peace, comprehensive peace education,* and *holistic peace education* already serve as frameworks which unify education in the areas of human rights, peace, development, and environment.

Additionally, one can look to development education (Sterling, 1996; Selby, 2000) for evidence of this convergence of environmental and social concerns in education. According to a 1992 UNICEF definition of the goals of development education, it should promote the development of attitudes and values, such as global solidarity, peace, tolerance, social justice, and environmental awareness, and facilitate the acquisition of knowledge and skills which will empower learners to promote these values and bring about change in their own lives and in their communities, both locally and globally (cited in Fountain, 1995).

Global education is a field which has also presented a synthesis, primarily, of peace, development, human rights, and environmental education (Greig, Pike, & Selby, 1987), focusing especially on the interdependence and interrelatedness of local, national, and global issues. The aims of this approach, which is said to take into account the needs of both person and planet, are set out by S. Greig, G. Pike, and D. Selby (1987), as follows:

- Students should understand the principles of ecology, that is, the dynamic nature of ecological systems and how their stability can be threatened by the actions of humankind.

- Students should appreciate what other cultures have to offer—that is, an awareness and appreciation of diverse, cultural viewpoints and experiences . . .

- Students should have a concern for justice, rights, and responsibilities.[11]

PURPOSE AND CONTENT OF THE ANTHOLOGY

This anthology intends to consider how peace education and environmental education can appropriately respond to the social and environmental crises that threaten the survival of all life and cultures that make up the Earth community. It focuses specifically on the interconnectedness that exists between these two sets of problems. The review of selected literature has brought to our attention the voices of those who explicitly advocate a convergence of these fields; it has also revealed the outlines of an emerging overlap between the theoretical and curricular development of the two fields. However, as noted above, though it bears repeating, this overlap should not be understood to reflect a majority view on the part of members of either field regarding the need to integrate education for social and ecological peace, nor does it shape common practice. Therefore, while committed to the diversity of educational responses and not advocating an integration of the two fields into one, the anthology seeks to further explore the manner of such a convergence. That is, how can each of these specializations in education incorporate into their curricula and learning activities the goals, knowledge and/or skills of the other so as to help learners understand and respond in an integrated manner to the social and ecological problems of our time ? Thus, the anthology aims to:

1. further refine the emerging understanding of how to integrate education for social and ecological peace;

2. extend awareness of this understanding beyond the critical core of educators represented in the review;

3. illustrate how understanding can be translated into educational practice.

While each chapter contributes to this threefold aim in a unique manner, conceptually the chapters are linked in theory and/or practice by the recognition of the reciprocity that exists between social and ecological peace and its antithesis, social and ecological violence.

P. Mische (chapter 1) focuses on *ecological security*. The chapter considers the significance of security in human and societal development and how requirements for security have changed over time. It then illustrates the two-way linkage between war and environmental degradation to argue that *ecological security* is at the core of human security. Thus, chapter 1 describes the *social context* which together with the *educational context* outlined above provide the rationale for the anthology. Finally, educators are challenged to facilitate a radical new learning—to re-inhabit the Earth responsibly and overcome habits of war and violence. According to Mische, this new learning will require exchanging existing paradigms and worldviews for an understanding that peace and ecological sustainability are critical to authentic security and authentic community. The chapters that follow take up this challenge.

F. C. Verhagen (chapter 2) presents a framework that educates for *contextual sustainability*, the notion that the integrity of the natural world is essential to the achievement of social peace and that, reciprocally, a society characterized by peaceful relationships among humans provides the context for the achievement of ecological sustainability. The chapter describes the components of the framework: its ideological foundations—cosmogenesis, biocentrism, and bioregionalism, and value concepts—ecological sustainability, social justice, active nonviolence, and participatory decision making. It proposes the development of a transdisciplinary standard as a strategy for incorporating the framework into the curriculum in middle schools, acknowledging the need to work for educational change by taking advantage of contemporary trends in education. In making ideological foundations one component of the educational content of the framework, the chapter thus responds to the need, expressed in chapter 1, to educate towards a change in existing worldviews with the value concepts, the second component of the framework, guiding related behavioral changes.

A. Brenes-Castro (chapter 3) describes an *Integral Model of Peace Education* which was developed as part of a broader educational initiative organized by the United Nations University of Peace to support efforts towards post-conflict peace-building in Central America. Peace, universal responsibility, and community are values that are central to the Model. Peace, the core value and overall goal, is understood in terms of harmonious relationships with the self, others, and with Nature. The other two are normative values, shaping these relationships. The chapter outlines the contents of the Model, that is, the sets of specific values and traits that express peace within each of these relational contexts; it describes a series of ten didactic modules that have been designed to apply the Model for educational use in community development with groups involved in emancipatory struggles. The chapter concludes with an account of one such application in a densely populated marginal urban community in Costa Rica. Chapter 3 is also based on an explicit

biocentric worldview but, additionally, on the core assumptions that all humans aspire to live in peace with one another and in a sustainable relationship with the
biosphere and that there are universal values that shape a culture of peace but that
the expression of these values will be culture specific. Thus, values are also central
to Brenes' conceptual framework.

L. Sauvé and I. Orellana (chapter 4) also focus on education in communities
characterized by emancipatory struggles. The chapter first outlines the authors' assumptions about the nature and purpose of environmental education and describes convergences between environmental and peace education. However, its
central concern is whether socially critical environmental education can be justified in the context of emancipatory struggles—in communities where social conflicts are so serious that they overshadow environmental concerns. Based on their
experience with an environmental learning project with such communities in
Colombia, Brazil, and Bolivia, they describe and provide examples of the use of
the *learning community* as the context and method for enabling groups involved in
conflict to learn how to take action to improve and transform both the social and
environmental conditions in their community. Thus, they re-conceptualize environmental education in social terms as directed towards the achievement of a culture of peace characterized by harmonious relationships among humans and with
Nature and in personal terms as emancipatory—developing critical, creative, and
courageous individuals who are able to collaborate in this work. Building upon
chapter 2 and 3, which provide frameworks intended to determine the content of
an integrated approach to education for social and ecological peace, they propose
a methodological innovation which would facilitate it.

A. Wals and Fanny Heymann (chapter 5) also focus on environmental education in nonformal settings, but in this chapter, two themes, introduced in earlier
chapters, are central to facilitating community education, that is, (1) that expressions of social peace and/or sustainable living are context specific, and (2) that conflict can play a key role in the process whereby such expressions are developed,
accepted, and implemented. Focusing, therefore, on the role of conflict as it is manifest in determining what sustainable living should entail in a particular context,
A. Wals and F. Heymann first outline varying contexts for decision making about
sustainable living in terms of the extent to which they allow and foster self-determination and openness. They then argue that these varied "spaces" will give rise to
conflicts whose outcome can be best facilitated through social learning, understood
as a collaborative process of deconstructing and reframing the views or frames held
by individuals or groups in conflict with one another. They outline the steps of a
methodology for facilitating this process, that is, *dialogical deconstruction*, whose goal
is the creation of frames participants will hold in common and which, therefore,
lead to a more open discussion about and resolution to issues of concern. Like the

"learning community," "dialogical deconstruction" is another methodological innovation for education in settings characterized either by the potential for conflict or in an actual state of conflict. However, Wals and Heymann's point of emphasis is the *process* of social learning, not its content nor a context that will facilitate it, an approach they also recommend for education in formal settings.

A. L. Wenden (chapter 6) advocates the need to include *perspective development*, an acquired set of organized assumptions and values about a social reality, as a learning objective in a curriculum that would integrate education for social and ecological peace. The chapter first provides the rationale for doing so—arguing that perspective development receives scant attention in peace and environmental education and that values, the basic components of a perspective, have a pervasive and profound influence on human thought and action. She then proposes and defines the values that should be the core components of a perspective for analyzing and evaluating social and ecological realities, that is, nonviolence, social justice, ecological sustainability, intergenerational equity, and civic participation. Thus, as is the case with the F. C. Verhagen framework and the Brenes-Castro model, values are assigned a central role in education for social and ecological peace. Moreover, chapter 6, as do earlier chapters (e.g., 4, & 5) also addresses the question of methodology, providing guidelines for perspective development that would promote critical reflectiveness, and the use of analytic and imaging skills—all essential to an autonomous application of a value-based perspective.

I. Harris and P. Mische (chapter 7) also address the need for an integrated approach to learning objectives in peace and environmental education. Identifying the two fields as within the tradition of education for social responsibility, they first outline some of their commonalities and differences. The chapter then describes the content of concepts that integrate ecological balance and a sustainable peace. It explains how environmental learning, specifically an understanding of natural systems, enhances concepts of peace highlighting both its dynamic and communal nature and how peace strategies, that is, prevention, peacemaking, peacekeeping, and peacebuilding, can be applied to environmental crises. In this way chapter 7 provides peace educators with an expanded understanding of what is entailed in the achievement of peace while, at the same time, making environmental educators aware of strategies for preserving environmental integrity. Furthermore, by introducing the notions of environmental peacemaking, peacekeeping, and peacebuilding the chapter responds to the need, advocated in chapter 1, to educate for an enhanced understanding of what ecological security entails.

Almost all of the chapters in the anthology refer to the Earth Charter. In chapter 8 P. B. Corcoran expands our knowledge about and appreciation of the significance of this document, which has been included in a list of inspirational documents, such as the Magna Carta, which have profoundly influenced the direction of human society. The chapter describes the sources of the values that constitute the Charter and the consultation process whereby they were incorporated into several drafts, and ultimately, the final document. It considers two educational uses of the Earth Charter and provides illustrative examples of how the Charter has been used for educational purposes in diverse settings. Focusing on the educational uses of the Earth Charter, this last chapter provides a restatement of the theme which has determined the aims and purpose of the anthology and which, therefore, underlies the individual chapters, that is, the interdependence, even indivisibility, as the author of this chapter writes, among environmental challenges, human rights, and peacemaking. At the same time, it also provides a framework, a comprehensive framework of values and ethical principles, for guiding an integrated approach to education that would focus on this connectedness between social and ecological realities.

NOTES

1. E-mail communication from a social scientist in Serbia to J. Myers-Walls sent to Peace Education Commission Listserv, April 25, 1999.

2. See L. Brock (1992) for an analysis of some causal and instrumental linkages between war or direct physical violence and the environment.

3. Excerpted from *The summary profile of the case submitted to the International People's Tribunal on Human Rights and the Environment* by Research International on behalf of the People of the Essequibo Riverian Area of Guyana and *The Report of the Guyana Society for the Protection and Preservation of the Environment* (1997).

4. Adapted from V. M. Kotlyakov, (1991), The Aral Sea Basin, *Environment*, 33 (1): 3–14.

5. Excerpted from S. Bliss, (2002), Western States, *Tom Paine. Common Sense*, http//www.tompaine.com/dispatch.

6. Excerpted from J. W. H. Mellor, (1988), The intertwining of environmental problems and poverty, *Environment*, 30: 8–30.

7. Writing in a similar vein, M. Gronemeyer (1996) suggests that pedagogical principles that characterize the ecological movement should be applied to peace education.

8. See J. Palmer (1998) for other precursors and/or contributors to environmental education.

9. Sustainability as understood at the UNCED and in earlier documents meant that in providing for their needs, contemporary societies should not endanger the resource pool needed for future generations to meet these same needs (e.g. WCED, 1987).

10. J. Fien and D. Tilbury (2002) list the following as terms used to refer to sustainability education, that is, education for sustainable living, education for sustainability, education for sustainable development, education for a sustainable future, and environmental education for sustainability. Education for sustainability is the term used in this introduction.

11. For an overview of specific areas of convergence between peace, development, human rights and environmental education, see S. Greig, G. Pike and D. Selby, (1987), Earth rights (London: Kogan Page co-published with World Wildlife Fund); and A. Wals, (1999), Stop the violence, in L. Forcey and I. Harris (eds.) Peacebuilding for adolescents [pp.239-262] (New York: Peter Lang).

REFERENCES

Ahearn, S. (1994). Educational planning for an ecological future. In B. Reardon & E. Nordland (Eds.), Learning peace: The promise of ecological and cooperative education (pp. 121-148). Albany, NY: State University of New York.

Bjerdstedt, A. (1990). Towards a rationale and a didactics of peace education. In A. Bjerdstedt (Ed.), Education for peace in the nineties (pp. 45-72). Peace Education Reports No. 1. School of Education. Malmo, Sweden: Lund University.

Bjerdstedt, A. (Ed.). (1992a). Peace education around the world: Some expert interviews. School of Education. Malmo, Sweden: Lund University.

Bjerdstedt, A. (Ed.). (1992b). Peace Education: Perspectives from Malta and England. Peace Education Miniprints No. 25, 12-21. School of Education. Malmo, Sweden: Lund University.

Bjerdstedt, A. (Ed.). (1993a). Peace education: A conversation with Haim Gordon, Israel. Peace, Environment and Education, 4 (2), 12-19. School of Education. Malmo, Sweden: Lund University.

Bjerdstedt, A. (Ed.). (1993a). Peace education: A conversation with Swee-Hin Toh, Canada. Peace, Environment and Education, 4 (2), 20-32. School of Education. Malmo, Sweden: Lund University.

Bjerdstedt, A. (Ed.). (1993b). Views of peace education: Interviews with the five former Secretaries of the Peace Education Commission. Peace, Environment and Education, 4 (3), 41-45. School of Education. Malmo, Sweden: Lund University.

Bjerdstedt, A. (Ed.). (1994a). Peace education: Perspectives from Costa Rica and Japan. *Peace Education Miniprints No. 62*, 3–20. School of Education. Malmo, Sweden: Lund University.

Bjerdstedt, A. (Ed.). (1994b). Peace education: A conversation with Linden Nelson, California Polytechnic State University. *Peace, Environment and Education*, 5 (2), 55–64. School of Education. Malmo, Sweden: Lund University.

Bjerdstedt, A. (Ed.). (1994c). Peace education: A conversation with Takehito Ito, Wako University, Tokyo, Japan. *Peace, Environment and Education*, 5 (2), 47–54.

Bliss, S. (2002). Western States: A grasshopper invasion—A warning signal but is anybody listening. *Tom Paine.Common Sense: A Public Interest Journal*. Retrieved August 1, 2002 from http//www.tompaine.com/dispatch

Braus, J., & Wood, D. (1994). *Environmental education in the schools: Creating a Program that works!* Rock Spring, GA: North American Association of Environmental Education.

Brock, L. (1992). Security through defending the environment: An illusion ? In E. Boulding (Ed.), *New agendas for peace research: Conflict and security reexamined* (pp. 79–102). Boulder, CO: Lynne Rienner Publishers.

Brock-Utne, B. (1989). *Feminist perspectives on peace and peace education*. Oxford: Pergamon Press.

Burns, R. J., & Aspelagh, R. (1996). Approaching peace through education. In R. Burns & R. Aspelagh (Eds.), *Three decades of peace education around the world: An anthology* (pp. 25–70). New York: Garland Publishing, Inc.

Byrne, J. (2000). From policy to practice: Creating education for a sustainable future. In K. Wheeler, & A. Perraca Bijur (Eds.), *Education for a sustainable future: A paradigm of hope for the 21st century* (pp. 35–72). New York: Kluwer Academic.

Castro, L. (2001). *Peace education: A teacher-training manual*. Center for Peace Education. Quezon City, Philippines: Miriam College.

Educators for Social Responsibility. (1998). *Nuclear weapons: Acceptance or abolition? A resource guide*. New York: Educators for Social Responsibility, New York City.

Fagan, G. (1996). Community-based learning. In J. Huckle & S. Sterling (Eds.), *Education for Sustainability* (pp.136–148). London: Earthscan Publications Ltd.

Federico, C. M., Cloud, J., Byrne, J., & Wheeler, K. (2001). Kindergarten through twelfth-Grade. In J. C. Dernback (Ed.), *Stumbling toward sustain-*

ability (pp. 607–623). Washington, DC: Environmental Law Institute, 1616 P Street, NW.

Fien, J., & Tilbury, D. (2002). The global challenge of sustainability. In D.Tilbury, R. Stevenson, J. Fien, D. Schreuder (Eds.), *Education and sustainability: responding to the global challenge* (pp 1–12). Gland, Switzerland and Cambridge, United Kingdom: IUCN.

First Mindanao Congress for Peace Educators. (2000). Cotabato Declaration on Education for a Culture of Peace. *International Journal of Curriculum and Instruction: Special issue-Education for a culture of peace, 2* (1), 121–125.

Flogaitis, E. (2000). The contribution of environmental education in sustainability. In A. Jarnet, B. Jickling, L. Sauvé, A. Wals, & P. Clarkin (Eds.), *A colloquium on the future of environmental education in a post modern world* (pp. 97–99). Available from *Canadian Journal of Environmental Education*, Yukon College, Box 2799, Whitehorse, Yukon, Y1A 5K4.

Fountain, S. (1995). *Education for development: A teacher's resource for global learning.* Portsmouth, NH: Heinemann.

Galtung, J. (1964). Editorial. *Journal of Peace Research, 1.*

Goldstein, T., & Selby, D. (2000). *Weaving connections: Educating for peace, social and environmental justice.* Toronto: Sumach Press.

Greig, S., Pike, G., & Selby, D. (1987). *Earth rights: Education as if the planet really mattered.* London: Kogan Page co-published with the World Wildlife Fund.

Grundy, L., & Simpkin B. (1996). Working with the youth service. In J. Huckle & S. Sterling (Eds.), *Education for sustainability* (pp. 123–135). London: Earthscan Publications Ltd.

Gronemeyer, M. (1996). The ecological movement: A new field for peace education. In R. Burns & R. Aspelagh (Eds.), *Three decades of peace education around the world: An anthology* (pp. 211–222). New York: Garland Publishing, Inc.

Harris, I. (2002). Conceptual underpinnings of peace education. In G.Salomon & B. Nevo (Eds.), *Peace education: The concept, principles and practices around the world* (pp. 15–26). New Jersey: Lawrence Erlbaum Associates.

Hicks, D. (1988). Understanding the field. In D. Hicks (Ed.), *Education for peace* (pp. 3–19). London: Routledge and Kegan Paul.

Hicks, D. (2000). Hope, human and wild: Contributions to a culture of peace. *International Journal of Curriculum and Instruction: Special issue-Education for a culture of peace, 2* (1), 47–64.

Hopkins, C., & McKeown, R. (2001). Education for sustainable development: An international perspective. In D. Tilbury, R. Stevenson, J. Fien, D. Schreuder,

(Eds.), *Education and sustainability: Responding to the global challenge* (pp. 13-24). Gland, Switzerland & Cambridge, United Kingdom: IUCN.

Hutchinson, F. (1992). Making peace with people and planet: Some important lessons from the Gandhian tradition in educating for the 21ˢᵗ century. *Peace, Environment and Education, 3* (3), 3-14.

Hutchinson, F. (1996). Educating beyond violent futures. London: Routledge and Kegan Paul.

IUCN/UNEP/WWF (1991). *Caring for the Earth: A strategy for sustainable living.* Gland, Switzerland: IUCN.

Kaza, S. (1999). Liberation and compassion in environmental studies. In G. Smith & D. Williams (Eds.), *Ecological education in action: On weaving education, culture and the environment* (pp. 143-160). Albany, NY: State University of New York Press.

Kotlyakov, V. M. (1991). The Aral Sea Basin: A critical environmental zone. *Environment, 33* (1), 4-38.

Maxwell, A. M. (2002). Educating for peace in the midst of violence: A South African experience. Paper presented at the 19th conference of the International Peace Research Association (IPRA), Suwon, South Korea.

Mellor, J. W. (1988, November). The intertwining of environmental problems and poverty. *Environment, 30,* 8-30.

Mische, P. (1991). The Earth as peace teacher. In E. Boulding, C. Brigagao, & K. Clements (Eds.), *Peace, culture, and society: Transnational research and dialog* (pp. 133-145). Boulder, CO: Westview Press.

Mitina, V. (1994). New thinking: Its application for a new learning. In B. Reardon & E. Nordland (Eds.), *Learning peace: The promise of ecological and cooperative education* (pp. 45-66). Albany, NY: State University of New York Press.

NGO International Forum. (1992). Treaty on environmental education for sustainable societies and global responsibility. ICAE Tel: 5511 62-7053; Fax: 5511 3457.

Nordland, E. (1994). New world-new thinking-new education. In B. Reardon & E. Nordland (Eds.), *Learning peace: The promise of ecological and cooperative education* (pp. 1-20). Albany, NY: State University of New York Press.

Orellana, I., & Fauteux, S. (2000). Environmental education: Tracing the highpoints of history. In A. Jarnet, B. Jickling, L. Sauvé, A. Wals, & P. Clarkin (Eds.), *A colloquium on The future of environmental education in a post modern world* (pp. 2-12). Available from *Canadian Journal of Environmental Education,* Yukon College, Box 2799, Whitehorse, Yukon, Y1A 5K4.

Orr, D. (1992). *Ecological literacy: Education and the transition to a postmodern world*. Albany, NY: State University of New York Press.

O'Sullivan, E. (1999). *Transformative learning: Educational vision for the 21st century*. London: Zed.

Paden, M. (2000). Education for sustainability and environmental education. In K. Wheeler & A. Perraca Bijur (Eds.), *Education for a sustainable future* (pp. 7–15). New York: Kluwer Academic.

Palmer, J. (1998). *Environmental Education in the 21st century*. London: Routledge and Kegan Paul.

Pike, G. (2000). A tapestry in the making: The strands of global education. In D. Selby & T. Goldstein (Eds.), *Weaving connections: Educating for peace, social and environmental justice* (pp. 218–241). Toronto: Sumach Press.

Quebec Association for the Promotion of Environmental Education. (1997). *Montreal Declaration on Environmental Education at the Planet'ERE Forum*. International Francophone Forum on Environmental Education from the Perspective of Sustainable Development. Montreal, Canada, 1997.

Reardon, B. (1988). *Comprehensive peace education*. New York: Teachers College Press.

Reardon, B. (Ed.). (1988a). *Educating for global responsibility*. New York: Teachers College Press.

Reardon, B. (1994a). Learning our way to a human future. In B. Reardon & E. Nordland, (Eds.), *Learning peace: The promise of ecological and cooperative education* (pp. 21–44). Albany, NY: State University of New York Press.

Reardon, B. (1999). Peace education: A review and a projection. *Peace Education Reports No. 17*. Malmo, Sweden: School of Education, Malmo University.

Reardon, B. (2000). Education for a culture of peace in a gender perspective: A prototype study unit for teacher education. *International Journal of Curriculum and Instruction: Special issue-Education for a culture of peace, 2* (1), 33–46.

Reardon B., & Nordland, E. (Eds.). (1994) *Learning peace: The promise of ecological and cooperative education*. Albany, NY: State University of New York Press.

Sauvé, L. (2000). Environmental education between modernity and post modernity: Searching for an integrating framework. In A. Jarnet, B. Jickling, L. Sauvé, A. Wals, & P. Clarkin (Eds.), *A colloquium on the future of environmental education in a postmodern world* (pp. 44–56). Available from *Canadian Journal of Environmental Education*, Yukon College, Box 2799, Whitehorse, Yukon, Y1A 5K4.

Selby, D. (2000). Global education: Toward a quantum model of environmental Education. In A. Jarnet, B. Jickling, L. Sauvé, A. Wals, & P. Clarkin (Eds.), A *colloquium on The future of environmental education in a post modern world* (pp. 139-146). Available from *Canadian Journal of Environmental Education*, Yukon College, Box 2799, Whitehorse, Yukon, Y1A 5K4.

Sitarz, D. (Ed.). (1998). *Sustainable America: America's environment, economy and society*. Carbondale, Illinois: Earth Press, *Chapter 9*.

Stapp, W. B. (1969). The concept of environmental education. *The Journal of Environmental Education, 1* (1), 30-31.

Sterling, S. (1996). Education in change. In J. Huckle & S. Sterling (Eds.), *Education for sustainability* (pp. 18-39). London: Earthscan Publications Ltd.

Sloan, D. (1982) (Ed.). *Education for peace and disarmament: Toward a living world*. New York: Teachers College Press.

Synott, J. (1994). Peace education report from Australia: Implications of some recent developments. *Peace, Environment and Education, 5* (1), 32-36.

Toh, S. H. (1988). Justice and development. In D. Hicks (Ed.), *Education for peace* (pp. 122-142). London: Routledge and Kegan Paul.

Toh, S. H., & Floresca-Cawagas, V. (1987). *Peace education: A framework for the Philippines*. Quezon City, Philippines: Phoenix Publishing House, Inc.

Toh, S. H., & Floresca-Cawagas, V. (2000). Educating towards a culture of peace. In D. Selby & T. Goldstein (Eds.), *Weaving connections: Educating for peace, social and environmental justice* (pp. 365-388). Toronto: Sumach Press.

Udayakumar, S. P. (1993). Peace education in the post-cold war era: An interview with Johan Galtung. *Peace, Environment, and Education, 4* (4), 58-62.

Verhagen, F. C. (2001). The Earth Community School (ECS) model of secondary education: Contributing to sustainable societies and thriving civilisations. *Journal of Social Alternatives, 21,* 11-17.

Verhagen, F. (Fall, 1999). The Earth Community School: A back-to-basics model of secondary education. *Green Teacher, 59,* 28-31.

Vriens, L. (1990). Peace education in the nineties: A reappraisal of values and options. In A. Bjerdstedt (Ed.), *Education for peace in the nineties* (pp. 7-23). Malmo, Sweden: School of Education, Lund University.

Wals, A. (1999). Stop the violence: Conflict management in an inner-city junior high school through action research and community problem solving. In L. Forcey & I. Harris (Eds.), *Peacebuilding for adolescents: Strategies for educators and community leaders* (pp. 239-262). New York: Peter Lang.

Wahlstrom, R. (1991). Growth towards peace and environmental responsibility. *Theory into practice, 67,* 1–78.

Wilke, R. J. (1993). *Environmental education teacher resource handbook: A practical guide for K–12 environmental education.* Millwood, New York: Kraus International Publications in cooperation with the *National Science Teachers Association.*

WCED. (1987). *Our Common Future.* Oxford: Oxford University Press.

Zuber, R. (1994). Economic leadership in an age of diminishing superpower prerogatives. In B. Reardon & E. Nordland (Eds.), *Learning peace: The promise of ecological and cooperative education* (pp. 189–210). Albany, NY: State University of New York Press.

CHAPTER 1

Ecological Security

New Challenges for Human Learning

Patricia M. Mische[1]

Many hundreds of people were killed in India in May, 2002, not by terror-ists (although it was alleged that terrorists were crossing into India from Pakistan); not in a war (although Pakistan and India were threatening war, including with nuclear weapons), and not from old age, hunger, or poverty (although these put them at greater risk). The real killer was a record breaking, 124° heat. Back up a few years to 1995, in Chicago, New York, and other cities in the United States, re-lentless, record breaking heat killed many hundreds of people then too. My hus-band was among the casualties. The 13 hottest years since records began to be kept have all occurred since the 1980s. Global warming has moved from scientific hypothesis, to prediction, to killing reality. The cause is not Nature, but what humans are doing to Nature.

Ecological security is not an abstraction, nor is it only for a few scientists and environmentalists to ponder. Threats to ecological security are a clear and present danger striking at the heart of human survival. They need to be considered on a par with military, terrorist, and economic threats as matters of utmost priority for security. They need to be considered as part of the matrix of national and global se-curity, because the issues included in a society's definition of security are given top political priority and sufficient allocation of resources. They generate the heroic effort and expertise needed to effectively resolve them.

This chapter, therefore, takes up the challenge of pondering ecological se-curity. It considers the significance of security in human and societal development and in human learning, and examines some of the linkages (and also some antag-onisms and contradictions) between ecological, economic, and military security, asserting that ecological security is at the core of true human (and national and global) security. It considers some ways in which environmental degradation may cause civil strife and warfare, and conversely, how warfare and its preparation cause environmental degradation concluding that ecological security is a prerequisite for peace, and peace is a prerequisite for ecological security. Finally, it also asserts that ecological security requires a fundamental change in concepts of security, in international relations, and in education and learning.

THE SIGNIFICANCE OF SECURITY IN A SOCIAL SYSTEM

Security is commonly defined as "freedom from danger; safety." It is related to the basic need for survival—a need so primal it is intrinsic in all human beings and societies—indeed in all species. In animals, survival is instinctive, but for human animals, with their longer infancy and greater vulnerability, instinct alone is not enough; the means to survive must be learned and taught to succeeding generations. It is believed that the brain was pushed to greater capacity and complexity by humans' need to learn and to teach themselves how to survive amid the more powerful forces of nature. Humans lacked the strength of the elephant, the speed of the gazelle, and the tree-swinging agility of chimpanzees. Such relatively weak creatures, therefore, had to depend on one another for their mutual survival, and this required that they learn to cooperate and, when necessary, subordinate individual desires to the common good. Initially their interdependence and cooperation for survival was undertaken in kinship-based hunting and gathering groups. Later, as technologies, economies, and the focus of security changed and interdependencies expanded, so did the size and structure of governance systems that groups developed to assure their security: from clans to larger tribes, horticultural and pastoral societies, city-states, kingdoms and traditional civilizations, to the nation-state, regional, and international systems of today. Each expansion to larger security groups entailed expanded loyalty systems and modes of cooperation. A key organizing principle in all these social structures was cooperation for mutual security and survival in the face of expanding interdependencies.

However, within living systems, including human social systems, security is not a fixed or steady state; it functions more like a catalyst or organizing principle guiding the overall direction toward survival and life within a dynamic evolutionary process. But a variety of choices may be available for getting there, some more viable, effective, or satisfactory than others. That different plant and animal species—indeed whole ecosystems—have evolved in particular ways with particular characteristics has been greatly affected by how they adapted to different, sometimes changing, requirements for security and survival. The same applies to human societies. The choice humans make about how to organize for security affect the whole social fabric at unconscious as well as conscious levels.

A security system is a total system: it shapes the myths and archetypes, identity and belief systems, structures of thought, leadership requirements, and gender roles, as well as political, economic, and social systems. It affects the social status of different members in a society, who is valued and who marginalized, who chosen to lead and who to follow. All are greatly affected by a society's perceptions of who can best assure its security and who is a burden or threat to it; who needs to be protected and who can best protect. In a social system where the primary threat is perceived to be military, those chosen to lead are likely to be those with the most militarily advantageous characteristics. In a social system facing environmental threats, a different set of leadership qualities may be required and valued.

HISTORICAL CHANGES IN CONCEPTS OF SECURITY

Within the framework of the nation-state system, national security has been thought of in military terms as the capacity of a state to deter, thwart, or win a war against other states or, in the case of civil war, against rebel forces within a state. More recently, terrorist attacks have led to an extension of the definition of war to include state efforts to thwart military threats by non-state actors who are spread among multiple states around the world. But regardless of the major actors, in the long sweep of human history, organized warfare is relatively new. Historians estimate that the war system began to emerge only about 10,000 years ago. As Margaret Mead has asserted, warfare is a human invention, and it can be uninvented. Earlier human groups may have demonstrated capacities for violence and aggression, but there is no evidence that organized warfare was the locus of group security. Instead, for millions of years human societies organized for security against other perceived threats to their existence.

People's perceptions of what constitutes these *perceived threats* to their survival and the security systems they have developed to meet them have varied over time and in different geographical regions. In general, however, there have been two major historical periods, and we may now be entering a third. In the first and longest period, human security systems focused primarily on the life-giving and life-taking powers of Nature—*what nature could do to humans*. Earthquakes, tornadoes, hurricanes, floods, droughts, blizzards, and excessive heat and cold threatened human survival. On the other hand, life-giving powers in water, trees, animals, and plants could nurture human life—in body and spirit. Early human societies developed whole systems related to their experience of these life-giving and life-threatening powers. The creative powers of Nature were often associated with a mother who could give birth and suckle new life. Leadership went to those—male or female—who seemed most skilled in interpreting, mediating, and securing the life-giving forces and in protecting against the forces that threatened human life. A central challenge in human learning was how to recognize and bring individual and community lives into harmony with the more powerful forces of Nature.

In the second period the primary locus of threats shifted from the biosphere to the sociosphere—*what human groups could do to one another and the rise of organized warfare*. Some historians suggest that organized warfare may have originated as a consequence of environmental degradation. When deteriorating environmental conditions—whether from natural or human causes—led to food shortages, some groups resorted to raiding and plundering from their neighbors. Initially these raids may have been sporadic, limited to periods of scarcity, and did not constitute a war system. But over time, possibly in prolonged periods of scarcity, and/or when this plundering paid off in the form of increased food, wealth, power, and prestige for the plunderers, whole systems began to develop around it, transforming the structures of thought, belief, myths, culture, economic and political structures, leadership requirements, gender roles, and definitions of social status within warring societies. Groups that were invaded, raided, and conquered, if not killed or enslaved, gradually developed a war system also to defend against aggression. Eventually the war system spread worldwide until it was near universal. Over time enmity, fear, and xenophobia were institutionalized, given ideological and political content (e.g. "Better dead than red"), and built up until they constituted mega-threats which were met by mega-weapons and supported by mega-myths so pervasive that the whole world hung on the verge of mutual assured destruction. Although the Cold War is over, the underlying world system remains largely a war system. The faces of "the enemy" may change, as exemplified in wars against terrorism, drugs, ethnic or racial groups, and "infidels," but the structures of thought and belief that sustain the war system remain entrenched, reproducing themselves through the ongoing process of socialization.

At the same time, a new class of threats has emerged suggesting the emergence of a third historical period, one that requires a new way of thinking, organizing, and learning/teaching for human security. Once more the threats have to do with Nature, but this time not with what Nature can do to humans, but rather with *what humans are doing to Nature* and, in turn, how the adaptations Nature makes in response to human assaults affects the prospects for future human survival.

NEW THREATS TO SURVIVAL:
THE NEED FOR ECOLOGICAL SECURITY

Humans have affected the ecosystems in which they have been dwelling from the beginning of hunting and gathering societies to modern times. Sometimes these impacts have been relatively benign, at other times quite destructive. Evidence exists in all world regions from all historical periods of past human harm to the environment.[2] However, in the past, this harm was usually local in scale and did not exceed the Earth's long-range healing capacity. In the twentieth century, however, human harm to the environment escalated to a new global scale and complexity that exceeded sustainable limits and altered the Earth's functioning integrity.

Social and Economic Impact of Growth

The indicators of this emerging new period are stark. In the 100 years from 1900 to 2000, human populations multiplied almost four times, from 1.6 billion to six billion. The global economy multiplied 17 times from an annual output of U.S. $2.3 trillion in 1900 to $39 trillion in 1998. The growth in economic output for just three years—from 1995 to 1998—exceeded that in the 10,000 years starting from the beginning of agriculture up to 1900 (Brown & Flavin, 1999). Per capita income quadrupled, from U.S. $1,500 to $6,600, with most of this increase coming in the second half of the century. Life expectancy increased from 35 years in 1900 to 66 years in 1999 (Brown & Flavin, 1999). More food was produced in the twentieth century than ever before, and human products poured into the global market place—and into the Earth's biosphere—at a record rate.

In one sense, these aggregate figures represent tremendous human success. Advancements in education, science, medicine, industry, and technology made it possible for more people to live longer, healthier, and more productive lives. But the aggregate figures obscure underlying inequities. The social and economic disparities are already evident. While most of the population growth was in the poorest countries of the world, most of the economic growth was in the richest. In short, one-fifth of the world population reaped the social and economic benefits of global economic growth, while another one-fifth at the bottom struggle to survive with little or no access to safe water, adequate nutrition, housing, health care, employment, or education These inequities portend serious conflicts and wars in the future.

Environmental Cost of Growth

As for the environmental costs, though they have not been fully calculated, we know the following:

- In the twentieth century, the Earth lost close to 50% of its original forest cover. This deforestation led to increased flooding, soil erosion, the depletion of water tables and aquifers, followed by drought and famine. Deforestation also diminished the Earth's capacity to absorb carbon emissions that cause global warming.

- A fivefold increase in fossil fuel use since the 1980s contributed to atmospheric concentrations of CO_2 that are now at the highest level in 150,000 years and contributing to a rise in world temperatures. The increased heat has killed elderly and other vulnerable segments of the human population, caused drought, flooding, and alterations in the food-producing capacities of some regions.

- The production and use of ozone-depleting gases has caused a hole in the stratospheric ozone layer undermining its ability to protect humans and crops from solar ultraviolet radiation.

- Whereas soil formation exceeded soil erosion through most of the Earth's evolution, in the twentieth century a combination of over-plowing, overgrazing, and deforestation reversed the ratio. A threshold of unsustainability was crossed, and now each year the Earth loses millions of tons of topsoil, depleting its fertility and undermining its food-producing capacities (Brown, 1998).

- The twentieth century also saw more toxic and radioactive pollutants dumped into the air, water, and soil than in all previous centuries combined. Access to safe, affordable water has become the major issue and preoccupation of one-fifth of the world's people. And already evidence is found of damage to the sperm count, fertility, and human gene pool resulting from these pollutants (Bertell, 1985).

- In the twentieth century human activities also caused a wave of mass species extinctions unequaled by all previous generations combined. It has been calculated that in the three centuries between 1600 and 1900, humans accounted for the loss of one species every four years. After 1900 the rate began increasing to one a year, and by 1979, to one a day. Depending on whose calculations are used, by 1999 the estimated losses in biodiversity were between 1,000 to 27,000 species lost each year.[3] With the rapid destruction of tropical rain forests (the habitat for between 70 to 90 percent of species), the Earth may lose as many as half of all remaining species in the coming decades. Such a mass extinction will surpass the "great dying" of the dinosaurs and thousands of other species some 65 million years ago. Evolutionary processes may generate new species, but this may take millions of years, longer than since the time humans first came into existence (Quammen, 1999).

Cost of Growth to Future Generations

For the first time in history, humanity is capable of universal and irreversible harm to the planet and the human gene pool. We, who have evolved out of the Earth's creative processes and who depend on the functioning integrity of those processes as the bottom line for our own survival, are now intervening in those processes in ways that are altering the course of planetary evolution and, therefore, undermining the chances for our own species to survive. The question before us is not whether the Earth will survive. As it always has through its long evolution, the Earth will adapt to crises and changing conditions and continue in its evolution. The question is whether humans will be able to survive the evolutionary adaptations that the Earth makes in response to human assaults.

Children and future generations are especially vulnerable. Children are more vulnerable than adults to pollutants and unborn children the most vulnerable of all, especially in the embryonic stages when organs begin to form. Girl children are born with all the ova they will ever produce. The genetic mutations from environmental pollutants may not show up in the affected child, but later, they appear in genetic mutations in the next or even subsequent generations. Human development—emotional, social, and spiritual—may also be affected after birth. Children who grow up on an impoverished Earth may also be impoverished in body, mind, and spirit. For our very humanness is greatly affected by the life communities in which we are nurtured. If we were to grow up on a desolate environment devoid of life, such as the moon, we would be very different beings than those who grow up in a vibrant, living Earth. We are stealing the future from our children and grandchildren, and making them pay the costs—possibly with their very lives—of our ecological irresponsibility. This may be one of the worst forms of criminal behavior, akin to child abuse and infanticide.

Time to Choose a New Direction

Some of the ecological harm already done is irreversible, but future harm can be prevented if the world community acts quickly and effectively. Most of today's crises have been caused by human actions. Human volition was involved and human volition can be activated to prevent further harm. There is still a narrow margin of time to make a difference. However, that margin of time diminishes daily. Once today's environmental crises, with their interactive and compounding effects, go beyond a certain point, they will take on a life of their own beyond the range of human volition to remedy.

INADEQUACY OF EXISTING SYSTEMS AND WORLDVIEWS

Existing international systems have not effectively redressed the trans-boundary aspects of this global ecological and economic disequilibrium. The United Nations (UN) and its related agencies evolved in the shadows of World War II and the Cold War. A generation of world leaders was guided by perceptions of security that were tied to their memories of that war and to the exigencies of the bipolar world order that evolved with the Cold War. For more than four decades, international relations, inside and outside the UN, were dominated by these perceptions of security. These were the very decades in which today's crisis of growth was mounting, with attendant population pressures, economic inequities, and environmental crises. Many of these crises might have been dealt with sooner and more effectively had they not been subordinated and obscured by narrow Cold War perceptions of national and global security. Although some progress was made in establishing na-tional and international laws for environmental protection during this time, including the first World Conference on the Human Environment in Stock-holm in 1972, the constraints of the war system greatly limited what could be achieved.

However, with the ending of the Cold War, hope that ecological issues would come to the fore rose. The 1992 Earth Summit in Rio de Janeiro, which was the first world conference after the Cold War ended, brought together an un-precedented number of heads of government and governmental and nongovern-mental groups. Treaties on biodiversity and climate change were signed; Agenda 21, a comprehensive program of action for environmental protection and sus-tainable development into the twenty-first century, was adopted. But the achieve-ments and hopes of the Earth Summit were soon eclipsed by lingering wars in the Middle East, the former Yugoslavia, Rwanda, and then, after the tragic events of September 11, 2001, the United States war on terrorism.

Thus, despite the evidence of grave ecological threats, many governments still subordinate ecological security to military security. Most in the corridors of government are not prepared to think about, much less effectively respond to global ecological threats. They were schooled in narrow, military or economic views of security; they have not yet learned how peace and economic security are linked to ecological security. They do not understand that, on the one hand, en-vironmental degradation leads to conflict and war, and on the other, war is a cause of environmental degradation. We are currently moving on a downward spiral that is increasingly untenable. The true security and well-being of the human community now requires that the linkages between ecological security and peace be understood.

ECOLOGICAL DEGRADATION AND
SCARCITY AS CAUSES OF WAR

War and civil strife often follow environmental degradation and scarcity. Recent examples include conflicts and wars in the Middle East (where water, productive land, and oil are critical), Somalia, the Sudan, Ethiopia, the Philippines, Papua New Guinea, Haiti, Honduras, and El Salvador to name only a few. Today there are more than 10 million environmental refugees—people who have left environmentally depleted homelands in search of productive land, food, water, and other vital resources. These migrating populations often conflict with people whose territories they enter. In the twenty-first century, as increasing populations compete for diminishing resources, we can expect even more environmental refugees, conflict, and warfare.

Of course, wars are not "caused" by Nature in any true sense. The "causes" of war lie in the sphere of human interactions and the ways societies choose to deal with environmental conditions they create or in which they find themselves. Nor should the role of environmental factors in conflict build-up be viewed in isolation, but as interactive with cultural, religious, psychological, political, economic, and other factors. Moreover, not all groups go to war in the face of adverse conditions, whether those conditions are environmental, economic, political, or sociocultural. Even if a crisis sparks conflict, it may not lead to war. Faced by crises, some groups may choose to cooperate in a search for constructive solutions, or they may choose from a wide spectrum of other behaviors short of violence or warfare.

However, it is clear from history that environmental crises have sometimes been a significant factor in the build-up of conflicts that have spilled over into violence and war (Westing, 1986; Starr, 1991; Homer-Dixon & Blitt, 1998). Environmental factors in past wars have included (1) competition for natural resources; (2) the overuse and depletion of shared resources by one or more groups in a bioregion, affecting others who also depend on the resources (often exacerbated by class, ethnic, religious, or other divisions); and (3) environmental degradation (e.g., pollution, soil erosion, deforestation, loss of biodiversity) that impoverishes the living space and undermines a society's physical, economic, social, or spiritual quality of life. Although these environmental factors are listed separately here for ease of discussion, in fact, they often overlap or are different aspects of a single ecological problem.

Competition for Resources as a Cause of War

Among possible environmental factors in wars, the most obvious up to now has been competition for natural resources. The resources at stake in past wars have included both living and nonliving, renewable and nonrenewable resources and have ranged from mineral and other raw materials to energy supplies, food and timber sources, sea or land passages, land rich in topsoil, and waters rich in fish. Even when groups or countries don't acknowledge such resources as the "cause" for which they are fighting (resource wars have often been "justified" on other grounds), they may be significant underlying factors.

Scarcity and/or mal-distribution are often factors in conflict over a key resource. Natural resources tend to be distributed unevenly around the world, with some regions and countries with sufficiency and others in short supply or totally lacking one or more resources perceived as vital to their well-being. The scarcity and mal-distribution may also run along class, ethnic, or religious lines, increasing the potential for conflict. At least four types of resource scarcity may contribute to conflict[4]: (1) physical scarcity (the resource is only available in finite amounts); (2) geopolitical scarcity (the resource is distributed unevenly around the world so that some regions depend on others for access or deliveries); (3) socioeconomic scarcity (unequal distribution of property rights or purchasing power to obtain resources within or between societies); and (4) environmental scarcity (a previously abundant and naturally renewable resource is made scarce by environmental degradation when a group fails to manage the resource in a sustainable way, for example, contamination of water, soil, or air) (Rees, cited in Libiszewski, 1992). The type of scarcity affects the issues, parties, and dynamics of a conflict, and thus, also the requirements for resolving it. There may also be more than one type of scarcity involved, compounding the complexity of the conflict and its resolution.

But not all conflicts over natural resources involve scarcity. Even the discovery of resources not used in the past or new sources of vital resources providing an increased supply can be a source of conflict, especially when agreements on access rights have not yet been worked out between potential users. In such cases, nations may fight to gain control of or to prevent other nations from controlling access to the new resources. A "cause" of conflict here is not scarcity but a lag in intergroup norms or international agreements for equitable sharing.

The desire to gain or control natural resources has been a major factor in expansionism and colonial conquests from ancient times to the present. The process of annexing and colonizing other territories and the resources on them may not always have involved warfare or other forms of *physical* violence, but it inevitably involved *structural* violence—the domination and exploitation of other peoples and their environments, including the wholesale looting of natural resources. Perhaps just as inevitably, the victims of structural violence will revolt. For thousands of years, wars of independence have been fought not only for political autonomy, but also for sovereignty over natural resources.

State University of New York Press
90 State Street, Suite 700
Albany, NY 12207-1707

We take pleasure in sending you this review copy of

EDUCATING FOR A CULTURE OF SOCIAL
AND ECOLOGICAL PEACE

By: Anita L. Wenden

Publication date: August, 2004

Price: $75.50 HC, $25.95 PB

Please send two copies of your review to

STATE UNIVERSITY OF NEW YORK PRESS
90 STATE STREET, SUITE 700 ALBANY NY 12207

In the twentieth century alone, millions of people were killed in wars over natural resources. The following are only a few identified by Arthur Westing (1986):

- *The First World War of 1914–18.* Natural resource aspects included population pressures in Central Europe; territorial rivalries, for example, over the iron-rich Lorraine area; Germany's goal of access to oil; and conflicts over colonies in resource-rich areas of Africa, Asia, Pacific islands, and so forth.

- *The Chaco War of 1932–35.* Paraguay and Bolivia fought for control of the Gran Chico wilderness area. They thought (incorrectly) that it contained oil.

- *The Second World War of 1939–45.* Natural resource aspects included population density in Germany (a justification given by Germany). Germany annexed the iron-rich Lorraine area of France, the agriculturally and iron-rich Ukraine in the USSR, and the nickel-rich Petsamo (now Pechenga) region of Finland. Germany pillaged Poland's timber resources. Japan's expansionism was likewise motivated largely by a scarcity of indigenous resources.

- *The Algerian War of Independence of 1954–62.* A colonial war in which France fought, in part, to continue its hold on Algerian oil deposits.

- *The Congo Civil War of 1960–64.* A civil war in large part fomented by Belgian and other foreign interests so as to protect their investments in copper and other minerals.

- *The Third Arab-Israeli War of 1967.* Israel conquered parts of Egypt, Jordan, and Syria, gaining much-needed water and oil.

- *The Nigerian Civil War of 1967–70.* Attempts by the Eastern region (Biafra) to secede were thwarted by the government. At stake were rich deposits of oil.

- *The Anglo-Icelandic Clash of 1972–73.* Icelandic gunboats drove away British trawlers that refused to recognize Iceland's unilateral extension of its coastal fishing rights from 22 to 93 kilometers from its shores.

- *The Falkland/Malvinas Conflict of 1982.* Argentina and the United Kingdom both claimed ownership of the islands, which are attractive for the surrounding fishery resources and potential offshore oil deposits.

Many other wars could be added to Westing's list, including the 1991 War with Iraq after it invaded Kuwait. At stake, in this case, were the oil fields of Kuwait.

Environmental Degradation and Resource Depletion as Causes of War

Although less research is available on the role of environmental degradation and resource depletion, they have also been factors in civil strife and warfare. When one group depletes or pollutes a shared resource, such as a river or aquifer, the cause of the resulting conflict is obvious. But in other cases, such as soil erosion, deforestation, and desertification, the contending parties may be less aware of the environmental factors in their hostilities, pointing instead to the economic effects of the degradation, such as poverty, unemployment, and hunger.

Recent examples where environmental degradation and resource depletion contributed, along with other factors, to social upheaval and conflict include Ethiopia, Haiti, El Salvador, Somalia, and the Philippines, to name only a few. According to the Ethiopian Relief Commission, the primary cause of the 1975 famine in Ethiopia and the resulting mass migrations and other social upheavals was not the long drought, but the accumulated consequences, over the years, of resource degradation and of the increase in human and animal populations (Macneill et al., 1991). Haiti provides another example. Mass deforestation and soil erosion (down to bedrock in many parts of the country) resulting in hunger and economic crisis led to civil strife and more than a million boat people—approximately one sixth of the country—fleeing (USAID, cited in MacNeill et al., 1991). El Salvador experienced years of civil strife and insurgency warfare after depleted soil, water, and forests could no longer support increasing populations. So many Salvadorans began crossing the border seeking a better life in Honduras that by 1969, when Honduras began expelling them, illegal Salvadorans comprised 12% of the Honduran population. In reaction to the expulsions, El Salvador invaded Honduras, demanding (successfully) that Honduras allow existing Salvadorans to stay, and trying (unsuccessfully) to force Honduras to accept future immigrants (Westing, 1986). Decades of insurgency warfare in the Philippines were catalyzed in part by massive deforestation, mono-cropping, unsustainable agriculture, and the failure of land reform, contributing to hunger, unemployment, and mass migrations of poor peasants into fragile mountain lands where they clashed with indigenous peoples.

In the above and similar cases, rapid population growth, political corruption, and gross inequities in the distribution of wealth, power, and resources were interactive with environmental degradation in the conflict build up. Such gross inequities increase the likelihood of conflict and warfare. When the deprivation and suffering are shared relatively evenly among a population, people may be less likely to consider the system unfair and thus less likely to revolt. But when they perceive great inequities, with some people reaping most of the benefits and others most of the misery resulting from environmental degradation, there will be greater likelihood of revolt especially if these groups are defined by differences in class, race, ethnicity, or religion. This is because the system itself will be seen as unjust and illegitimate (Boulding, 1978; Mische, 1991b).

WAR AS A THREAT TO ECOLOGICAL SECURITY

If environmental degradation has led to warfare and untold human deaths the converse is also true: War, and preparations for war, have become increasingly damaging to the functioning integrity of planet Earth.

Wars in the TwentiethCentury

Sometimes environmental harm is a side effect of war that is written off as "collateral damage" or a "necessary cost" of national security. At other times damage to the Earth is a deliberate strategy undertaken to demoralize an enemy or deprive them of food, water, habitat, livelihood, escape, or refuge. For example, in the 1991 Gulf War, a key resource, oil, was not only a cause of war, but also a weapon and target. Millions of barrels of oil were deliberately poured into the sea, and the oil fields of Kuwait set ablaze by Iraqi forces, with enormous ecological damage in sea, land, and air environments. Added to this was the "collateral" damage inflicted by both allied and Iraqi forces through massive bombing, sea- and land-mining, and deployment of troops and military equipment in fragile desert systems.

But the Gulf War was hardly the only time warfare has been environmentally destructive. Protracted warfare in Vietnam turned one-third of the country into a wasteland, pockmarking farms with 2.5 million bomb craters and defoliating forests with 50 million liters of Agent Orange. Between 1945 and 1982, Vietnam lost over 80% of its original forest cover. Fighting in Afghanistan during the Cold War destroyed centuries-old irrigation systems and left the land filled with hundreds of thousands of landmines. Following the tragic events of September 11, 2001, Afghanistan's already war-scorched land was subjected to repeated bombing; mountains were leveled to flush out terrorists who might be lurking in caves. In Central America and the Philippines during the 1960s–1970s, government counterinsurgency forces used "scorched earth" policies, destroying crops and razing forests in the pursuit of rebels.

Ecological Impacts of Weapons Systems

The environment has been a war casualty since ancient times, but in the twentieth century, war and war preparation became ever more environmentally destructive. Moreover, inasmuch as the Earth is a total, living system or life community of which humans are a part, whatever befalls the larger community of life befalls humans. Thus, the ecological impacts of weapons systems, that is, nuclear, chemical, and biological weapons of mass destruction, must be seen as posing tremendous threats both to the environment and to humans.

Even if such weapons are never used in a war, their very production, testing, and stockpiling cause ecological damage, which, in turn, affects human viability. According to United Nations data, by 1980 the nuclear powers had conducted some 1,233 nuclear tests globally, destroying desert ecosystems, vaporizing some Pacific islands and rendering others uninhabitable, and contaminating air, water, soil, plant, and animal life (Bertell, 1983; 1984; 1986). Within this life community, humans are at the top of the food chain, where pollutants become increasingly more concentrated. It is no wonder then that human populations are suffering increased incidence of cancers, birth defects, and many other ill-health effects from the environmental impacts of weapons and weapons production. The victims of the atomic bombing of Hiroshima and Nagasaki numbered about 328,000 (including the 155,521 civilians who died immediately, 147,033 who died between September 1945 and January 1950 from radiation induced diseases and other bomb injuries, and thousands of cancer victims and genetically damaged offspring). Since then, the global victims of fallout from nuclear weapons production, stockpiling, and testing have been estimated at more than 16 million. Among the peoples of the Marshall Islands, who experienced high levels of radiation exposure from 68 nuclear bomb tests in their region, whole family lines have died out, with some of the survivors rendered sterile or unable to give birth to viable offspring (Bertell, 1983, 1986). Weapons developed in the name of protecting people now pose one of the gravest threats to the whole Earth Community—to the existence of natural life and to human existence. Radioactive food, fish, air, water, all impact human health and the human gene pool.

Ending the Cold War has not ended the nuclear threat. Although the United States and Russia agreed on cuts, thousands of nuclear weapons are still stockpiled, primarily by the United States and Russia, but also the United Kingdom, France, and China. Pakistan and India now have nuclear weapons and periodically threaten their use, and several other countries have, or are on the threshold of having a nuclear-weapons capability, including Israel, Iraq, Iran, Libya, and North Korea. Some thirty countries have operating nuclear power reactors and access to fissionable materials, and 24 countries, most in the Third World, have or are developing long-range rockets that can be used as ballistic missiles armed with nuclear or chemical warhead (Nye, 1993). Political uncertainties feed fears that nuclear weapons and fissionable materials will end up in the hands of terrorists or renegade states.

Before the 1990s such "unconventional" weapons were in a separate category of thought from "conventional" armaments. Their use was considered "unthinkable" because of the mass human death toll and environmental destruction that would result, not only immediately, but also by long-term contamination of soil, food, water, air. However, the lines of separation became blurred in the 1990s when an offspring of nuclear weapons was used in "conventional" wars in the Persian Gulf, Bosnia, and Yugoslavia. Armor-piercing ammunition was introduced utilizing depleted uranium (DU)—depleted because it is the waste from uranium processing. DU is more radioactive than uranium in its natural state because the uranium is more concentrated in the waste. DU emits an alpha particle with a radioactive half-life of 4.5 billion years. Like other heavy metals, such as lead, DU is also chemically toxic. The radioactive and chemical toxics in DU cause cancers, respiratory and kidney diseases, chromosomal damage, birth defects, and more. The illness called "Gulf War syndrome," contracted among troops in that war, is believed to have been caused by exposure to DU (Fahey, 1999, and Bertell, 1999).

According to the U.S. Army Environmental Policy Institute, DU is a low-level radioactive waste which must be disposed of in a licensed repository (Bertell, 1999). DU-contaminated soil is supposed to be scraped up and containerized. By the end of the Gulf War some 640,000 pounds (290,000 kilograms) of depleted uranium had contaminated equipment and soil in Saudi Arabia, Kuwait, and southern Iraq. Because these clean-up costs are estimated in the tens of billions of dollars, they are unlikely to be undertaken (Fahey, 1999). No international law is in place requiring such cleanup of battlefields. Without a way to hold governments who wage war legally responsible for the environmental cleanup and its costs, it is unlikely that there will be any cleanup. And without an international agreement prohibiting the use of depleted uranium, it will proliferate, poisoning ever more land, water, and people with radioactive contaminants.

Land mines is another type of weapon that continues to devastate environmental health long after hostilities cease. Although many governments have now ratified a ban on land mines, millions of active mines remain implanted in the Earth rendering once productive land unusable for food production or other human needs and killing or dismembering unsuspecting children.

Effects of Global Militarization on Resources

Military activities are undermining ecological security not only through weapons systems that degrade, destroy, or contaminate the Earth, but also by the

inordinate use of resources. Worldwide, militaries consume amounts of nonrenewable natural resources far beyond those used in the civilian sector. In the
United States, the Pentagon is the single largest oil consumer, and possibly the
largest worldwide. In 1989 alone, the United States Department of Defense pur-
chased 200 billion barrels of oil for military use. This could have run all U.S. public transport systems for 22 years (Science for Peace, 1992). An F-16 fighter jet
consumes almost twice as much gas in one hour as the average United States mo-
torist uses in a year. The same is true abroad. One-fourth of the world's jet fuel
and 9 percent of global iron and steel are consumed by the military. Worldwide,
militaries consume more aluminum, copper, nickel, and platinum than the entire
civilian Third World (Science for Peace, 1992). Thus, militaries contribute to
scarcity and exacerbate conflicts that are caused by scarcity. It is a vicious circle,
with militaries then being given more and more resources to quell more conflicts
over the scarcities they have caused.

Militaries also control increasing amounts of the world's land, water, and
airspace, leaving less for use by increasing populations, and inflicting serious damage to ecosystems. Globally, they control between 750,000 and 1.5 million square
kilometers of land (not including areas used by arms-producing companies). The
United States military alone controls land areas within the United States equiva-
lent to the entire state of Virginia, plus more than 8,000 kilometers of land in
other countries. Lands used for military training usually suffer severe damage, including destroyed vegetation and wildlife habitats, soil compression and erosion,
and water and soil contamination (Science for Peace, 1992).

The effects of militarization on the Earth's atmosphere and climate can only
be roughly estimated. German environmentalist Gunar Seitz calculated that 6 to
10% of global air pollution was from military activities (Science for Peace, 1992).
The Worldwatch Institute estimated that military activities were responsible for
10% of the carbon dioxide emissions that produce global warming. Militaries
have also produced a large share of the chlorofluorocarbons (CFCs) and other
gases that are depleting the Earth's ozone layer. According to Science for Peace, the
United States military alone is responsible for half of the use of CFC-113 worldwide and a major user of Halon 1211, both of which cause ozone depletion.
Worldwide, militaries have used more than two-thirds of all CFC-113, and many
other ozone-depleting substances, some with no civilian counterpart (Science for
Peace, 1992).

Militaries have also produced extensive hazardous wastes. Besides the radioactive contaminants from nuclear weapons production and testing, these have
included pesticides, polychlorinated biphenyls (PCBs), cyanides, phenols, acids, al-
kalies, metals, fuels, and explosives, all of which can undermine environmental
and human health (Science for Peace, 1992). Although many countries have

adopted environmental protection laws, too often the military are held to lesser standards than the civilian population or not made to comply at all. In the United States, for example, some 15,000 hazardous waste sites appear on active and former Department of Defense properties. But according to the Center for Defense Information (CDI), the majority of these facilities do not meet federal and state hazardous waste control requirements. Environmental contamination was revealed at seventeen nuclear warhead factories in twelve states (CDI, 1989).

Finally, we can add to these effects of global militarization the co-optation for military uses of incredible financial, scientific, and technological resources that could be better applied to advance ecological sustainability and economic well-being.

ECOLOGICAL SECURITY AND PEACE ARE INSEPARABLE

It is evident that, whatever use the war system may once have had, it is now inimical to true human security. It is destroying the ecological foundations for human survival. Thus, *the advancement of world peace is essential to ecological security*. Paradoxically, the converse is also true. As ecological systems are degraded and natural resources diminished, economic tensions and civil strife increase, and so does the temptation to use military force. Thus, *ecological security is essential to world peace*. In short, *ecological security is a prerequisite for peace; and peace is a prerequisite for ecological security. The two must be pursued as an inseparable whole.*

Although ecological security is becoming ever more critical, it cannot be achieved through conventional approaches to national security. Unlike military or economic threats, environmental threats cannot be defined by traditional national security ideology. Nor can they be resolved through conventional competition for power. A more powerful state or arsenal is no added advantage. Domination will not bring salvation. Bombing delivers no victories; it only increases the damage and delays a remedy. National sovereignty offers no protection against transboundary environmental threats. The Earth does not recognize sovereignty as we now define it. Thus, a whole new way of thinking is required to assure ecological security.

CHALLENGES TO HUMAN LEARNING

In the past, when groups exceeded the limits of environmental sustainability in a particular location, they moved to new territorial frontiers. But now there are few uninhabited territories capable of supporting human populations, and many countries are loath to absorb more refugees. The moon does not offer promising prospects for habitation, and other planets alive like Earth have not yet been found. But the habit of looking for a new frontier to resolve economic and environmental limits is deeply imbedded. In the absence of new territorial frontiers, some look to new technological frontiers, and while environmentally friendly technologies may help resolve some, they cannot resolve all our environmental problems. However, there is one promising new frontier for redressing environmental crises: the new frontier of mind, spirit, and consciousness—the territory of human learning.

New Frontiers in Learning

Humans have evolved through continuous learning and adaptation in the search for survival and well-being. But today it is not only *human* well-being that requires deepened human consciousness and learning; the Earth's well-being also requires it. The significance of the challenge to human learning before us was foreseen by the French paleontologist, Teilhard de Chardin and the Russian academician, Vladimir Vernadsky. Although both died before today's ecological crises were fully apparent, they postulated the incredible responsibility humans had for the Earth's further evolution. As they saw it, the emergence of the human was a continuation of Earth's evolution: Humans were *from* the Earth and *of* the Earth. Their bodies were comprised of the Earth's elements in the same proportion as they existed in the Earth. But they were the Earth in a new, macrophase of its development: the phase of consciousness. Through humans the Earth was able to arc back on itself in self-reflection. Humans were not the culmination of evolution, for the Earth would continue in its development, but increasingly this development would take place on the other side of this new threshold, that is, in the realm of mind, spirit, and human consciousness and this, in turn, would affect evolutionary dynamics. In this view the emergence of the human was an event of incredible magnitude The Earth had entered a period of *co-evolutionary* dynamics in which the fate of the Earth was increasingly a matter of human choice.

The implications of this for human learning are profound. We can help the Earth to flourish, or we can render it uninhabitable for future human generations. But there has been a tragic lag in our development. We have not yet developed the consciousness, wisdom, moral maturity, or ethical systems to use our new powers in ways that will enhance rather than diminish the prospects of life on Earth. We have not yet developed a global culture of co-evolutionary or ecological responsibility—or its extensions in global public policy and law—that will help the Earth sustain its functioning integrity. A failure to develop an adequate consciousness and ethic related to this responsibility would be a failure of the greatest magnitude. The challenge is no less than to learn and teach one another how to re-inhabit the Earth in new, more responsible ways as contributing members of the community of life. Constructive membership in this community requires that we also learn to rise above past, narrow definitions of security and old habits of war and violence and understand that peace and ecological integrity are critical to true security and true community.

The greatest hurdle in meeting this challenge is how to awaken the human community, and especially educators and policymakers, to the fact that we face a major challenge to human learning that goes beyond anything we have seriously considered to date. We, educators, must awaken and revivify humanity. We must lead new generations to a deeper awareness, wisdom, and knowledge of our fundamental and inextricable relationship with the Earth community and generate the creativity needed for renewing the total Earth community—human and non-human. We must develop a new mind, a new humanity in vital relationship to the Earth. We are not talking about the physical development of a new brain, but about a new *mind*, a new way of seeing and being, of *learning to be* in the world as responsible, creative members of the community of life, with co-responsibility for the next stages of planetary evolution. This is no small challenge for educators and educational policy, but we have not yet even begun to grasp its gravity, scope, and depth.

The challenge is not just for schooling and literacy. These may, of course, be helpful. But it is not the unschooled and illiterate who are perpetrating the gravest environmental harm; it is rather those who have been schooled in patterns of unquestioning consumption, waste, and ignorance of their integral relationship to the Earth and each other; it is those who have been schooled in narrow views of national security and violence and who view militarism as a way to achieve it regardless of the ecological or human costs. Given that few schools or adult education programs have even begun to undertake the kind of social and environmental learning required to effectively redress environmental threats, schooling in itself is no guarantee of ecological responsibility. A central challenge before us, then, is to develop a *pedagogy of ecological responsibility*. This applies to all types of learning, whether formal, nonformal, or informal; at early-childhood, elementary, secondary, or adult-education levels; in family, school, or community settings.

A pedagogy of ecological responsibility must be commensurate to the needs of our times. It must respond to the scale and complexity of the destruction humans have wrought on the environment, a destruction unprecedented in history. It will need to facilitate learning that goes much deeper than simply superimposing facts about peace and the environment on top of existing paradigms and worldviews. If we are to find long-lasting solutions to environmental crises and militarism we need to get at the unconscious thought structures, ideologies, and world views that guide our harmful choices and behavior, and learn to re-inhabit the Earth in deepened consciousness and attunement to the life of the Earth and of one another. We must learn to embrace our common dependency and shared responsibility for Earth's functioning integrity and for a revivified humanity that is part of a vibrant community of life. We must come to understand at a deep and profound level, in the very marrow of our bones, that the Earth is like a single cell in the universe, and humans are not over this cell, but part of it. We will live or die as this single cell lives or dies. It will be no trivial matter to change the underlying structures of thought in which we have been schooled, and which at deep and often unconscious levels affect our fundamental patterns of seeing and being on the planet, but there is little margin for error.

NOTES

1. Parts of this chapter have been discussed in previously published articles written and copyrighted by Patricia Mische, that is, (Mische, 1989a; 1989b; 1991a; 1992a; 1992b; 1992c; 1993; 1994; 1995; 1998).

2. A good summary of this research can be found in Andrew Goudie, "The Changing Human Impact," in L. Friday & R. Laskie (Eds.), (1989), *The fragile environment* (Cambridge: Cambridge University Press).

3. J. Tuxill (1999) uses the figure 1,000 per year. Norman Myers, in his speech at Eco Ed, an international conference on Environment and Development held in Toronto, October, 1992, estimated 27,000 per year.

4. These distinctions from Judith Rees are discussed in S. Libiszewski (1992).

REFERENCES

Bertell, R. (1999). Gulf War Veterans and Depleted Uranium. In *Depleted Uranium: A Post-War Disaster for Environment and Health*. Amsterdam: Laka Foundation.

Bertell, R. (1983). Early war victims of World War III: Testimony at 1983 Nuremburg Tribunal. *Breakthrough, 5* (1).

Bertell, R. (1984). The Health of the Oceans. *Breakthrough, 5* (4).

Bertell, R. (1985). *No immediate danger: Prognosis for a radioactive Earth*. Summertown, TN: The Book Publishing Company.

Bertell, R. (1986). An Appeal for the Marshall Islands. *Breakthrough, 7* (3) 28–29.

Boulding, K. (1978). *Stable peace*. Austin, TX: University of Texas Press.

Brown, L. (1998). The future of growth. In L. Brown, C. Flavin, & H. French (Eds.), *State of the World 1998: A Worldwatch Institute report on progress toward a sustainable society* (pp. 3–20). New York: W.W. Norton & Company.

Brown, L., & Flavin, C. (1999). A new economy for a new century. In L. Brown, C. Flavin, & H. French (Eds.), *State of the World, 1999: A Worldwatch Institute report on progress toward a sustainable society* (pp. 3–21). New York: W.W. Norton & Company.

Center for Defense Information (CDI). (1989). Defending the environment: The record of the U.S. military. *The Defense Monitor, 18* (6).

Depleted uranium: A post-war disaster for environment and health. (1999). Amsterdam: Laka Foundation.

Fahey, D. (1999). Depleted uranium weapons: Lessons from the 1991 Gulf War. In *Depleted Uranium: A Post-War Disaster for Environment and Health*. Amsterdam: Laka Foundation.

Goudie, A. (1989). The changing human impact. In L. Friday & R. Laskie (Eds.), *The fragile environment* (pp. 1–21). Cambridge: Cambridge University Press.

Homer-Dixon, T., & Blitt, J. (1998). Ecoviolence: Links among environment, population, and security. Lanham, MD: Rowman & Littlefield.

Libiszewski, S. (1992, July). What is Environmental Conflict? *Occasional Paper No. 1, Environment and Conflicts Project (ENCOP)*. Center for Security Studies and Conflict Research, Swiss Federal Institute of Technology, Zurich, Switzerland.

MacNeill, J., Winsemius, P., & Yakushiji, T. (1991). *Beyond interdependence: The meshing of the world's economy and the Earth's ecology*. Oxford: Oxford University Press.

Mische, P. M. (1989, Summer/Fall). Ecological security in an interdependent world. *Breakthrough*. 7–17. New York: Global Education Associates.

Mische, P. M. (1989, October). Ecological security and the need to reconceptualize sovereignty. *Alternatives, 14* (4), 389–427.

Mische, P. M. (1991a). The Earth as peace teacher. In E. Boulding, C. Brigagao, & K. Clements (Eds.), *Peace, culture, and society: Transnational research and dialog* (pp. 133–145). Boulder, Co.: Westview Press.

Mische, P. M. (1991b). *Perceptions of social justice as a variable affecting conflict or co-operation, war or peace in a social system: The 1986 people's revolt in the*

Philippines as a case study (Ph.D. diss.). New York: Columbia University Teachers College.

Mische, P. M. (1992a). Toward a pedagogy of ecological responsibility. *Convergence: Journal of the International Council for Adult Education, 25* (2), 9–25.

Mische, P. M. (1992b). National sovereignty and international environmental law. In S. Bilderbeek (Ed.), *Biodiversity and international law* (pp. 105-114). Amsterdam: IOS Press.

Mische, P. M. (1992c). Security through defending the environment. In E. Boulding (Ed.), *New agendas for peace research* (pp. 103-120). Boulder, CO: Lynne Rienner Publishers.

Mische, P. M. (1993). Ecological factors in war, peace, and global security. *Viewpoint*, 3–16. The Wisconsin Institute: A consortium for the Study of War, Peace and Global Cooperation.

Mische, P. M. (1994, Fall). Peace and ecological security. *Peace Review, 6* (3), 275–284.

Mische, P. M. (1995). Ecological security in a new world order: Some linkages between ecology, peace and global security. In *Non-Military Aspects of International Security* (pp 155-195). Paris: UNESCO, 1995.

Mische, P. M. (1998). *Ecological security and the United Nations system: Past, present future.* New York: Global Education Associates.

Nye, J. Jr. (1993, February). A cloud that lingers. *World Monitor, 30.*

Quammen, D. (1999, October). Planet of weeds: Tallying the losses of Earth's animals and plants. *Harper's Magazine,* 57–69.

Science for Peace. (1992). *Taking stock: The impact of militarism on the environment.* Preliminary report. Vancouver, 1992.

Starr, J. (1991, Spring). Water wars. *Foreign Policy,* No. 82, 17–36.

Tuxill, J. (1999). Appreciating the benefits of plant biodiversity. In L. Brown, C. Flavin, & H. French (Eds.), *State of the World 1999: A Worldwatch Institute report on progress toward a sustainable society* (pp. 96-114). New York: W. W. Norton & Company.

Westing, A. (Ed.). (1986). *Global resources and international conflict.* Oxford: Oxford University Press.

CHAPTER 2

Contextual Sustainability Education

Towards an Integrated Educational Framework for Social and Ecological Peace

Frans C. Verhagen

Our individual self finds its most complex realization within our family self, our community self, our species self, our earthly self, and eventually our Universe self.

—Swimme & Berry (1992, p. 268)

Pulitzer prizewinning journalist Ross Gelbspan (1998) notes that throughout history, it has been philosophers, religious leaders, and revolutionaries who have asked us to "reexamine our relationships, our purposes, and the way we live," but that "now we are being asked by the oceans" (p. 171). Certainly, the present sorry state of Nature that is characteristic of the "Petroleum Interval" in the Earth's history, particularly the global warming of her atmosphere with its rising ocean levels, extreme weather conditions, excessive droughts and floods, melting glaciers and reduced crop yields, leaves humankind no choice except to re-examine all aspects of its habitation on this planet as a matter of great urgency.

Since the early 1970s environmental education (EE) has responded in various ways to this urgent need, as is evidenced, for example, in the histories of the member organizations of the North American Environmental Education Association (Archie & McCrea, 1996; Palmer, 1998). However, it is only in the last decade that sustainability education (SE) emerged as an alternative to these earlier responses. Its earliest history can be traced back to sustainability theory in international development, which found its earliest expression in the 1970 Club of Rome's publication *Limits to Growth* (Meadows, Randers, & Behrens III, 1972). Presently, there are many types of sustainability education. Some cover a set of *topics* to promote an understanding of sustainability, (e.g., Lawrence Hall of Science, 2000); others aim to teach *behavioral change* for sustainable living (e.g., VanMatre, 1990).

This chapter will present yet another approach to sustainability education, that is, contextual sustainability education (CSE). In contrast to the above approaches, CSE is *a conceptual framework* that is intended to guide both environmental and peace education in efforts to respond to the social and ecological problems and challenges of our times. As a *framework for peace and sustainability education*, CSE is based upon the premise that the integrity of the natural world is not one issue among many, but the comprehensive frame of all, without which social peace cannot be achieved. However, it also recognizes that ecological sustainability—the integrity of the natural world—can be achieved only within the context of a society whose norms are defined by social justice, active nonviolence and participatory decision making. As an *educational framework*, CSE is based upon the notion from critical pedagogy that "education is not neutral" but operates within a system of prevailing powers that establish "official knowledge" (Freire, 1970; Steiner, Krank, McLaren, & Bahruth, 2000; Apple, 2001). Therefore, CSE challenges the existing anthropocentric assumptions that underlie contemporary education, emphasizing the need for a biocentric orientation that makes the human species a member of the web of life, not its master or, even, its manager. It provides an alternative to the neoconservative and neoliberal philosophies that are still dominant in many societies and their educational systems (Apple, 2001).

The chapter will describe the components of the CSE framework—its ideological foundations and value concepts—and outline a strategy for incorporating it into the curriculum of formal educational institutions, particularly those of the middle grades in public schools in North America. It is hoped that it will be a contribution to the political task of educators to care skillfully for our shared world by placing education within the sustainability debate and education for sustainability at the center of the education debate.

CSE FOUNDATIONS AND VALUE CONTENT

Ideological Foundations

Ideologies, according to Van Dijk (1999), are the "basic frameworks for organizing the social cognitions shared by members of social groups, organizations, institutions" and as such they "mentally represent the basic social characteristics of a group, such as their identity, tasks, goals, norms, values, position, and resources"

(p. 18). Whether they are explicitly or implicitly adhered to or not, ideologies provide the foundation for educational theories, frameworks, curricula, school administration and, even, school architecture. Their influence in education is recognized by C. A. Bowers (1997) who recommends that "rethinking the ideological foundations of education" should be an essential first step in educational renewal. Similarly, D. W. Orr (1994) notes that reformers of problems in education often fail to identify and resolve the problem of education itself because they do not recognize how education is also subject to a community of often implicit assumptions. The following makes explicit the ideological basis of the CSE framework.

A Universe Story for the 21st Century. Throughout human history questions of origin and purpose have been raised and answered in order to bring meaning to human existence. Local religions, some of which developed into world religions, have answered most of these questions in their creation stories, which can be considered to constitute their cosmologies or meaning systems. In the prescientific age, knowledge of natural processes was scant. Therefore, these religious answers were satisfactory; the cosmologies were functional. However, cosmologies based exclusively on insights from world religions are no longer functional for contemporary times. A literal understanding of the Adam and Eve story as an explanation of the origin of natural and human life on Earth may have been acceptable in premodern times, but it falls short in the face of the theory of evolution. To be relevant and functional, a contemporary cosmology should include insights derived from scientific advancement, especially from the fields of astrophysics and evolutionary biology.

Essential to such a functional cosmology is "a sense of *cosmogenesis*," that is, of an unfolding rather than a static cosmos (Swimme & Berry, 1992, p. 2–3). It is only in modern times through the advances in the space and biological sciences that we have begun to develop such a time-developmental mode of consciousness, experiencing time as an evolutionary sequence of irreversible transformations. Until the present, human cultures have experienced and celebrated Nature's seasonal changes in a spatial mode of consciousness, experiencing time as ever-renewing seasonal cycles. However, now we know that the unfolding of the Universe started with the Big Bang, which evolved into galaxies, solar systems, planets. We are able to date the sequence of these cosmological events and trace the evolution of life, which has resulted in an astounding biological and cultural diversity on planet Earth. These scientific achievements have changed our mode of consciousness and our understanding of the role of the human species, which should now be defined within this evolutionary sequence. That is, unlike earlier cosmologies which placed humans at the top rung of the hierarchical ladder of beings (the Scala Naturae), which they were expected to dominate—in the Adam and

Eve story humans were to name the animals, a clear sign of dominance—now humans are considered part of an evolutionary process and members of the Unity of All Beings (Swimme & Berry, 1992; Lonergan & Richards, 1988).[1] As members of this web of life, they are no longer to manage and exploit the Earth, but to manage *with* the Earth and assist, support, and strengthen the Earth's cycling of matter, webbing of life and flow of energy (Susskind, 2000).

Educational Implications. The notion of cosmogenesis has important educational implications for student identity development. Besides their social identities based on gender, ethnicity, and social-economic status, students should be guided in the development of an ecological identity—a planetary and a cosmic self, based, respectively, upon their status as Earthlings and fellow inhabitants of the Universe. They should learn that they are part of an evolving Earth and an evolving Universe; they are "star stuff" given that the hydrogen and helium gases of the earlier Universe have chemically combined in the formation of their own bodies. Educational curricula should aim to help them understand the complexity of their individual identities. As the B. Swimme and T. Berry (1992) quotation (p. 1) points out, our individual identity is realized "within our family self, our community self, our species self, our earthly self, and eventually our Universe self"(p. 268). (For similar views see Thomashow, 1996; Naess, 1989). Second, the notion of cosmogenesis suggests that students be helped to understand the dynamic and evolutionary nature of all reality, that is, how evolution takes place biologically, chemically, geologically and how this dynamic is also at work in human culture and in a person's maturing process. This view of reality greatly differs from the predominantly static view of reality that is reflected in creationism or intelligent design formulations and extends our understanding of evolution beyond the notion of biological evolution on planet Earth. Rather, natural, social, and personal life are presented as one interrelated evolving reality with a cosmic dimension.

A Biocentric Worldview. A biocentric worldview places the Earth's webbing of life, her cycling of matter, and flow of energy in a central position. Human life is derivative, for it depends on those three life-support processes. Humans are considered a member of the web of life, and together with other life forms constitute the Earth community. Their task is not to subjugate or even manage Nature, but to manage with Nature (Botkin, 1990). Such a biocentric consciousness is often present in primal peoples' philosophies of which most Native American cultures are a part. Chief Seattle's often quoted statement is an example, that is, "We did not weave the web of life; we are only a strand in it." It also appears in the Biophilia theory, which emphasizes the innateness of humans to Nature (Wilson, 1996), the ecological unconscious theory, which considers the Earth to be inscribed in us (Roszak, 1993), the affinity for life theory (Orr, 1994).

Educational Implications. Placing the Earth's rather than humanity's well-being at the center of learning and instruction will, first of all, require the re-purposing of present learning and instruction: predominantly anthropocentric goals that focus on human welfare should be substituted by biocentric goals that place the well-being of planet Earth and all her life forms first.[2] Second, approaches to the teaching of the various school subjects will need to be changed. For example, in social studies, economics, and technology classes, notions of success, progress, and growth should be redefined to take planetary well-being into account. Students should be led to understand the limitations of the GNP as a measurement of economic progress and to consider Earth productivity measures, such as increases/decreases in fish stocks, in top soil, in grasslands . . . as an alternative (Berry, 1990) and to discuss the contents of a General Progress Index, which places greater emphasis on planetary well-being than do the anthropocentrically oriented indices of human development, happiness or well-being. In this way, they could come to understand that human health is not possible on a sick planet and that economic activities are to be subservient to the ecological requirements of a healthy planet, an understanding that is in opposition to the still prevailing neo-classical economic systems where ecological considerations take a secondary place (Prugh, Constanza, & Daly, 2000).

In a language arts class, an educator can contrast biocentrically oriented metaphors, for example, Nature as web and Nature as mother, with anthropocentrically oriented metaphors, for example, Nature as a machine and as a storehouse. These can be subjected to critical scrutiny to show how they suggest different views of the Earth and of humans' relationship with her. The relationship with the Earth implied by everyday expressions, such as "killing two birds with one stone," which are anthropocentric in meaning, can also be the focus of student discussion, leading to the identification of substitute words that express less violence to Nature. The language arts curriculum can also introduce biocentric ways of marking the term *Earth*, for example, through capitalizing the term, referring to Earth as a "she" or a "her." (More advanced ways of marking can be found on www.ecolinguistics.org.).

Bioregional Environmentalism. Bioregional environmentalism is the third ideological component of the CSE framework. According to Canadian political scientist Robert Paehlke (1989), who has tracked the history of the main political theories in North America over the last two centuries, environmentalism is emerging as the organizing principle of societies in the twenty-first century.

Though theories of environmentalism vary in their emphases, all have in common the premise that the integrity of the natural environment is not one issue among many, but as noted earlier, the comprehensive frame for all other issues. They also agree that societies are to be organized on the principle of Earth wellbeing because all life, including human life, depends upon the maintenance and restoration of the Earth's life-support processes and services.

Bioregional environmentalism adds the notion that humans are to be living within the opportunities and limits of their local biophysical region, that is, the region that is typically determined by its watershed. Long-range planning, according to bioregionalists, is to be done on the basis of maintaining and strengthening the watershed rather than on the level of political jurisdictions of a state, county, or city, which often have come about by the vagaries of history. Examples of such planning are the operations of the Oregon Watershed Councils or New York City's watershed policies (Prugh et al., 2000). Another aspect of bioregional planning and living is the reliance on local staples rather than their importation from distant areas with the resulting increase in pollution and reduction of strength of local economies. For example, apples grown locally should not be imported from elsewhere simply because an ecologically inefficient pricing system has made them cheaper to buy. Living bioregionally also means that the inhabitants of the watershed acquire a sense of place. This not only includes an awareness and appreciation of the geological features of the watershed, but also of the flora and fauna of the region and of the local cultural heritage which is based upon these biophysical features. (See Berry, 1990; Traina & Darley-Hill, 1995; Sale, 1991; Smith & Williams, 1999 for bioregional awareness indices).

Educational Implications. Education based on bioregional environmentalism would assist students in developing a sense of place. To this end, emphasis would be placed on understanding and appreciating the immediate surroundings of the bioregion and on maintaining and, as will often be the case, restoring the local watershed. It would also mean helping students to become rooted in the region, proudly making it part of their identities. (For recent examples of such bioregional education, see Springer, 1994; Lappe & Lappe, 2000; www.csf.org).

It must be emphasized that bioregional education is not intended to be education for chauvinism, ethnocentrism, isolation, or autarchy, all forms of education in which local issues are not connected with national and global concerns. Authentic bioregionally oriented education should be like a local ecological system, which is linked to larger ecosystems and, in final instance, with the Earth's total ecosystem. In the same way, education that emphasizes a sense of place would help students to learn about the causes and consequences of local social and ecological problems and challenges and to connect these to their national and global counterparts. It would be global in scope. Bioregional education would also prepare students for critical action and engagement. While learning to "think globally," they would also be encouraged to "act locally" by joining locally or electronically based organizations that work to promote a bioregional vision of sustainability. In thus linking social and ecological problems and challenges, and in encouraging action to respond to them, students will be more motivated and an already cooperative school climate strengthened, perhaps even resulting in higher scores on standardized tests. (See Lieberman, 1998 for test outcomes in EIC (Environment in Context) Schools.)

Value Content

In agreement with an increasing number of educators, who acknowledge that education is not value free (e.g., Freire, 1970; Apple, 2001), the second main component of the CSE framework consists of four values: ecological sustainability, social justice, active nonviolence and participatory decision making. These four values, which interact dynamically, will be defined and explained in terms of what they imply for human relationships and extended, where practicable, to the Earth-human relationships. Selected illustrations related to food will suggest how youngsters in the middle grades can be helped to understand and appreciate these values as guides to action.

Ecological Sustainability. Ecological sustainability is defined, here, as the ability of the Earth and all her life to survive and thrive by maintaining and strengthening the dynamic integrity of her cycling of matter, webbing of life, and flow of energy. It is the core value of the CSE framework.

Applied to an economy, ecological sustainability implies that it (the economy) function in support of the environment and that environmental factors take a leading role in economic decision making (Chambers, Simmons, & Wackernagel, 2001, p. 5–7). This view stands in contrast to anthropocentric views in the technocratic sustainability literature, which consider sustainable (economic) development as meeting "the needs of the present without compromising the ability of future generations to meet their own needs" (WCED, 1987).[3] Ecological economists (Elkington, 1998; Daly, 1996; Hawken, 1993 and other members of the International Society of Ecological Economists) have pointed to the three minimum requirements of economies that are necessary to sustain the Earth's life-supporting processes. That is, an economy should not use up all the resources that the global ecosystem provides or undermine the delivery by the Earth of her ecological services of photosynthesis, atmospheric gas regulation, climate and water regulation, soil formation, and pest control. Nor should an economy overwhelm the waste-absorbing capacity of the Earth (Prugh et al., 2000). These minimum requirements are further elaborated in the Earth Charter[4] which advocates that we protect and restore the integrity of Earth's ecological systems, with special concern for biological diversity and the natural processes that sustain life (principle 5); prevent harm as the best method of environmental protection and, when knowledge is limited, apply a precautionary approach (principle 6); adopt patterns of production, consumption, and reproduction that safeguard Earth's regenerative capacities, human rights, and community well-being (principle 7) ; and advance the study of ecological sustainability and promote the open exchange and wide application of the knowledge acquired (Principle 8).[5] Ecological sustainability also includes the notion of a thriving planet. That is, it is not sufficient to ensure that the Earth's life-support processes are not diminished; they must also be strengthened. In their story of cosmogenesis, Swimme and Berry (1992) refer to this latter notion as celebration, referring to the Universe as "a single, multiform, sequential, celebratory event" (p. 264).

The following are suggestive of educational activities that can be used to help urban pre-adolescents understand and experience ecological sustainability.[6] *Pictures* of dead zones caused by the runoff of pesticides and nitrates, as the leftovers of nitrogen fertilizers (e.g., in the Gulf of Mexico) and pictures of clear rivers near organic farms with no pesticides or fertilizers can be used to introduce the differences between unsustainable and sustainable agriculture. Students can, then, be asked to read *case studies* of farmers who stopped productivist agriculture and went to multifunctional or sustainable agriculture (See case studies in Lappe & Lappe, 2002). Questions based on these accounts could have students determine how the two approaches to farming were different; the difficulties the farmers faced in each case; the results of both approaches and why farmers chose these different approaches.

A third activity would be to have students work in groups to prepare a *report on one of the major food sources*, for example, agriculture, animal husbandry, aquaculture, and genetically modified food production, indicating what it is, who owns it, and how it is financed. Group reports would be followed by a discussion of the extent to which each food source is ecologically sustainable, and as a way of demonstrating their learning the groups could draw a concept map, schematically representing the relationships between the various aspects of the food sources they had researched. Finally, students can be asked to identify two places from which they may purchase food in their neighborhood, to research the source of this food and determine its sustainability (i.e., of the food source).[7]

Social Justice. Social justice is a value that refers to the right relations between humans in their various social groupings be they based upon income, gender, geography, race, religion. Right relations means upholding the rights of all, without discrimination, to a natural and social environment supportive of a human quality of life. Generally, when these relations refer to fair sharing of resources, they are called distributive or economic justice; to non-discriminatory siting of major polluting or NIMBY (Not in My BackYard) facilities, environmental justice[8]; to fair decision making in the distribution of those resources, democratic justice.

There has been a clear progression in the refinement of our understanding of the relationship between social justice and ecological sustainability. In 1975, the Nairobi Assembly of the World Council of Churches included in its principles of environmental action the promotion of a "sustainable, just, and participatory society." The World Conservation Union's (IUCN, 1987) report, "Conservation With Equity," and NGO contributions at the 1992 Earth Summit emphasized the value of sufficiency as a standard for organized sharing and noted that basic floors and definite ceilings should be set for equitable and "fair" consumption, arguing that the Earth is able to provide for everyone's need, but not for everyone's greed, a norm reflected in the often-quoted statement: "Live simply, so that others can simply live." Social justice was extended from fairness in consumption to fairness in decision making about consumption by D. Hessel (cited in Dernbach, 2002), who points to the need for "Socially just *participation* (author's italics) in decisions about how to obtain sustenance and to manage community life for the good in common and the good of the commons" (p. 596–7). Finally, according to the Earth Charter March 2000 benchmark draft, the eradication of poverty should be considered an ethical, social, and environmental imperative (Principle 9) and economic activities and institutions at all levels should promote human development in an equitable and sustainable manner (Principle 10). Thus, social justice has developed from the notions of distributive justice and sufficiency to that of democratic justice and, most recently, to the notion of integrated social justice where equity and sustainability are considered essential.

Again, examples related to food can be used to help youngsters understand the different types of social justice. To introduce students to the notion of *economic justice,* a large pizza pie can be brought into the class by the teacher and students divided into two groups representing the North or high-income countries (20% of the students in the class) and the South or low-income countries (80% of the students in the class). Then, the pizza is divided in two parts, 80% of the pizza going to the North or high income countries, which only make up 20% of the world population and the remaining 20% going to the South or low-income countries which make up 80% of the world population. Student groups could first discuss how they feel about the apportionment of the food and why. Reports of their small group discussions should be shared with the whole class. Using ideas provided by students, the teacher could then lead a class discussion to help students clarify their understanding of economic justice. Students can also consider the apportionment of the pizza pie from a local level. Are there groups in their local community that would receive the smaller piece of pizza? the larger piece? In a final exercise in this introduction to the notion of economic justice, student groups can be asked to discuss why food is distributed inequitably, whether the uneven distribution and access to food is acceptable and if not, to list the reasons why.

To help students develop an understanding of *environmental injustice*, they can be asked to identify sites in their community where food-processing plants are located or where food-related toxic wastes have been dumped. Working in groups they can find out why/how this came to be. These local case studies can then be used as a basis for a discussion on environmental justice and on ways to redress this local injustice. (See the section on participatory decision making for an example of how students can be introduced to the notion of democratic justice.)

Active Nonviolence. Active nonviolence refers to the resistance toward social and ecological evils in order to reduce or remove them. A total of over 250 forms of nonviolent protest have been identified.[9] These include marches, boycotts, picketing, sit-ins, and prayer vigils. In his advice to the antiglobalization movement—many people prefer to emphasize the movement's positive goals and label it the social justice movement—David Cortright (2002) emphasizes the importance of nonviolent action in demonstrations and other forms of assertive action, pointing out that it ensures morality of action and generates political support. According to Cortright:

> The choice of nonviolence should not be left to chance. It must be integrated into every element of the global justice movement. It should be publicly proclaimed as the movement's guiding principle and method. . . . The most radical and effective forms of social action are those that heighten the contrast between the just demands of the global justice movement and the brutal actions of the police. Only by preserving nonviolent discipline can the movement occupy and hold the moral high ground and win political support for necessary social change. (p. 13-4)

Nonviolent action changes the consciousness of persons and organizations involved as became evident in the civil rights movement in the United States (www.thekingcenter.com). By exercising self-control and not engaging in violent responses to the various forms of discrimination, black Americans gained self-esteem and strength. Their changed consciousness gradually changed the consciousness of those in power, both locally and federally. The latter were forced to reflect on the nonviolent strength and courage of the black population and came to recognize the injustices that had been perpetrated upon their fellow Americans.

Examples that show how social violence leads to ecological degradation abound though the connection does not seem to be usually made in the peace education literature (cf. for example, Steger & Ling, 1999; www.thekingcenter.com). Wars are probably the most dramatic examples, and while their short-term ecological effects are directly and immediately observable, their long-term effects are not. Consider, for example, the future consequences on the land, water, and air of the depleted uranium tipped bombs used in the war on Kosovo, including the unloading of unused bombs in the Adriatic sea as planes returned from Kosovo to Italy. Social violence on a smaller scale, such as conflicts between neighborhood gangs, can also have adverse impacts on the local ecology, when, as a result of these fights, arson increases air pollution, or the dumping of undesirable objects in the local waters increases water pollution. Violent behavior among humans both during war and nonwar situations may also lead to cruelty to animals, who are part of the local ecology. The Earth Charter's principle 15 reminds us that violence towards animals should be avoided and that all living beings are to be treated with respect and consideration.

Teaching students the skills necessary to resolve conflicts nonviolently is one approach to teaching active nonviolence. Many schools in the United States of America have *programs in conflict resolution* to reduce fighting and violence among students. Students, faculty, and parents are trained to make these programs work, as is the case with the STOP program of Educators for Social Responsibility. Students can also study the civil rights movement in the United States of America and the *Gandhi independence movement* in India and evaluate its effectiveness. A third example would be to *study food riots*. Students can analyze cases of food riots to consider their effectiveness in the short and long term. They may then devise a role-play of the situations that led to a food riot devising a nonviolent approach to resolving the problem. The debriefing after the role plays should also include a discussion of the potential short- and long-term effects of active nonviolence to resolving the problem.

Participatory Decision Making. Participatory decision making ensures that all stakeholders in a particular issue are represented in a fair and effective way. As noted earlier, participatory decision making is a form of democratic justice. The Earth Charter's principle 13 lists the following characteristics of a fair and effective decision-making process. It refers to the need for transparency and accountability in governance, for access to justice and the need to eliminate corruption in all public and private institutions; the right of everyone to clear and timely information; freedom of opinion, expression, peaceful assembly, association, and dissent; and effective and efficient access to administrative and independent judicial review. The benefits of participatory decision making are many. It builds companionship, trust, cohesion, and unity. It leads to a readiness to dialogue, to openness in listening, and by using the insights and abilities of many, it will often produce a better result.

The process of participatory decision making depends very much on the culture and the approach to socioeconomic development of a particular society. In large nation-states in Western societies, such decision making mostly takes place by representative government while smaller jurisdictions, such as the Cantons in Switzerland, are able to achieve this in direct assembly. In non-Western agricultural societies, participatory decision making can take place in a great variety of ways. An Ashanti chief in Ghana, who consults with his elders, is one example. Having an assembly of villagers together in a long house in Sumatra to decide issues of social or ecological importance is another. Whatever the cultural form for decision making, however, to be participatory the process must take into account the characteristics outlined by the Earth Charter's principle 13 (p. 63), and the outcome must benefit all the stakeholders. As for participatory decision making on a global level, one can look to the United Nations. There 191 member states in the hundreds of UN and UN-affiliated agencies struggle to decide how best to develop international processes and institutions to ensure a sustainable future for planet and people. Borrowing from Barber's concept of strong democracy, T. Prugh, R. Constanza, and H. Daly (2000) argue that local politics or civic engagement on the local level is the best preparation for decision making on a global scale in respect to sustainable future issues.

Participatory decision making is generally considered to take place only among humans, but according to CSE, all living creatures have the right to participate in the decision-making process in matters pertaining to their well-being. This form of participatory decision making is called "biocratic" (Berry, 1990). The Endangered Species Act is an example of biocracy in that the law is giving an endangered species the right to be heard (to vote) through the voices of its protectors (Daly & Cobb, 1989; Steger & Ling, 1999).

Case studies of communal approaches to food production, access, and distribution, which highlight participatory decision making in communities in various continents in overcoming hunger and landlessness can be used to help students understand the meaning and value of participatory decision making. They can serve as the basis for developing role-plays, which would provide students experience in joint decision making and an understanding of democratic justice. Debriefing after the role-plays would consider the advantages of participatory decision making. Further discussion would have students imagine the consequences should certain groups involved in the stories and the role plays not be given an equal opportunity. The micro-credit movement of the Grameen Bank in

Bangladesh, the preservation of seed ownership by the Navdanya movement in India, the green consumer campaign by the Co-op America organization, the banning or at least the labeling of genetically modified foods by many Vermont towns in their Annual Town Meetings (www.ise.org) provide the basis for such role plays (Lappe & Lappe 2002).

THE CONTEXTUAL SUSTAINABILITY EDUCATION FRAMEWORK

The ideological foundations and value concepts that constitute the CSE framework are schematically represented in figure 2.1 in three concentric circles that show the relationship among the values and between the values and the foundations. Ecological sustainability is in the inner circle. It is surrounded by the other three values in the second circle to indicate that ecological sustainability is the core value but that it can only be realized in the context of a society characterized by its supportive values—social justice, active nonviolence, and participatory decision making. The three ideological foundations, cosmogenesis, biocentrism, and bioregionalism, are located in the outer ring to indicate that the four values are to be rooted in these foundational beliefs.

FIGURE 2.1
Contextual Sustainability Education (CSE)

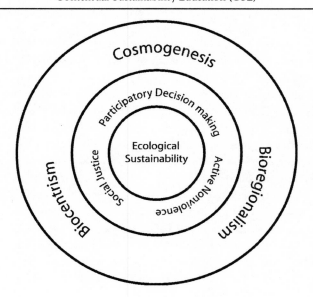

IMPLEMENTING CONTEXTUAL SUSTAINABILITY EDUCATION

While the activities described above can be organized by individual teachers, in order for CSE to be integrated into the curriculum of a school district in a coherent and systematic fashion, a trans-disciplinary standard is necessary.

Rationale

While the United States has been the forerunner in setting standards in education (Sacks, 1999; U.S. Department of Education, 2002), it seems that the adoption of standards in education is now spreading to many other countries. Standards provide teachers with guidelines for organizing the main contents of the curriculum and for determining the levels of performance to be achieved in those content areas. For the latter purpose, standards are translated into rubrics that spell out in great detail the required components of a project or program. Used as a measure of educational progress, standards also provide school systems with a basis for making schools accountable. Progress is usually measured by high-stakes tests, which, together with other assessment measures, determine whether students are below the standard, approaching the standard, meeting the standard, or exceeding the standard and, therefore, whether or not they can be promoted. Increasingly, these tests include more free response questions than multiple choice questions which far better measure a student's understanding of a particular topic. Teachers are mandated to teach according to those standards that are specific to their particular subject area, though often with little curriculum support and staff development. As a result and because of an overemphasis on high-stakes tests, teachers "teach to the tests" overusing review books and sample tests rather than engaging in education for critical thinking and action that leads to an informed and involved citizenry.

Notwithstanding this ever widening use (and abuse) of standards, veteran standards expert Robert J. Marzano (cited in Scherer, 2001) and others have pointed out that there is a lack of "focus and coherence" in the present standards. From the perspective of CSE, this may be because technical standards in the subject areas are not related to the broader social and ecological issues that challenge our society now and in the future. The challenge, therefore, is to develop a coherent set of standards that are organized according to a principle that is able to make this link and to provide students with an understanding of these issues as they relate to and are manifest in the various subject areas that make up the school curriculum. To some extent this challenge is met by the Applied Learning standards and by STS (Science, Technology and Society) modules that relate subject-specific standards to society. However, they lack a wider vision, are often only tangentially covered in a school's curriculum, and not systematically included in tests. As for the programs that were and are developed by the U.S. Global Change Research Program (Mortensen, 2000), however laudable, they are outside a school's curriculum and do not possess a strong cohesive framework that integrates social and ecological realities.

What is needed, therefore, is a transdisciplinary standard that will enable students to make those links, both intellectually, affectively, and behaviorally. The CSE framework could bring such focus and coherence to the standards movement providing it with direction, motivation and inspiration. Unlike the pragmatic approach recommended by some whereby one is advised to relate environmental education instruction to standards now required by the schools (Bentley, 1998), CSE is presented as an overarching standard—a comprehensive frame for the other standards, providing an integrated perspective on social and ecological values by which students can critically assess past, present, and future events, processes, technologies presented by the specific standards in the subject area.

The Standard

Formulated for the middle grades, the CSE standard reads as follows. Students will

1. develop an understanding of the connections between social and ecological processes and events;

2. become aware of their assumptions about social and ecological issues and of the values that underlie those assumptions;

3. be able to critically assess the benefits and/or ill effects on society and the environment of biocentric and anthropocentric worldviews;

4. recognize and appreciate their identity as Earth and Universe beings, that is, their ecological selves;

5. assess events, trends, technologies, and actions, using the values of ecological sustainability, social justice, active nonviolence and participatory decision making to determine their adverse or beneficial impacts on the well-being of planet, people, and other species and their contribution to social and ecological peace;

6. develop and apply a vision of socially and ecologically sustainable futures based upon the five values that directs their basic decisions in respect to personal, economic, and political matters.

The placement of the CSE standard in a particular curriculum is important. Subject matter in middle schools is organized either in an integrated curriculum with team teaching and block scheduling or in a subject-specific curriculum with the school day broken down into short periods devoted to one subject area. In either type of curriculum, the CSE standard should be the introductory standard. However, in a school with an integrated curriculum, where teachers jointly devise their curriculum units based upon the standards in their particular areas, there is more likely to be a need for a common framework or organizing principle that would make their collaboration more effective. Thus, the CSE standard is more likely to be adopted and implemented at the beginning of units of learning in such schools than in schools with subject-specific curricula. Of course, if a school's mission statement were structured on the basis of the CSE framework, teaching to the CSE standard would be greatly facilitated however the curriculum is organized.

The name of the standard is also important. It must be labeled in terms that clearly reflect its content. With this in mind the CSE standard could be labeled as "Envisioning a Sustainable Future," "The Sustainability and Peace (S&P) Standard," "The Earth and Peace Literacy (EPL) Standard." The latter label has been used by the author for several years and is the basis for a module he has developed for the beginning of the school year (Verhagen, 1999).

Each standard consists of content, curriculum support, and methods of assessment (American Federation of Teachers, 2001). The *content* of the CSE standard is based on the foundations and values described in earlier sections of this chapter. They, in turn, determine its learning objectives, that is, having students (1) understand the Universe story and its implications for their identity, (2) develop a biocentric worldview, and (3) understand how to live bioregionally.

A second major learning objective would be to help students develop an understanding of each of the values, their behavioral and affective implications and the reciprocal nature of ecological sustainability *and* social justice, active nonviolence and participatory decision making. Thirdly, as suggested by the UNESCO work plan of 1997, they should learn to use these values to envision "alternative ways of development and living, evaluating alternative visions, learning how to negotiate and justify choices between visions" (Mortensen, 2000, p. 34).

Curriculum support for the CSE standard should provide a selection of topics related to the components of the framework. (For lists of such topics, see, for example, Chiras, 1994; Huckle & Sterling, 1996; Sitarz, 1998; Verhagen, 1999; Wheeler & Bijur, 2000; Tilbury, Stevenson, Fien, & Schreuder, 2002; the many links on the website of the Sustainability Education Center <www.sustained.org>). The CSE standard would utilize the "process of interactional discovery" as a *method of assessment*, that is, students' oral interaction in class and their written reflections in a journal (Dawson cited in Jacobs & Jacobs-Spencer, 2001). In addition, their achievement could be further assessed by administering a survey at the beginning of the school year and one at the end, the comparison of which would be a more scientific way of determining the impact of the CSE standard upon their thinking and affect.

Working Through Major Educational Organizations

To implement the CSE standard in the middle grades it is essential to work through national or local organizations dealing with teacher accreditation, middle schools and the various subject areas such as science, language arts, and so forth.

Teacher Accreditation Organizations. In the United States it is the task of the National Council for the Accreditation of Teacher Education (NCATE) to set standards according to which a teacher education department is evaluated and accredited. NCATE's membership includes national organizations of colleges, teacher unions, and specialty organizations, such as the North American Association of Environmental Education (NAAEE).

Among the six standards it uses for institutional accreditation, it emphasizes the importance of the one that deals with the "conceptual framework(s)" which an institution has to develop. This standard could serve as an entry point for the inclusion of the CSE framework, which could then spell out a teacher's ecological responsibilities and provide a framework for course development. Thus, the standard would enhance NCATE's "Vision for a Professional Teacher for the 21st Century" which defines a professional teacher as one who has developed the knowledge and skills "to succeed as a *responsible citizen* (author's italics) and a contributor to the new economy" (NCATE, 2002, p. 4).

National Middle Schools Associations or Federations. In the United States, the organization that deals with middle schools is called the "National Middle School Association (NMSA)." Its website (www.nmsa.org) reports that it has over 30,000 members representing principals, teachers, central office personnel, professors, college students, parents, community leaders, and educational consultants across the United States, Canada, and 45 other countries. NMSA "welcomes and provides support to anyone interested in the health and education of young adolescents". Its list of publications contains a Watershed document for integrative learning (Springer, 1994), which could serve as a basis for introducing the CSE framework.

Standard Setting Committees of Professional Organizations. The principal national professional organizations of teachers engaged in the teaching of science, math, language arts, social studies have standard-setting committees which employ a draft consultation process to develop their particular standards, both content and performance standards. A minimalist way to participate in their drafting processes is to present comments, particularly by pointing to the need for a standard that can bring coherence among the often long lists of subject-specific standards. A middle way is to make presentations at the conferences of their professional organizations, so that members themselves can either engage in drafting or in commenting on a CSE standard. A maximalist approach is to become a member of the consultation draft committee and actually engage in negotiating an introductory CSE standard.

CONCLUSION

To restate the challenge issued at the beginning of the chapter, the state of the Planet requires that we reconsider our relationships, our goals and our manner of living. The Worldwatch Institute (2001) adds to this the broader imperative to "accelerate the shift to sustainability." CSE, an integrated framework for social and ecological peace education, intends to provide an educational response to this challenge. It outlines a cohesive set of values and foundational beliefs that are intended to shape a contemporary understanding of peace that takes into account both social and ecological realities. While the Earth Charter principle 16 defines peace as "wholeness created by right relationships with oneself, other persons, other cultures, other life, Earth, and the larger whole of which all are a part," CSE defines peace as contextual sustainability, pointing to the social and ecological context within which this wholeness is made possible.

CSE aims to be transformative rather than reformist in vision and goal. It challenges the foundations of most contemporary educational efforts, the goals of which do not explicitly and substantially include a vision for a sustainable future. It points to questions educators ought to ask in respect to the contested meanings of progress, freedom, sustainability (Davison, 2001). It is explicitly biocentric and as such represents a shift away from the still prevalent mechanistic and anthropocentric paradigm that shapes education in general, and, to a lesser extent, environmental education. This paradigm shift means that education's mode of learning and instruction is to be re-oriented and re-purposed. Only such repurposed education is able to contribute to the profound transformation of consciousness that is needed in the face of the enormous ecological and social challenges that humanity faces in the twenty-first century (Berry, 1990; O'Sullivan, 1999).

Furthermore, while the CSE framework is offered as a means of linking the educational efforts of peace and environmental education, it also allows for the inclusion of a broad range of perspectives and multiple knowledge bases, such as civics/patriotism education, global/development education, character/moral education. By expanding their goals to include those of the CSE framework, these concentrations will be enhanced while at the same time contributing their own theoretical and practical disciplinary achievements to CSE. Finally, the CSE framework is a dynamic framework that is to be refined by ongoing reconceptualization and reflection not only of educational theory and practice, but also of the evolving character of sustainability theory and practice. It is hoped that it will lead to the "stimulation of an ethos/system, within which continuous motivation, renewal and rebirth can occur" (Dottin, 2001) and that it will, thus, contribute to the necessary "eco-social revitalization of education and culture that can solve the accumulating modern crises of ecological degradation and social inequities both within and between nations" (Bowers, 1997).

NOTES

1. The expression Unity of Being refers to the unity that exists in the Universe, while the expression Unity of all Beings refers to the unity of the web of life on planet Earth.

2. It is the absence or presence of this biocentric orientation that determines whether a particular type of sustainability education approach is reformist or transformative.

3. Being a political compromise, the term "sustainable development" carries an "intentional fuzziness" (IUCN, 2002). Given its "ambiguities and tensions," M. Bonnett (1999) argues that it cannot be taken as "a statement of policy," but that sustainability as "a frame of mind" may have positive and wide-reaching educational implications. This view of sustainability as a frame of mind is similar to CSE's concept of ecological self.

4. Based on a global consensus, the Earth Charter is a statement of an integrated set of values, which is intended to provide humanity with an ethical guide for dealing with its present and future social and ecological problems and challenges. It should also become a basic document in sustainability education. See chapter 8 and www.earthcharter.org for more information.

5. While these requirements outline the general contents of ecological sustainability, as the authors of IUCN (2002) demonstrate and as chapter 5 argues, implementing ecological sustainability is always a matter of local adaptation.

6. The author recognizes that pedagogical tasks and activities, such as those provided here and elsewhere in the chapter for illustrative purposes, will be implemented in educational systems that are still mostly based upon implicitly held mechanistic, technocratic, linear, fragmentary values that support a world that is deeply ecologically unsustainable, socially unjust within and between countries,

technologically oriented, and politically dominated by large transnational corporations. However, it is his belief that this does not discount the need to introduce students to these basic beliefs and values nor their effectiveness in initiating behavior changes in their lives.

7. See K. Todd (2003) for a quiz that students may take to determine the size of their "ecological footprint," that is, to determine how large a share of Earth's resources they absorb.

8. Extending the value of justice to the Earth to emphasize fairness to the Earth community and the Earth's life-support processes is called "Earth justice" (Rasmussen, 1996). The term eco-justice seems to be used interchangeably with Earth justice. Strictly speaking, this type of justice is part of the ethical dimension of ecological sustainability.

9. The King Center for Nonviolent Social Change in Atlanta, Georgia (www.thekingcenter.com) has translated the 250 forms into six principles and associated steps for achieving nonviolence.

REFERENCES

American Federation of Teachers. (2001, Winter). Making standards matter: Sixth annual assessment of the standards movement. *American Educator.*

Apple, M. W. (2001). *Educating the "right" way: Markets, standards, god, and inequality.* New York: Routledge Farmer.

Archie, M., & McCrea, E. (1996). *Environmental education: Past, present, and future.* Paper presented at the 1996 National Environmental Education Summit, Burlingame, California.

Bentley, M. (1998). *Environmental education in the new standards: A constructivist appraisal.* Paper presented at the 1998 NAAEE conference, Atlanta, Georgia.

Berry, T. (1990). *Dream of the earth.* San Francisco: Sierra Club.

Bonnett, M. (1999). Education for sustainable development: A coherent philosophy for environmental education? *Cambridge Journal of Education, 29* (3), 313–324.

Botkin, D. B. (1990). *Discordant harmonies: A new ecology for the 21st century.* New York: Oxord University Press.

Bowers, C. A. (1997). *The culture of denial: Why the environmental movement needs a strategy for reforming universities and public schools.* Albany, NY: State University of New York Press.

Chambers, N., Simmons, C., & Wackernagel, M. (2001). *Sharing nature's interest: Ecological footprints as an indicator of sustainability*. London: EarthScan.

Chiras, D. D. (1994). *Environmental science: Action for a sustainable future. Fourth Edition*. Redwood City, CA: Benjamin/Cummings.

Cortright, D. (2002, February 18). The Power of nonviolence. *The Nation*.

Daly, H. (1996). *Beyond growth: The economics of sustainable development*. Boston: Beacon Press.

Daly, H. E., & Cobb, J. (1989). *For the common good: Redirecting the economy toward community, environment and a sustainable future*. Boston: Beacon Press.

Davison, A. (2001). *Technology and the contested meanings of sustainability*. Albany, NY: State University of New York Press.

Dernbach, J. C. (Ed.). (2002). *Stumbling towards sustainability*. Washington, DC: Environmental Law Institute.

Dottin, E. S. (2001). *The development of a conceptual framework: The stimulation for coherence and continuous improvement in teacher education*. Lanham, MD: University Press of America.

Elkington, J. (1998). *Cannibals with forks: The triple bottom line of 21st century business*. Stony Creek, CT: New Society Publishers.

Freire, P. (1970). *Pedagogy of the oppressed*. New York: Seabury Press.

Gelbspan, R. (1998). *The heat is on: The climate crisis, the cover-up, the prescription*. Cambridge, MA: Perseus Publishers.

Hawken, P. (1993). *The ecology of commerce: A declaration of sustainability*. New York: Harper Collins.

Huckle, J., & Sterling, S. (Eds.). (1996). *Education for sustainability*. London: Earthscan.

IUCN. (1987). *Conservation with equity*. Geneva, Switzerland.

IUCN. (2002). *Education and sustainability: Responding to the global challenge*. Geneva, Switzerland.

Jacobs, D. T., & Jacobs-Spencer, J. (2001). *Teaching virtues: Building character across the curriculum*. Lanham, MD: Scarecrow Press.

Lappe, F. M., & Lappe, A. (2002). *Hope's edge: The next diet for a small planet*. New York: Putnam.

Lawrence Hall of Science. (2000). *Science and sustainability*. Berkeley, CA: The Regents of the University of California.

Lieberman, J. (1998). *Closing the achievement gap*. Retrieved in January 2002 from http://www.seer.org.

Lonergan, A., & Richards, C. (1988). *Thomas Berry and the new cosmology*. Mystic, CT: Twenty-Third Publications.

Meadows, D. M., Randers, J., & Behrens III, W.W. (1972). *Limits to growth*. New York: Universe.

Mortensen, L. L.. (2000). Teacher education for sustainability: 1. Global change education: The scientific foundation for sustainability. *Journal of Science Education and Technology*, *9* (1), 27–36.

Naess, A. (1989). *Ecology, community and lifestyle*. D. Rottenberg, Trans. New York: Cambridge University Press.

National Council for Accreditation of Teacher Education (NCATE). (2002). Professional standards for the accreditation of schools, colleges and departments of education: 2002 edition. Retrieved December, 2002, from www.ncate.org

Orr, D. W. (1994). *Earth in mind: On education, environment, and the human prospect*. Washington, D.C.: Island Press.

O'Sullivan, E. (1999). *Transformative learning: Educational vision for the 21st century*. Toronto: University of Toronto Press and London: Zed Books.

Paehlke, R. (1989). *Environmentalism and the future of progressive politics*. New Haven, CT: Yale University Press.

Palmer, J. A. (1998). *Environmental education in the 21st century: Theory, practice, progress and promise*. New York: Routledge and Kegan Paul.

Prugh, T., Constanza, R., & Daly, H. (2000). *The local politics of global sustainability*. Washington, DC: Island Press.

Rasmussen, L. (1996). *Earth community, earth ethics*. Maryknoll, NY: Maryknoll.

Roszak, T. (1993). *The voice of the Earth*. New York: Simon and Schuster.

Sacks, P. (1999). *Standardized minds: The high price of America's testing culture and what we can do to change it*. New York: Perseus Books.

Sale, K. (1991). *Dwellers in the land: The bioregional vision*. Philadelphia: The New Society Publishers.

Schäffner, C., & Wenden, A. (Eds.). (1999). *Language and peace*. Amsterdam: Harwood Academic.

Scherer, M. (2001, September). How and why standards improve student achievement: A conversation with Robert J. Marzano. *Educational Leadership, 59* (1), 14–18.

Sitarz, D. (1998). *Sustainable America: America's environment, economy and society in the 21st century.* Carbondale, IL: EarthPress.

Smith, G. A., & Williams, D. R. (1999). *Ecological education in action: On weaving education, culture and the environment.* Albany, NY: State University of New York Press.

Springer, M. (1994). *Watershed: A successful voyage into integrative learning.* Columbus, OH: National Middle School Association.

Steger, M. B., & Ling, N. S. (Eds.). (1999). *Violence and its alternatives: An interdisciplinary reader.* New York: St Martin's Press.

Steiner, S. F., Krank, H. M., McLaren, P., & Bahruth, R. E. (Eds.). (2000). *Freirean pedagogy, praxis and possibilities.* New York: Falmer Press, Taylor and Francis.

Susskind, A. (2000). *Dr. Art's guide to planet Earth : For earthlings ages 12 to 120.* VT: Chelsea Green Publishing Co.

Swimme, B., & Berry, T. (1992). *The universe story from the primordial flaring forth to the ecozoic era: A celebration of the unfolding of the cosmos.* San Francisco: Harper.

Thomashow, M. (1996). *Ecological identity: Becoming a reflective environmentalist.* Cambridge, MA: MIT Press.

Tilbury, D., Stevenson, R. B., Fien, J., & Schreuder, D. (Eds.). (2002). *Education and sustainability: Responding to the global challenge.* Belgium: IUCN Commission on Education and Communication.

Todd, K. (2003, January/February). Are you big foot? *Sierra*, 40–44.

Traina, F., & Darley-Hill, S. (Ed.). (1995). *Perspectives in bioregional education.* Troy, OH: NAAEE.

U.S. Department of Education. (2002). *No Child Left Behind Act.* United States of America Public Law 107–110. Retrieved December 11, 2003, from www.ed.gov/nclb

Van Dijk, T. (1999). Discourse analysis as ideology analysis. In C. Schäffner & A. Wenden (Eds.), *Language and peace* (pp. 17–36). Amsterdam: Harwood Academic Publishers.

VanMatre, S. (1990). *Earth education: A new beginning.* Greenville, WV: The Institute for Earth Education.

Verhagen, F. C. (1999, Fall). The earth community school: A back-to-basics model of secondary education. *Green Teacher*, 28–33.

Wheeler, K. A., & Bijur, A. P. (Eds.). (2000). *Education for a sustainable future.* New York: Kluwer.

Wilson, E. O. (1996). *In search of nature.* Washington, DC: Island Press.

World Commission of Environment and Development. (WCED). (1987). *Our common future.* Oxford: Oxford University Press.

Worldwatch, Institute. (2001). *State of the world 2001: A report about progress towards a sustainable society.* New York: W. W. Norton.

CHAPTER 3

An Integral Model of Peace Education

Abelardo Brenes-Castro[1]

During the decade of the 1980s, the University for Peace[2] supported efforts to achieve peace in the Central American region in many ways. It provided academic and political support to the National Councils for Reconciliation created by the 1987 Esquipulas II Peace Accords. In 1989 an international conference, *Seeking the True Meaning of Peace* (Brenes-Castro, 1991), organized under the auspices of the University, led to the formulation of the "Declaration of Human Responsibilities for Peace and Sustainable Development," which the Costa Rican government presented to the General Assembly in that same year (United Nations General Assembly, 1989). Research and seminars on the "peace zone" concept were also organized. These provided a foundation for the 1990 *Declaration of Puntarenas*, in which the Central American presidents, ". . . interpreting the aspirations of the Central American peoples, declared the Isthmus as a Region of Peace, Freedom, Democracy and Development." Within this political context, the governments of the region further acknowledged that the University for Peace should contribute to the postwar reconstruction phase that was beginning to emerge. Thus, in 1992 with the financial support of the European community, the University developed a program for the promotion of human rights and peace education in Central America.

Noting the success of the program, the government of Nicaragua proposed to the other Central American governments that the University for Peace be invited to carry out a more ambitious program. As a result, in 1994 it was agreed that the University would develop and implement the "Program for the Culture of Peace and Democracy in Central America." The Program was publicly launched in October 1994 by the presidents of Central America within the framework of the Central American Conference on Peace and Development.

During the first phase, the program promoted the development of values and behaviors that facilitate peaceful human relations and respect for human rights taking into account the ethnic and cultural diversity of the region. It also contributed to the establishment of consensus-building opportunities between institutions and persons of diverse opinions in each country and provided bridges for interchange and joint action between diverse organizations for the promotion of regional integration, sustainable development, and a culture of peace.

National Advisory Councils, with representatives from diverse social sectors, were created in each country for the purpose of orienting program officials on national challenges and opportunities for the construction of a culture of peace. They also served as democratic contexts for facilitating processes of dialogue on difficult and complex issues. With the participation of these councils, about fifteen communities throughout Central America were selected to participate in the community component of the program. They had either been involved in civil wars or had traditions of violence and suffered from socioeconomic exclusion and diverse social and developmental problems. The Program supported these communities through local councils by means of diverse educational and cultural activities and then disseminated those practices that had exemplary educational value to broader sectors, particularly through the action of another key component of the program—communicators and journalists. In 1996, based on the results of the first phase of the Program, a mandate was given to the University for Peace by the Central American governments to execute a second four-year phase—from 1997 to May 2001. During this second phase, the Program continued to focus on the construction of cultures of peace and democracy within the region.

The *Integral Model of Peace Education* (IMPE)[3] was formulated during the initial period of the Program with contributions from many specialists from diverse countries in Central America.[4] A series of 27 *Basic Texts on a Culture of Peace, Democracy and Sustainable Development* were produced with 24 accompanying didactic guides. These were adapted in each country for use at the community level, taking into consideration local cultural differences. During the second phase of the Program, the Model was adapted to formal educational systems, at primary, secondary and university levels. It was also used to develop new methodologies and educational texts.[5]

Having outlined the educational activities that led to the development of the Model, I will now provide a detailed description of the Model itself—its assumptions and normative frameworks, its main contents and pedagogical approach—concluding with an account of how it was applied in a marginal urban community in Costa Rica.

ASSUMPTIONS OF THE IMPE

The *Integral Model Peace Education* is based on the assumption that there are universal values foundational to the principles that shape a culture of peace, for example, those underlying the *United Nations Declaration and Program of Action for a Culture of Peace* (United Nations General Assembly, 1999) and *The Earth Charter*. However, it acknowledges that these values and principles can be expressed in diverse ways in different cultures. Moreover, there may be other values and principles expressed in the life practices of specific cultures that may differ from these universals. Therefore, the process of building a global culture of peace can best be approached through a continuous process of intercultural dialogue, within the context of an open consensus seeking process on what a universal culture of peace can mean. It is a historical process based on respect and dialogue between cultures for mutual enhancement and learning, which further assumes that the aspiration to live peacefully and in a sustainable relationship with our biosphere is, in effect, universal and that in all peoples we find individuals and groups who are seeking ways of realizing this aspiration. In this latter belief, the Model has been influenced by Mahayana Buddhism's belief in universal compassion as a prime motivating value for human development and its understanding of the interdependence of all phenomena.

In the case of Central America, it is further assumed that if people are given an opportunity to understand the nature of the violence and authoritarianism they have experienced, they will realize that it is not inevitable and that they can aspire to live in peace. Moreover, if this subregion takes on its collective responsibility to develop its potential as a region characterized by values such as peace, responsible freedom, democracy, and development of its human potential (the main values of *The Declaration of Puntarenas*), this could contribute substantially to forging a planetary civilization of peace and sustainability, a fundamental challenge for our generation.

However, it is also acknowledged that given the accelerated processes of economic globalization, it will be particularly difficult to gear the course of future development on the basis of endogenous determinants. It would require, on the one hand, that Central Americans be able to consolidate their cultural sovereignty, recognizing and valuing indigenous cultural values and expressions of cultures of peace, democracy, and sustainability. On the other hand, it would further require that the influx of values, lifestyles, and cultural patterns coming from the cultures of other peoples be viewed critically. Moreover, in the context of deeply asymmetric societies characterized by gross socioeconomic, political, and cultural inequities, as is the case of the Central American countries, this historical dynamic is driven fundamentally by a struggle between social groups following emancipatory agendas of development and groups who enjoy freedom of choice in regard to lifestyle (Giddens, 1991).

Given this context, the *Integral Model* views the role of dialogue as essential. Dialogue concerning which values and lifestyles can effectively lead to societies characterized by regional values and principles, such as those stated in the Central American political frameworks (e.g. *Declaration of Puntarenas* and *Alliance for Sustainable Development*), and by universal values and principles (e.g. the *United Nations Declaration and Program of Action for a Culture of Peace* and *The Earth Charter*) must be fostered within countries in the region. It is further assumed that this public dialogue can lead to a recognition of the worthiness of those groups whose lifestyles are in accord with such values and principles.

Finally, the *Integral Model* assumes a holistic vision of reality. Based on T. Berry and B. Swimme (1992), it sees the universe as a dynamic and creative totality characterized by diversity and interdependence between all beings and manifested as a continuous process of self-realization guided by three dynamics principles: differentiation, autopoesis, and cooperation. These principles are manifest in a particularly sublime way in humans. That is, we can assume that, in a certain sense, each person is singular and has a unique life mission (differentiation), and a self-reflective consciousness—a culmination of the whole history of the universe (autopoesis). Finally in his/her striving toward communion and love, each person recognizes a profound identity between and among all beings which leads to a deep sense of respect for each one (cooperation). The *Integral Model* interprets these three principles as jointly expressing "a spirit of community," a core value for peace. It assumes that an ideal human community would be characterized as follows:

• Membership in such a community allows for the satisfaction of vital needs for all its members.

• There is a commitment on the part of all its members towards the mutual protection, enhancement, and promotion of the common good of the community.

• The idiosyncrasy of each member is valued and her/his contributions are synergistically integrated within the diversity of the group.

• All members participate in the making of those decisions that affect the common well-being (Brenes, 2002, p. 28).

Finally, from this dynamic and creative view of the universe, there follows a vision of Planet Earth as a community of life that is auto emergent, auto propagating, auto nutritive, auto educational, auto governing, auto healing, and auto realizing (Berry, 1988). Within its natural history, humans emerge as a self-reflective consciousness through which life can reflect, celebrate, and create itself in an intentional manner.

NORMATIVE FRAMEWORKS

Universal Declaration of Human Rights

The fundamental normative framework for the *Integral Model* is provided by the *Universal Declaration of Human Rights*. Proclaimed in 1948, it is recognized as extraordinary for its acknowledgement by the universal community of nations that each person is a subject of fundamental rights. However, given that there is a very limited understanding of what freedom entails and given the egocentric sense of personal development that underlies contemporary culture, fraternity, mentioned as a duty in Article one of the *Declaration*, must be recognized as the value that is fundamental to sustaining a culture of peace. It entails a recognition of the need to balance the universal protection of each person, with each person's consciousness of his/her universal responsibility towards others, towards other living beings and towards the natural systems of the Earth.

The *Integral Model* assumes a holistic approach to human rights and freedoms, considering them as forming an interdependent and indivisible set. This holistic approach is clearly highlighted in the so-called third generation human rights, that is, the Right to Peace, the Right to Development, and the Right to a Healthy Environment.

The Right to Peace (United Nations General Assembly, 1984) can be considered as a synthesis of all human rights since peace is a condition for the full realization of all fundamental rights and freedoms for all persons. It also provides the foundation of an ethics of congruence between ends and means. The Right to Development is an alternative formulation of this holistic approach (see Sengupta, 2001). It emphasizes the dynamic nature of humans—the legitimate aspiration of each person and of all persons to achieve to the maximum their potential for self-realization. However, in the context of highly inequitable societies, the Right to Development, interpreted as the right of each and every person to achieve their fullest potential, entails distinct agendas. Thus, it is assumed that to the degree that individuals or groups enjoy real external freedom or autonomy of agency—that they can satisfy their primary survival needs and their secondary needs for a life with dignity, then those persons or groups have the power to choose a given lifestyle (life politics, following Giddens, 1991). On the other hand, to the degree that an individual's or group's ability to satisfy these needs is lacking, then their developmental agenda will be primarily of an emancipatory nature. This distinction provides a basis for justifying a principle of differentiated responsibility within a broader context of universal responsibility.

While viewing humans as the center of sustainable development, the Right to a Healthy Environment does stress that this is only possible if there is harmony with Nature (United Nations Conference on Environment and Development, 1992). These Third Generation human rights are sometimes called "Solidarity Rights" because they more explicitly express the need for all citizens, not only states, to fulfill their fraternal duties in order for there to be an effective defense and promotion of human rights for all. Seen from this perspective, there is a direct relationship between a holistic view of human rights and the principle of universal responsibility described below.

Earth Charter

The *Earth Charter* is a normative framework that was incorporated into the final version of the *Integral Model*. The principle of universal responsibility appears in paragraph five of *The Preamble to the Earth Charter*.[6] This principle is essential for the realization of the human rights and freedoms framework described above if it is understood as an awareness that the enjoyment of human rights and freedoms is based on fulfilling one's universal duty of fraternity. It (the principle) further urges us to recognize our global citizenship and our responsibility for caring for our fragile and interdependent ecosystem both in the present and in the future. Thus, in the *Earth Charter*, the principle of universal responsibility takes on added meaning including not only our relationship towards one another, but also towards future generations and towards the biosphere.

However, in a world characterized by deep inequities and power differences, the principal of universal responsibility would not have much practical meaning if not coupled with a principal of differential responsibility. "Universal responsibility," here, refers to the moral dimension of a global ethic that can be shared by all humans. "Differentiated responsibility" refers to the "capacity to respond," depending on our actual capacity to do so. Thus, although we may all be equally obliged to respond ethically to meet the challenges we face, our actual capacity to respond depends on the powers and resources one has at hand. *The Earth Charter* assumes this in stating that ". . . with increased freedom, knowledge, and power comes increased responsibility to promote the common good" (subprinciple 2b).

THE INTEGRAL MODEL OF PEACE EDUCATION

The *Integral Model* is a person-centered conceptual framework which considers "peace" as a state of integrity, security, balance, and harmony. These conditions are also seen as fundamental to self-realization. It is assumed that each person lives within three relational contexts: in relationship to the self, to others, and to Nature. Violence or peace can be expressed within each one. A culture of peace, therefore, needs to be constructed simultaneously in all these contexts, on ethical, mental, emotional, and action levels. The Model, which incorporates all three contexts, can be depicted as a circular, mandala-type graph (Figure 3.1).

"Peace" is at the core of the model; it is viewed as a result of harmonious relationships on all levels within the three contexts. The second concentric circle is

---

FIGURE 3.1

Fundamental Values and Traits of the *Integral Model of Peace Education*

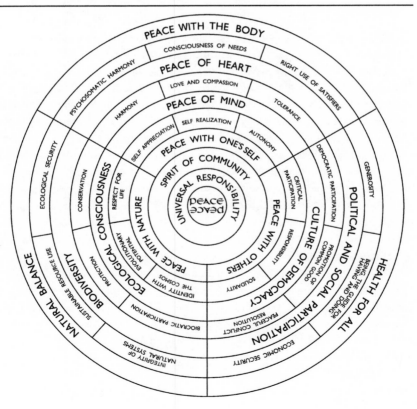

"universal responsibility," which as discussed above, is based on a holistic frame-work of human rights and duties thus implying that all humans are endowed with an ethical core, which is the basis of our sense of justice and which enables us to bal-ance our rights with our duties. The third concentric circle, "spirit of community," refers to the notion that "peace" requires an integrated consciousness that goes be-yond dualisms, for example, person/society, human community/community of life, inner/outer and mind/body. In other words, it is a view of personhood as part of the web of life. Around each of these axes, there are three interdependent dimen-sions (contexts): *Peace with One's Self, Peace with Others,* and *Peace with Nature.* Each dimension is specified in terms of three value domains. For example, "ecological consciousness," "biodiversity," and "natural balance" specify *Peace with Nature.* In turn, each value domain is specified in terms of traits. In the case of "natural bal-ance," these would be integrity of natural systems, sustainable resource use, and ecological security.

Peace with One's Self

Peace with the Body consists of bodily health based on psychosomatic har-mony. This entails the development of a consciousness of the organism's needs for physical, emotional, and mental health, and wise optimization of satisfiers for these needs, which reduces the impact that individual consumption has on the natural en-vironment. "Voluntary simplicity" is a value orientation that sums-up this approach to optimizing human needs. It is supported by extensive psychological research that suggests that the "consumer society" is driven by an "empty self" model of person-hood, which leads individuals to seek satisfaction of the need for participating in so-cial and natural communities by joining pseudo-communities of consumers, which ,in turn, lead to pseudo need satisfaction (Cushman, 1990; Durning, 1992).

Peace of Heart refers mainly to the satisfaction of psychological needs, which generates a sense of basic security and trust. To achieve this, the Model supposes that it is necessary to cultivate qualities such as love, compassion, and tolerance. True emotional gratification and security is to be met by identifying and using sat-isfiers based on these qualities. Moreover, as taught in the Buddhist tradition (Kelsang Gyatso, 1990), love, compassion, and tolerance can lead to liberation from those attachments and compulsions which cause negative emotions, such as anger, hate and envy, and which also sustain materialistic consumer lifestyles. This psychological substratum is the foundation for the development of relation-ships based on solidarity and generosity between humans. The overall result of this dimension of personal peace is a sense of *harmony.*

Peace of Mind refers to the potential for self-realization based on a con-sciousness of universal responsibility. This would include awareness of responsibility towards oneself—to achieve inner peace and to develop a meaningful mission in life and strive to fulfill it. Identifying one's life mission further requires an appreciation of (1) one's place in natural and human history; (2) the interdependence of all beings in the universe; (3) the nature of the present day global challenges; and (3) of the satisfaction of following a life course geared by a global ethic. Critical autonomy, the capacity to question one's society and culture, is necessary to making informed decisions in shaping one's life mission. Equally important is freedom derived from the possession and responsible use of personal powers, that is, functional autonomy (Doyal and Gough, 1991).

The values and traits that constitute this first dimension of the model, that is, *Peace with One's Self*, are the basis for the fostering of the values and conditions in the other two, *Peace with Others*, and *Peace with Nature*. At the same time, they are, to a certain degree, determined by them.

Peace with Others

Culture of democracy refers to the critical and responsible participation of all citizens in promoting the common good and security of all humans and the community of Nature. Given that we do not live in isolation and that our life projects are to a certain degree determined by collective decisions in our families, communities, nations, and the world as a whole, we need to be able to participate critically and autonomously in the making of decisions at all these levels. This requires respect for cultural and ethnic diversity as well as a commitment to respect and promote human rights for all, including future generations, that is, a sense of solidarity.

For political and social participation to promote the common good, love, compassion, and tolerance are essential. They provide the basis for effective democratic participation, that is, participation that will bring about equal and just opportunities for all; equity and solidarity between women and men; a commitment to nonviolence; peaceful resolution of conflicts; and participation in the development of social policies to promote the integral development of all.

Health for all is founded on the notion that all are responsible to contribute to the essential economic well-being of all persons by working for an economic system based on human generosity rather than on assumptions of scarcity. Such an economic system requires that citizens appreciate both nature's capacity to satisfy essential human needs and the limits of her bounty. It also requires that they be conscious of their true needs and oriented to the right use of satisfiers, in other words, to a sense of *being* which acts as a guide for *having* and *doing*. (See Max-Neef et al., 1986). In other words in a peaceful society, health is guaranteed for all and economic security is based on an adequate distribution of satisfiers for common basic human needs.

Peace with Nature

Ecological consciousness is based on a sense of respect for life in all of its forms and a sense of identity with the cosmos cultivated by going beyond dualisms, for example, mind/body and inner/outer world, and by understanding our interdependence within the community of life. It is a consciousness that leads to a commitment to foster the evolutionary potential of living beings. The *protection* and *conservation* of *biodiversity* is based on a recognition of the right of all living beings to exist, to enjoy a suitable habitat, and to develop their evolutionary potential. This implies *biocratic participation* (Berry, 1988), the right of all living beings to participate in the decisions that affect the community of life. The *balance of natural systems* is based on a commitment to protect the integrity of Earth's natural systems. This is achieved by environmental conservation and rehabilitation and by adopting sustainable forms of resource use in all activities of human production, consumption, and reproduction. The outcome, for humans, is ecological security.

As is the case with the dimension *Peace with Others*, the development of the personal traits and values that specify the dimension *Peace with Oneself* are the basis for achieving *Peace with Nature*. There is an intrinsic relationship between ecological and social sustainability and integrity as a fundamental orientation of personal development.

PEDAGOGY OF THE INTEGRAL MODEL OF PEACE EDUCATION

The *Integral Model* follows a critical constructivist pedagogical approach which seeks to create processes of reflection and dialogue for the purpose of generating, applying, evaluating, and disseminating cultural constructions of peace. The main application of the Model is through community-based workshops, which can be characterized as reflecting a methodology for collaborative inquiry (Bray, Lee, Smith, & Yorks, 2000) and one which educates through real life models of individuals and groups who portray peaceful and sustainable emancipatory agendas and lifestyles.

The description of the pedagogy that follows is based on the series of ten didactic modules entitled "Building a Culture of Peace in Our Community," designed primarily for promoters of community development, particularly in communities that have been involved in emancipatory struggles within Costa Rica.[7] Nonetheless, many of the components of this approach are also applicable to other groups who are interested in promoting cultures of peace.

Pedagogical Introduction to the Integral Model of Education for Peace (Module 1)

Module 1 presents the fundamental assumptions underlying the Integral Model (pp. 79–81) and its pedagogical orientation (described above). Participants are also given an overview of how the modules can be implemented, that is, sequentially or selectively, depending on the needs of a community.

Culture of Peace and Culture of Violence (Module 2)

Module 2 contains two didactic units. In the first one, students reflect on the nature of violence and learn to distinguish between direct, structural, and cultural forms of violence and the relationship between each. The presence of violence in their lives and environment and the emotions which these concerns evoke are reflected upon. The cause of violence is another topic that is considered. In the second unit students begin by considering the consequences of diverse thoughts and emotions related to violence and insecurity, how they affect their actions, and how these emotions can be transformed. Particular attention is given to despair, given its predominance in communities that experience social exclusion (Macy & Brown, 1998). Then, through relaxation and guided meditation, students experience states of inner peace and so learn that it is possible to transform negative emotions and thought patterns, including despair, into positive ones. The outcome is an evocation of aspirations to live in peace, that is, for a peaceful selfhood, peaceful human relationships, and peaceful relations with the natural environment. Students are then told that the rest of the modules will be devoted to considering ways of achieving these aspirations, called "*seeds for a culture of peace*," by developing their potential for the constructive transformation of reality for personal and collective development.

The Earth Charter (Module 3)

Module 3 introduces students to the relevance of the *Earth Charter* as a universal ethical framework for guiding personal and communal development on the basis of the principle of universal responsibility. Two themes included in the Preamble are emphasized, that is, how the processes of globalization and modernization are transforming the planet very rapidly and how there is an emerging sense of belonging to a single human family that faces common challenges within a broader Earth community. Students reflect on the significance of these challenges in their personal life and for their life community and on the implications for cooperation entailed by the interdependence that exists between diverse peoples.

The module also introduces the four main principles of *The Earth Charter*, which express the key components of the principle of universal responsibility. The first, "Respect Earth and life in all its diversity" implies that we need to understand our interrelationships and interdependencies within the community of life in this critical time period. The second, "Care for the community of life with understanding, compassion, and love" assumes that we should cultivate a higher level of knowledge, more akin to wisdom, as well as affective attributes and dispositions, such as "love" and "compassion." The third, "Build democratic societies that are just, participatory, sustainable, and peaceful," and the fourth, "Secure Earth's bounty and beauty for present and future generations," point to action-oriented values, which can be derived from and complement the values and attributes implied in the first two principles. Taken together, these values jointly provide a strong foundation for an ethics of universal responsibility and a rationale for the IMPE, which is presented in Module 4.

The Integral Model of Peace Education (Module 4)

The rationale for and the educational implications of the need to live according to an ethic of universal responsibility are explained in Module 4. Students are oriented to how the attributes and dispositions that are the basis of such an ethic are expressed and related to one another in the Model. They are also asked to compare their *seeds for a culture of peace* developed in Module 2, with the values and traits outlined in the *Integral Model* (see Figure 3.1). Experience doing this exercise with diverse groups and communities has repeatedly demonstrated that their visions and aspirations of peaceful selfhood, peaceful human relationships, and peaceful relations between humans and their natural environment are very similar to the values and traits of the *Integral Model*. To the degree that students perceive this to be the case, they will consider the use of the *Integral Model* as a guide for the educational processes developed in the rest of the modules to be validated.

Human Needs, Rights and Duties (Module 5)

Module 5 operationalizes the key values and themes of the *Integral Model* by guiding students in the construction of life projects, that is, their fundamental needs, their satisfiers, and powers required to achieve a life mission based on a consciousness of universal responsibility. Students first draw a life-size silhouette of themselves on paper and identify their needs and the satisfiers of these needs. Following J. Burton (1990) and L. Doyal and I. Gough (1991), needs are classified as follows: health needs, needs related to social acceptance, for example, love and belongingness; self-esteem needs; needs for self-realization and transcendence; needs for security, knowledge and personal power. Satisfiers are classified as singular, synergistic, destructive, inhibitive and as pseudo satisfying (cf Max-Neef et al., 1986). Students, then, evaluate their satisfiers according to whether they promote health, well-being, and self-realization, or have inhibitive or destructive effects, thus stifling need satisfaction. After having identified their needs and evaluated their satisfiers, the powers for fulfilling need satisfaction are identified, that is, various forms of thought, speech, and physical action. These are evaluated in terms of whether they promote peace, security, and community, or whether they lead to violence, insecurity, and social disintegration. (For a similar distinction between threat power, exchange power, and integrative power, see K. Boulding cited in Miall, Ramsbotham, and Woodhouse, 1999.)

To develop a life mission based on a consciousness of universal responsibility students must also be guided through meditations which are intended to facilitate three shifts in consciousness inspired by Buddhism (Batchelor, 1983; Dalai Lama, 1984; Kelsang Gyatso, 1990), that is,

1. *Equanimity.* Equanimity is the capacity to treat all human beings (and, on another dimension, all living beings) with an equal sense of benevolence, and at the same time to value the singularity of all persons and their inherent right to express that singularity in a unique life mission that contributes to a common good. This capacity also is fundamental for the development of *tolerance.* By treating one's enemies benevolently, it is possible to come to the realization that there is essentially no difference between one's friends and one's enemies and that the real enemy is the mental conditioning which leads us to react with fear or anger and violence.

2. *Equality of self and others.* Equality of self and others requires a shift from an egotistical orientation to a social and ecological orientation in which one realizes that life takes on its highest meaning when one orients one's freedom to serving the common good.

3. *Commitment to altruistic life practices.* Altruistic life practices are manifested as a channeling of one's life towards a universal agenda of emancipation for all humans from life conditions that create suffering, oppression, subjugation, and alienation, through nonviolent means.

Life projects are first constructed individually. In a second phase, participants identify commonalities among life projects, in terms of needs, satisfiers, and legitimate powers. This is first done by genders, then in a group as a whole. These commonalities are defined as the common good, the heart of the spirit of community.

The needs and the means of satisfying them that have been identified are then examined within the framework of human rights and freedoms. The values underpinning rights and freedoms refer to the basic universal needs which all humans have a right to satisfy if they are to live with dignity and seek happiness and self-realization. Human duties, which are equally important for the respect and promotion of rights and freedoms are, in turn, examined in relation to the powers for fulfilling need satisfaction considered as legitimate by the group. This perspective provides the group with an understanding of its moral and legal relationship within the broader civic community to which it belongs.

Emancipatory Politics and Life Politics (Module 6)

In Module 6 participants relate their personal and community life project to a broader framework of emancipatory politics and life politics (Giddens, 1991) within the perspective of universal responsibility. Emancipatory politics refers to those actions which promote effective enjoyment of human rights and freedoms understood in a holistic sense. As explained earlier (cf. pp. 81–82), part of the Integral Model's normative framework is the Right to Development, which stresses the indivisible and interdependent nature of the whole set of human rights and freedoms and which is the most widely accepted and inclusive expression of the contemporary approach to human rights (Sengupta, 2001). The module also teaches that our current historical challenge, on all levels of our relationships, is to forge a life politics whose central core values promote universal emancipation. Thus, the module stresses that we need not conform to prevalent models of human development promoted by economic globalization processes, particularly those based on compulsive consumption and work (Pilisuk, 2001). On the contrary, our challenge is to create new meanings for human development based on altruistic motivations. Fundamental conditions for achieving such an alternative approach to human development would include substituting our reliance on powers of dominance in seeking security and developing powers of love, compassion, and tolerance. Achieving internal freedom or critical autonomy is also required to liberate ourselves from fears, attachments, and compulsions which lead to egoistic life politics and inhibit our potential to create aspirations for a better world and the willingness and skills to make them real.

Local Development and Globalization (Module 7)

In Module 7, participants reflect on the processes of globalization and the implications that these processes have for local development. Strategies are developed to resist globalization's negative consequences and to take advantage of its constructive potential, particularly in relation to forging a greater sense of community in the human and natural domains.

Strategies and Life Projects for Fulfilling Emancipatory Politics and Life Politics (Module 8)

Module 8 is practically oriented. Its purpose is to support students in developing strategies for organizing themselves democratically and to forge a development plan to fulfill their emancipatory agendas and life politics. The heart of the module is the principle of the *spirit of community* (Peck, 1987) and what this entails in practice. Democratic leadership skills are given particular attention in this context.

Conflicts, Negotiation and Active Nonviolence (Module 9)

Module 9 addresses the nature and causes of human conflicts and the means for managing and resolving conflicts within the community. Following the Gandhian tradition (Bose, 1987), students are oriented to the possibility of pursuing their emancipatory agendas and life politics using nonviolent means, that is, to persuade one's adversary about the justice of one's cause, not to defeat him. To the degree that such strategies enable those in power to realize the truth and justice that sustain an emancipatory agenda, to that degree can this lead to a redirection of their life politics towards a greater sense of solidarity and community. Such a shift is, of course, also compatible with enlightened self-interest.

Processes of Communication and the Good News Concept (Module 10)

The importance of communication based on principles of truthfulness and empathy, both within one's community and in the broader social context, is stressed in Module 10. The right and duty to listen and speak are put forward as the foundation of a participatory democracy based on deliberative practices for channeling critical consciousness in seeking the common good. The need for cooperation between different cultural actors is also addressed so that the positive lessons emerging from nonviolent emancipatory struggles and peaceful, healthy, and sustainable lifestyles can be disseminated through multiple cultural communication channels. The Module presents basic tools for communicating these positive lessons.

AN EXAMPLE OF THE APPLICATION OF
THE INTEGRAL MODEL

Rincón Grande de Pavas, the mostly densely populated marginal urban community in Costa Rica, has had the reputation of being one of the most violent. It is located in the western section of San José between the Torres and Tiribí rivers, two of the most highly contaminated rivers in San José. In 1997, when the educational activities of the Central American Program for a Culture of Peace and Democracy began, this community was composed of approximately 4,500 inhabitants who lived on three square kilometers of land. Most of these people lived in poor housing, with little sanitation, economic, social, and recreational infrastructure, a lack of green areas and an accumulation of garbage in non-authorized places.

During 1997, the *Culture of Peace Program* collaborated with diverse governmental and nongovernmental institutions in Costa Rica to support the inhabitants of Rincón Grande de Pavas in the design of their development plan for the period 1998–2004. The *Integral Model of Peace Education* was one of the frameworks used to help the community identify their common aspirations, needs, and satisfiers, and to develop appropriate action strategies.

During 1998 and 1999, the *Integral Model* was used to organize multiple educational activities intended to meet the needs of the three main groups that compose the Educational Triangle, three groups responsible for education in the community, that is, community leaders, schools, and journalists. Some of these activities sought to foster cooperative relationships between these groups in order to (1) promote the *Development Plan of Rincón Grande de Pavas*; (2) transform the negative social image of Rincón Grande de Pavas that was dominant in Costa Rica; and (3) disseminate expressions of their emerging culture of peace and democracy building through the mass media.

In October 2000 when serious rioting took place, involving a clash between youth gangs in the community which led to the killing of one person, the conflict was diffused, in part, and the confrontation with the police between the youth groups and police ended thanks to the mediation of some of the community leaders who had been trained by the *Culture of Peace Program*. There was also a significant shift in the reporting policy of *La Nación*, the main Costa Rican daily newspaper. Instead of the traditional approach to reporting, which would have stigmatized the youth gangs and the community, most of the articles and editorials focused on the structural causes of violence that affected youth in communities, such as Rincón Grande de Pavas, and the common responsibility that all of Costa Rican society and the government had in finding solutions for the inhabitants of Rincón Grande de Pavas and similar marginalized communities. The urgent need to support the youth of these communities was stressed. Articles explained that the lack of opportunities for work and an educational system that is not geared to the specific needs of marginal youth meant that approximately 3,000 young persons in Rincón Grande de Pavas neither studied nor worked. As a result, it was written, many of them were caught-up in self-defeating life strategies, and belonging to a gang offered an alternative that gave some meaning and security to their lives.

The last phase of the work in Rincón Grande de Pavas, during 2000 and 2001, was aimed at helping the youth develop their own sense of community and a plan for development. Thirty-nine youths accepted an open invitation to attend a series of four one-day workshops. The group was quite heterogeneous. Approximately two-thirds were high school students; the other third belonged to the gangs.

The first day of the workshop was focused on their concerns, aspirations, and needs. Participants realized how divided they were and how this stifles their potential as a united movement. They also reflected on the negative social image they had in Costa Rica, which led to a desire to become known for who they truly are. Their main concerns were related to the violence in their community, which was mainly manifest in domestic aggression, assaults, and robbery in the streets, and in drug addiction and trafficking. This was understood as stemming in large part from the poverty of most of the community; the lack of opportunity for the youth to study and work; the contamination of the rivers, parks and empty lots; the lack of access to basic goods and services for the community, such as housing, recreational facilities, and health clinics. The effect of all this, they reflected, was sadness, fear, frustration, and anger.

By reflecting and sharing their concerns and aspirations in the second workshop, they realized that they had much in common and that by uniting themselves as a youth community, there was a better possibility of fulfilling these aspirations. Their sense of mission was summed up in the following quote from the *Youth Development Plan of Rincón Grande de Pavas, 2001–2003*:

> We are the youth of Rincón Grande de Pavas; we aspire that all youth in our community enjoy opportunities to develop all of their capacities as persons; that they have access to what they need to live with dignity and happiness; that they can become productive and responsible with themselves, with others and with nature. We are motivated to achieve a world in peace, just, united, with solidarity, without discrimination, without violence and without social problems. (p. 2)

Session three was devoted to identifying their personal powers, resources, and opportunities, as well as their vulnerabilities and the threats and obstacles they faced. Session four was dedicated to the design of their development plan, to organizing in committees in the areas of work, education, recreation and sports, culture, and health. Each committee identified specific goals for action. At the end of this session, they expressed their aspirations and goals as drawings, which were then used as the basis for the painting of a mural on the external walls of the Community Resource Center. An analysis of some of the specific panels of the mural permits an appreciation of the values and aspirations of the youthful artists, which are in consonance with the values and principles of the *Integral Model of Peace Education.*

The drawing in figure 3.2 seems to reflect what has been described above as a sense of universal consciousness. It depicts, according to one of the artists, ". . . the sun; it means that the sun is illuminating all of us equally and that light gives life to all, without distinguishing societies, nor who has more from who has less. . . . It also shows that we want a more organized community, more beautiful, without so much garbage. We painted it to demonstrate to the community that one day they too will have this light."

Another of the panels (figure 3.3) reflects their sense of autonomy and empowerment. "The drawing with the three hands working together depicts what we

---

FIGURE 3.2

Panel of "The Sun Illuminates Us All Equally"

FIGURE 3.3
Panel of "Hands Working Together"

are going to do, because we do not expect everything to be given to us. We are going to work and forge ahead with our own means," explained one of the artists.

The next panel (figure 3.4) shows the sense of appreciation and responsibility for key public services and institutions. "This hand that holds a school," explains one of the artists, "represents that this institution serves all of us and we must take care of it, because the school is a support that we enjoy from public institutions, such as the primary school, the high school, and the health clinic; these places are for the community and they serve us all."

The Youth Development Plan and the educational methodology that was used to create it were positively evaluated by a governmental commission that was created after the riots for the purpose of supporting the youth of Rincón Grande de Pavas. A decision was made to use it as a framework for the design of a governmental counterpart program that was to be set-up to respond to each of the five areas of the Plan, working jointly with the five youth committees that had been created. This collaboration continues fruitfully until the present.

Although the time set aside for the four workshops was too limited to develop many of the concepts and principles of the *Integral Model*, this case does

FIGURE 3.4
Panel of "Hand Holding School"

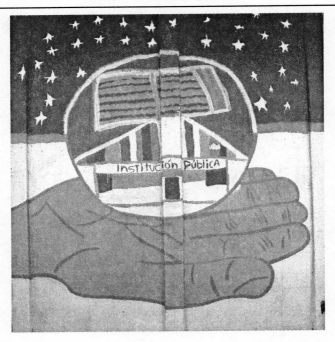

seem to demonstrate the validity of the fundamental assumption of this educational approach: if given an opportunity, people such as the participants from Rincón Grande de Pavas, will be able to transform patterns of despair and alienation into aspirations to live together as a community with a basic consciousness of universal responsibility.

NOTES

1. This presentation of the Integral Model of Peace Education draws partially on A. Brenes-Castro, (2002), The Earth Charter principles: Source for an ethics of universal responsibility, in P. Miller and L. Westra eds., *Just ecological integrity*, 26–36 (Oxford: Rowman and Littlefield Publishers, Inc.).

2. The United Nations University for Peace was created by the United Nations General Assembly in Resolution 35/55, December 5, 1980.

3. In this early version, the model was actually entitled *Integral Model of Education for Peace, Democaracy and Sustainable Development* and in earlier descriptions it is referred to by that name.

4. The main political framework for the selection of the IMPE's values, principles, and themes was provided by the *Declaration of Puntarenas* and the framework for policies of sustainable development of the *Central American Alliance for Sustainable Development*.

5. These texts included six didactic modules for popular education in Guatemala geared to the Guatemalan Peace Agreement and ten didactic modules entitled *Building the Culture of Peace in Our Community for Costa Rica*.

6. The Principle of Universal Responsibility (United Nations General Assembly, 1989) originated at the author's suggestion. Based on this contribution, he was invited to join the drafting committee of the *Earth Charter* (The Earth Charter Initiative, 2002) in 1998, and, subsequently, the principle was included in Paragraph 5 of the Preamble to the *Earth Charter*.

7. Though to a lesser degree than its Central American neighbor, there are significant socioeconomic inequalities and power differentials in *Costa Rica*.

REFERENCES

Batchelor, S. (1983). *Alone with others: An existential approach to Buddhism*. New York: Grove Weidenfeld.

Berry, T. (1988). *The dream of the Earth*. San Francisco: Sierra Club Books.

Berry, T., & Swimme, B. (1992). *The Universe story*. San Franciso: Harper San Francisco.

Bose, A. (1987). *Dimensions of peace and nonviolence: The Gandhian perspective*. New Delhi: Gian Publishing House.

Bray, J. N., Lee, J., Smith, L. L., & Yorks, L. (2000). *Collaborative inquiry in practice*. London: Sage Publications, Inc.

Brenes-Castro, A. (1991). *Seeking the true meaning of peace. Conference Proceedings*. San José: University for Peace Press.

Brenes-Castro, A. (2002). The Earth Charter principles: Source for an ethics of universal responsibility. In P. Miller & L. Westra (Eds.), *Just ecological integrity: The ethics of maintaining planetary life* (pp. 26-36). Oxford: Rowman & Littlefield Publishers, Inc.

Burton, J. (Ed.). *Conflict: Human needs theory*. London: Macmillan.

Cushman, P. (1990). Why the self is empty: Toward a historically situated psychology. *American Psychologist, 45* (5), 599–611.

Dalai Lama. (1984). *Kindness, clarity & insight*. Ithaca, New York: Snow Lion Publications.

Doyal, L., & Gough, I. (1991). *A theory of human need*. London: The Macmillan Press Ltd.

Durning, A. (1992). *How much is enough? The consumer society and the future of the Earth*. New York: W. W. Norton & Company.

Giddens, A. (1991). *Modernity and self-identity: Self and society in the late modern age*. Stanford, CA: Stanford University Press.

The Earth Charter Initiative. (2002). The Earth Charter. San José, Costa Rica: Earth Council.

Kelsang Gyatso, G. (1990). *Joyful path of good fortune*. London: Tharpa Publications.

Macy, J., & Brown, M. Y. (1998). *Coming back to life: Practices to reconnect our lives, our world*. Gabriola Island, BC: New Society Publishrs.

Max-Neef, M., Elizalde, A., Hopenhayn, M., and others. (1986). *Desarrollo a escala humana, una opción para el futuro*. Santiago: Centro de Alternativas para el Desarrollo.

Miall, H., Ramsbotham, O., & Woodhouse, T. (1999). *Contemporary conflict resolution*. Malden, MA: Blackwell Publishers Inc.

Pilisuk, M. (2001). Globalism and structural violence. In D. J. Christie, R. V. Wagner, & D. D. Winter. (Eds.). *Peace, conflict and violence: Peace psychology for the 21st century*. New Jersey: Prentice Hall.

Scott Peck, M. (1987). *The different drum: Community making and peace*. New York: Simon & Schuster.

Sengupta, A. (2001). *Third report of the independent expert on the Right to Development*. Submitted in accordance with Commission resolution 2000/5. Geneva: Commission on Human Rights, United Nations. E/CN.4/2001/WG.18/2.

United Nations Conference on Environment and Development. (1992). *The Rio Declaration on Environment and Development*.

United Nations General Assembly. (1984). Declaration on the Right of Peoples to Peace. Resolution 39/11. Retrieved December 2, 2003 from http://www.unhchr.ch/html/menu3/b/73.html

United Nations General Assembly. (1992). Report of the United Nations Conference on Evironment and Development. Annex I. Rio Declaration on Environment and Development. A/CONF.151/26(Vol. 1). Retrieved December 2, 2003 from http://www.un.org/documents/ga/confl51/aconfl5126-lannex1.html

United Nations General Assembly. (1999). Declaration and Programme of Action on a Culture of Peace. A/RES/53/243. Retrieved December 3, 2003 http://ods-dds-dds-ny.un.org/doc/UNDOC/GEN/N99/774/43PDF/N9977443.pdf?OpenElement

CHAPTER 4

Environmental Education

A Contribution to the Emergence of a Culture of Peace

Lucie Sauvé and Isabel Orellana

Our environments may be understood as socially constructed realities at the interface between Nature and culture. Environmental education seeks to shed light on and provide a critical appraisal of the complex webs of ecological and social relations that do and may emerge at this interface. It also seeks to re-establish the ties that bind people to each other, to the nonhuman world and, from a more global perspective, to our shared "home of life." It involves critical consideration of the close relationships between the three main ruptures that underlie the current socioenvironmental crisis: the rupture between individuals within a society, in the form of social disparity, inequity, abuse of power, and so forth; the rupture between societies, which both reflects and reinforces the first rupture; and the rupture between human beings and Nature, based on the denial of their own belonging to the web of natural life. The third rupture stems from the same set of attitudes and values as the first two, and all three feed back into each other, affecting each other synergistically.

The challenge for environmental education is to educate for profound cultural transformation, especially on the level of the third rupture, which separates human beings and Nature, so that the web of relations that link the individual, society, and the environment may be reestablished. This challenge is especially daunting in contexts of oppression, discrimination, and exploitation, which lead to social crises and direct violence. It is also considerable in situations in which psychosocial problems, such as those of young street workers, itinerants, or delinquents, arise. Can environmental education be justified in circumstances in which psychosocial concerns or social tensions are so grave that they overshadow environmental issues? How can it be deemed relevant in such conflict situations? What are the possible risks and benefits of promoting a socially critical environmental education in such contexts?

This chapter will present our thoughts on these issues and some elements of a response based on our own experience. First, we will synthesize the essential elements of our conception of environmental education and outline the historical, theoretical, and practical convergence between environmental education and the peace education. Then, we will underline the main social, environmental, and educational issues raised in the environmental education project, EDAMAZ, which challenged us to reconceptualize environmental education as a contribution to the construction of social peace. To this end and given the very conflictual contexts in which EDAMAZ evolved, the *learning community* appeared to be a singularly appropriate educational strategy, providing a crucible in which social and environmental concerns may be integrated; in which people may learn how to learn and to work collaboratively; and in which their capacity for living together may be nurtured. Relatively recent theory on and practical experience with the learning community suggests that it offers rich possibilities and relevant strategies for integrating peace and environmental education. Taking into account this potential, we will, therefore, put forward a reconceptualization of the *learning community* incorporating into the proposal some aspects of J. Dewey's and P. Freire's educational theories.

ENVIRONMENTAL EDUCATION: A PROPOSAL

Our conception of environmental education was developed gradually and discussed constantly over the course of our educational and research projects. It incorporates a number of complementary theoretical elements garnered from our exploration, experimentation, and critical analysis of the various trends of thought and practice that have emerged in the field of environmental education over the past 30 years[1] (Sauvé, 2002a; Sauvé & Orellana, 2001b).

(1) The *object of environmental education* is not the environment itself. Talk of education "about," "in or by," and "for" the environment, following A. M. Lucas's well-known typology, still does not take us to the core of environmental education: our own relationship to the environment. For each of us, this relationship is an idiosyncratic one, built-up over the course of an individual life experience, yet it is essentially mediated by the society one belongs to and is, therefore, culturally determined. What is required of environmental education, then, is that it take both personal and social aspects of human development into account.

(2) The *environment* is so complex a reality that it defies precise, comprehensive, and consensual definition. Rather than try to define it, our interest has

been in exploring the various ways it is perceived. These perceptions include the environment as Nature, to be appreciated and preserved; the environment as a resource, to be managed and shared; the environment as a problem, to be avoided or solved; the environment as a system, to be understood so as to improve decision making; the environment as a place to live, to get to know and improve; the environment as territory, a place one belongs to, a locus of cultural identity; the environment as landscape, to travel through and interpret; the environment as the biosphere, this "spaceship earth" in which we live together over the long term; and the environment as a community project, in which we become involved. It is through the totality of these interlinked and complementary dimensions that the relationship to the environment unfolds. If restricted to just one or another of them, environmental education remains incomplete and provides only a biased image of the relationship to the world (Sauvé, 2002b).

(3) One must bear in mind, furthermore, that *environmental issues*—the focus of many environmental education interventions—include social and biophysical components as well, and can, therefore, be understood only by analyzing the interests, visions, values, and power relations among the actors involved (Robottom & Sauvé, 2003). Consequently, it is most often more appropriate to speak about "socioenvironmental" issues. In *Cultivating Peace,* D. Buckles (1999) thus analyzes cases of social conflict over the use or sharing of natural resources; such conflicts are most often associated with the destruction of resources or with environmental problems. As E. Leff (2000) points out: "Failure to consider the social dimensions of environmental issues will give rise to either an idyllic or a catastrophist vision of the natural world that will prove incapable of engendering a critical understanding of socioenvironmental relations" (p.220).

(4) However, environmental education cannot be looked at only from a pragmatic problem-solving or issue perspective; it must be viewed as an *essential dimension of fundamental education.* It would be simplistic, therefore, to treat it as just one more type of thematic education: the environment is not a mere theme, but a vital reality of daily life. Environmental education is a core component of a human-development project. It involves more specifically one of the three spheres of interaction that are at the root of personal and social development (figure 4.1):

The central sphere is that of the *construction of identity.* This is the sphere of personal development, which is based on the individual's confrontation with him or herself, his or her characteristics, abilities, and limitations. Here one learns how to learn, how to define oneself, and how to relate to the other two spheres. This is the locus of development for self-esteem, autonomy, authenticity, integrity, reflectivity, and for responsibility to oneself—in terms, for example, of one's own rights and duties, health, and sexuality. It is where the search for harmony, serenity, and inner peace takes place.

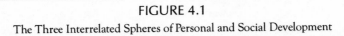

FIGURE 4.1

The Three Interrelated Spheres of Personal and Social Development

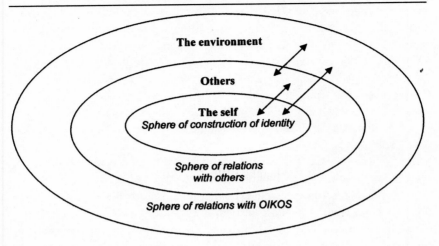

Source: L. Sauvé, (2001), L'éducation relative à l'environment. Une dimension essentielle de l'éducation fondamentale. In C. Goyer & S. Laurin, Entre culture, compétence et contenu: La formation fondamentale, un espace à redéfinir (pp. 293–318). Montreal, Canada: Logique.

The second sphere, the *sphere of otherness*, is very closely related to the first.
This is the sphere of interaction with other humans, whether with one person or
a social group: the "I" is shaped and defined through the "we" and the "you"
(Jacquart, 1999). In this sphere, one experiences both the advantages and difficulties of living with the other. Here one develops a sense of belonging to a group,
awareness of one's culture of reference, and a sense of responsibility towards others in the immediate surroundings and on a more global scale. This is where
peace, cooperation, intercultural, human-rights, and international-solidarity education take place. It is the locus of citizenship education, which involves learning
democracy, more specifically a "dialogical democracy," in which language is used
for mutual understanding and the other is perceived as being on the same level as
oneself and as an end in him or herself rather than as a tool (Miguelez, 1997). It
is here that one learns how to deal positively with conflict, to understand and accept difference, to make compromises when possible and seek consensus if need
be (Miguelez, 1997). It is where peace is constructed in an ongoing process of
interaction and dialog with the other.

It is in the third sphere that environmental education comes into play. This
is the *sphere of relations with the living place*, an area to which too little attention
has hitherto been paid in education. Here, the point of reference is *Oikos*, the

"home of life" that we share with each other and with other living beings. The *Oikos* (the Greek root of "eco-logy" and "eco-nomy") is formed and transformed at the interface between Nature and culture. It thus comprises the biophysical elements of the environment as they interact closely with the sociocultural aspects of the people living there. While the relationship with the world involves personal and private dimensions stemming from each individual's sensibility and life story, the relationship with the environment is essentially mediated by the sphere of interpersonal and social relations and thus determined by the culture of reference. This sphere involves a sense of otherness that goes beyond human otherness. It similarly involves another dimension of peace: one that concerns our relationship to Nature. The issue here is the extension of our sense of belonging and responsibility to the great network of living beings and the development of an ecocentric ethic: "an ethic centred on respect for life and not exclusively for human life, one that requires that the bounds of social responsibility be extended to include all the components of the web of life" (Leff, 2000, p. 228). It is in this sphere that a cosmology which gives meaning to the world and to our "being in the world" develops. Here, ecological education comes into play, and one learns how to get to know about one's "home of life" in all its diversity, richness, and complexity; how to integrate oneself into it; how to identify and define one's human niche in the global ecosystem; and how to fill it properly and harmoniously. Economic education also takes place here, as one learns to manage one's consumption patterns, to improve and properly use the shared space and common resources. To sum up, people learn to become responsible guardians, users, and builders of *Oikos*, our shared "home of life." The issue is not one of "managing the environment," but of "managing" our own individual and collective relationship with it. Environmental education sheds light both on the impact that individual and collective ways of being and doing have on the environment, and on the environment's influence on people's quality of being and ways of life. It also underlines the fact that the values that govern our relations with the environment are the same ones that govern our relations with each other. Thus, it is important to nurture not just respect for others and other living beings, but also a fundamental sense of responsibility that includes care and solidarity.

(5) Given this comprehensive educational perspective, environmental education should therefore not be considered a mere tool for solving environmental problems by trying "to change civic behavior." Such an instrumental, behaviorist approach to environmental education reduces its educational scope. Similarly, while ecocivism—regarding civil rights, and duties, and responsibilities towards the environment—may be useful for regulating social behavior in the short term, it cannot replace a holistic environmental education, which aims at the optimal development of individuals and social groups in relation to their environment. More

than a civic moral issue, it is a matter of *constructing a fundamental ethic*. Our conduct must be deliberate and based on ethical choices.

(6) Environmental education advocates a *critical approach* to social, environmental, and educational realities. While seeking to identify the positive aspects of a situation, such an approach also focuses on its possible limits, deficiencies, ruptures, inconsistencies, interplay of power, and the like, in order to bring about the transformation of realities that pose problems.

(7) This critical approach involves *adopting a praxis* that integrates action with reflection; critical examination must be directed from within and be at the heart of the process of experimentation of environmental and pedagogical situations. Such reflection can then yield the elements of a theory of personal and social relations with the environment and a pedagogical theory for environmental education.

(8) Given that the environment is something that is shared and that the relationship to it is socially constructed, environmental education calls for a *cooperative approach* both to learning and to taking action. The object is to learn to live together in a shared space and to build a healthy and congenial environment that is based on a common vision of what constitutes an optimal living place.

(9) Environmental education seeks to contribute to *ecodevelopment* in order to improve both people's quality of life and the quality of the environment, two integrally related poles of an *endogenous alternative development*. The issue is one of re-establishing the close bonds between the community and its living place and enhancing the bioregion's distinctive characteristics and possibilities, that is, the talents and culture of its inhabitants and its natural resources. The local population is encouraged to get involved in its environment and to live in harmony with it, making the most of its potentialities, while respecting not only its limits but its integrity as well. The object is not to hasten the advent of a "global village" governed by the rules of globalization and contributing to the expansion of monoculture but rather to stimulate development of a "globe of interlinked villages" (Morris cited in Nozick, 1999), each of which becomes self-sufficient in some ways and contributes to "biocultural" diversity.

(10) Finally, if we are to understand "development" in this way, environmental education clearly cannot be circumscribed by the proposition of sustainable development, in which it has little more than instrumental value, promoting an ideology that, though sharply disputed, remains hegemonic. The concern for sustainability may seem justifiable in the present context of the crisis of security that characterises our "risk societies" (Beck, 1992); it cannot, however, become the basis of a fundamental ethic for guiding human experience. The notion of sustainable development reduces the environment to the status of a resource reservoir for satisfying human needs and supports a con-

ception of development centred on economic growth and thus on competitiveness and inequity (Rist, 1996). Even when redefined in terms of a type of alternative development, the value of sustainability, in the sense of "tolerable" and "long lasting," does not stand up to ethical analysis. The alternative proposal of an ethic of responsibility seems richer and more profound, involving, as it does, not only civic responsibility but also a fundamental responsibility based on critical awareness, lucidity, care, and solidarity that binds beings to acting (Sauvé, 2001). Rather than sustainable development, we prefer to think and act in terms of the *development of responsible societies*.

Michèle Sato, a Brazilian environmental educator and researcher, puts forward a definition of EE that includes a number of these elements (Sauvé, Berryman, & Villmagne, 2002):

> The conception of environmental education is deeply rooted in a field of values that are more or less objectified; it is part of historic processes and specific contexts that give it a "polychromatic" character. Environmental education is part of a reflective, political, and critical vision that influences educational choices and determines human development, which is intrinsically linked to the environment. (p. 95)

ENVIRONMENTAL AND PEACE EDUCATION: AN INTERFACE

On the basis of the foregoing presentation of the main elements of the theory of environmental education, which we adopt in our research projects and upon which we base our educational interventions, we are able to identify the many points where environmental education coincides with peace education. Indeed, they appear as two essential, complementary, and closely interlinked dimensions of contemporary education. The environment is a highly political object, that is, one "having to do with public affairs." It is a shared territory and a common resource for life, a locus for the construction of group identity that calls for involvement by communities or social groups in problem solving and in conceiving and carrying out collective projects aimed at improving conditions of the living place. It is, therefore, important to learn how to share, discuss, negotiate, live together, build together, and develop the attitudes and skills linked to the practice of a "dialogical democracy." These same issues are of major importance in the field of peace education.

It is, furthermore, important to recognize and analyze the close relationships between environmental problems and social conflicts, which often give rise to each other:

Conflicts based on natural resources, particularly land, water and forests, are of a universal nature. In every country, people have competed to gain access to the natural resources they need or that they want to appropriate for subsistence or to improve their way of life (Buckles & Rusnak, 1999, p. 2).

D. Buckles and R. Rusnak (1999) point out that such conflicts bring into opposition people of different social classes, such as landowners and peasants, political leaders and populations, men and women, people of different cultures, and so on. The causes may vary. People may suffer when a local resource is damaged by human activity elsewhere in the region, for example, by upstream pollution of a river. Common resources may be the subject of internal social tensions stemming from divergent interests, involving policy issues, economic opportunism, and abuse of power. Resources may be damaged or may diminish, or they may become harder to get to, and the resultant scarcity may give rise to conflict. Finally, the cultural dimension of resource use may give rise to ideological, interethnic, and ultimately political struggles. Awareness of the close connections between environmental issues and social-conflict situations leads us to consider it relevant and even necessary to combine the objectives and integrate the processes of environmental education with those of peace education. The significant points of convergence between these dimensions of contemporary education make their integration even more relevant.

Historic Convergence

Both movements in peace education and environmental education gained momentum in the early 1970s mainly in relation to the formal institutional involvement of UNESCO (1974, 1976). The object was, on the one hand, to avoid a third world war and, on the other, to counter the depletion of natural resources and solve the serious environmental problems that had recently come to light. Though given impetus by a situation of insecurity and crisis, peace education and environmental education have, however, outgrown their initial instrumental purposes. Over the past few decades, they have given rise to significant ethical and educational reflection that has led to recognition of peace and environment as essential dimensions of education and core elements of a fundamental educational project aimed at the emergence of a "culture of peace" and the development of responsible societies. P. Weil (1994) thus speaks of "an art of living in peace with oneself, with others, and with the environment."

Axiological Convergence

A comparison of S. Rasseck's (1996) observations and UNESCO's (1976) proposals shows that the movements in both peace and environmental education stress value education, for example, responsibility, respect, solidarity, care . . . , and have adopted the same five categories of general objectives: awareness, knowledge acquisition, attitude and value development, the development of skills and abilities, especially skills related to critical thinking and information and communication processes, and taking individual and collective action.

Convergence with Regard to Strategic Issues and Limiting Factors

S. Rasseck (1996) and L. Sauvé (1997) observe the same problems related to peace education and environmental education. Both face difficulty in being incorporated in formal curricula and teacher training, with particular regard to interdisciplinarity, values education, and the issue of evaluation. They both have to deal with the limited availability of resources and the need to create partnerships with other actors in the "educational society."

Convergence of the Main Trends of Educational Interventions

Over the course of their development, the movements in peace and environmental education have given rise to different educational intervention and research trends. Comparing I. Robottom and P. Hart's (1993) analysis of the trends in environmental education with X. Jares's (1999) analysis of trends in peace education (figure 4.2), one notes the similarities between the categories they identify and describe. These categories echo N. Carr and S. Kemmis's (1986) analysis (inspired by Habermas) of educational trends in general.

The socially critical trend in environmental education, which corresponds to our theoretical choices presented earlier in this chapter, is consistent with the socio-critical trend in peace education, and, indeed, in dealing with crucial contemporary environmental and peace issues, it seems highly relevant to adopt a critical posture and pursue transformation. However, a research or intervention project that assumes this posture is hard to implement; it has to confront traditional education, and to question established social power and privilege. Moreover, as indicated by the experience of the EDAMAZ project, which we shall deal with below, a socially critical environmental education becomes all the more challenging in situations of major social conflict.

THE EDAMAZ PROJECT: A CHALLENGING
EDUCATIONAL CONTEXT

The EDAMAZ project (*Educación ambiental en Amazonia*-Environmental Education in Amazonia) brings together in a partnership the University of

FIGURE 4.2

Major Trends in Environmental Education and Peace Education: A Convergence

Trends	Environmental Education (Robottom and Hart, 1993)	Peace Education (Jares, 1999)
Technical-positivist	• Acquisition of knowledge *about* the environment • Behaviourist approach • Goals are predetermined, prescribed, not discussed. • Knowledge is objective and exogenous. • Educators, books or experts are the keepers of knowledge. • Learners are passive. • Pre-existing solutions to predefined problems	• Centered on objective and measurable phenomena concerning peace • Negative conception of peace as the absence of war • Cognitive approach; education must be neutral • No critical questioning of structures • Educators are experts transmitting information. • Learners are passive receivers.
Hermeneutico-interpretative	• Activities in the environment • Constructivist approach • Goals are predetermined but often negotiated. • Knowledge is intuitive, subjective, experiential. • Educators organize guided activities in the environment. • Learners are active; they learn through environmental experiences. • Exogenous interpretation of the environment	• Centred on subjective interdependence • Peace is the absence of war and of violence. • Intersubjective learning processes • Affective and cognitive approaches • No critical questioning of structures • Educators co-ordinate interactions and learning. • Learners participate actively in learning.
Socio-critical	• Action *for* the environment • Socially critical, reconstructivist approach • Goals are critiqued, negotiated. • Collaborative emergent knowledge derived from inquiry • Educators participate in inquiry process. • Learners participate in a collective problem-solving process.	• Centred on a positive, comprehensive and systemic conception of peace • Conflict may be creative. • Cognitive, affective, moral, and political approaches • Questioning of structures from an emancipatory perspective • Educators are researchers, agents of social criticism and agents of social change. • Interaction between educational institutions and society • Learners are active and involved participants.

Québec at Montréal and three Latin-American institutions—the University Gabriel-René-Moreno (Bolivia), the Federal University of Mato Grosso (Brazil), and the University of Amazonia (Colombia). The purpose of the project is to pro- mote environmental education as a contribution to the ecodevelopment of com- munities and social groups. The main phase (1996–2001)[2] was devoted to the conception, implementation, and evaluation of contextually relevant profes- sional development programs in this field, particularly in rural and disadvan- taged urban areas (Sauvé and Orellana, 2001a). Each program was designed by the members of the regional participating university team and adapted to the local context. All the programs, however, adopted the same experiential, critical, reflective, and collaborative approach to professional development.

Supported throughout by colleagues and professors from the university EDAMAZ team, the students of these programs, mainly teachers and commu- nity leaders, are asked to develop environmental education competencies by conceiving and experimenting with projects in their own school, village, or neighborhood. In an initial phase, the participants conduct an analysis of their milieu leading to a critical diagnosis which becomes the basis for developing a contextually relevant environmental education proposal. The teachers and com- munity leaders develop intervention projects centred on community action, join- ing together children, parents, and other members of the community in a participatory dynamic to improve socioenvironmental conditions in their milieu. The projects are discussed with colleagues and undergo improvement and change after further discussion, reflection on selected readings, and experimen- tation. Throughout the process, participants are invited to adopt a socially criti- cal and reflective stance so as to gradually develop a theory of environmental education that is transformative and meaningful for the specific context in which they practise.

Implementation of such an approach to professional development, which clashes with traditional school practices and calls for innovation, courage, and commitment, would be difficult in any context. But the EDAMAZ project was par- ticularly challenging specifically because of the unstable and uncertain socioenvi- ronmental context in which it evolved, a context in which environmental issues can easily be understood as causes or consequences of diverse situations of vio- lence and social tension. For a majority of people there, survival is an everyday concern. Lack of resources, low socioeconomic status of teachers, inequity, politi- cal tensions, and crisis associated with insecurity—all come into play. As a result, halfway through the project, very serious manifestations of latent social conflicts arose in the different regions where the EDAMAZ project was underway.

In Bolivia, bids by multinationals to privatize and control water gave rise to major protests. At issue were the social and ecological consequences of integrating local economies into a "unified market," which implies not only orienting production towards export but also the intensified exploitation of natural resources and people. In addition, Bolivian *cocaleros* (small coca farmers) found their crops destroyed by aerial spraying with a range of toxic chemicals. Citing demographic pressure, the complexity of the ecosystem, and the wish to protect biodiversity, the Bolivian government's "Dignity Plan" "relocated" 15,000 families from the coca-producing Chapare region. Ecological arguments are forgotten, however, when the question is one of exploiting the region's rich hydrocarbon resources with major investments by transnational oil companies. As a result, groups opposing the use of political and economic power to abuse people and land are being organized among the *cocaleros*, raising the spectre of guerrilla warfare.

In Brazil, there were long lasting national strikes involving public universities and a movement among the dispossessed rural populations to regain land and improve their working and living conditions (the *Movimento sem terra*). They mobilized to occupy and take possession of land; they also set up camps and laid siege to public agencies and multinationals to exert pressure on the government to alleviate their extremely insecure economic situation and undertook action to protest against the destruction of the environment, creating havoc in fields of genetically modified crops, for example.

In Colombia, where 80% of the world's cocaine is produced, the EDAMAZ team found itself in the middle of a civil war and of conflicts over the traffic in drugs. Aerial spraying of so-called illegal crops with a whole range of extremely toxic chemicals, including Monsanto's product RoundUp[3] among others, polluted bodies of water and endangered the health of peasant communities. Clashes between guerrillas, the armed forces, paramilitaries, and drug traffickers led to the forced displacement of people to the outskirts of cities into makeshift settlements that lacked basic health-care facilities.

In such a conflictive context where any critical posture is liable to annoy one or another of the factions on the ground, we learned that education itself may be seen as an object of suspicion; critical intellectuals may be seen as enemies of the formal leaders, or of the army, or of the "revolution"; and more specifically, environmental education, which calls for a critical analysis of social practices and power structures, may come to be seen as a subversive activity. In 1995, for example, Colombian university professor Alberto Alzate Patiño was assassinated. He was a regional leader in environmental education who advocated a critical approach to social and environmental discourses and proposals. He encouraged the involvement of teachers, students and members of the community in bioregional development projects aimed at enhancing local governance and the autonomy of social groups (Alzate Patiño, 1993). In our environmental education project, the call for socially critical and transformative action corresponded closely to Alzate

Patiño's thinking and practice. We were thus led to question the point of pursuing the EDAMAZ activities in situations in which people's main focus of attention was to stop violence and to regain their dignity and security. How was environmental education to be conceived in circumstances in which survival is a daily concern? We held intense discussions with our Latin American partners about the relevance and role of environmental education in such contexts, the ethical implications of pursuing the project, and the consequent conception and practice of environmental education we should adopt.

In fact, at the time that these issues became so acute, our Latin-American partners were already deeply engaged in the EDAMAZ Project, which they saw as a crucible for socioenvironmental and educational change. Therefore, they ultimately decided to continue with these activities and reorient environmental education towards the recovery of hope, in a context in which the lack of hope, though often unfortunately justified, is a major part of the problem. They decided to proceed carefully, however, and to concentrate on collective action projects aimed at solving concrete and immediate local problems. The focus of such projects would not be explicitly or a priori a critical appraisal of the political situation, although it appears to be at the root of most current socioenvironmental problems, nor, in principle, an attempt to penetrate the extremely complex psychosocial problematics of the situation. Rather, in an essentially pragmatic approach, the focus would be on concrete and realistic projects to restore and preserve aspects of local socioenvironmental conditions.

It was assumed that learning to work together and to pool skills and resources so as to find concrete solutions to crucial common problems (water quality, sanitary conditions, gardens of medicinal plants, etc.), people with different viewpoints and political allegiances might gradually come to know and understand each other better, and in this way, recognize and clarify the divergences in their visions of the world, values, and priorities, and identify the possibilities for sharing concerns about common problems and the search for solutions. The hypothesis was that this pragmatic approach might create the conditions for the parties to learn how to initiate a real dialogue, to adopt a critical stance towards inherent conflicts and to build on their experience to progressively achieve social transformation. The success by some pressure groups in bringing about the withdrawal or change of political decisions, such as the one in Bolivia regarding water privatization, was an encouragement to pursuing local action and helped to recover hope. What was ultimately intended by the EDAMAZ project was to empower local groups so that they could take action to improve the socioenvironmental conditions of their own milieu, while progressively constructing social peace.

Taking these considerations into account, we chose to center the dynamics of EDAMAZ on the strategy of the learning community, which lays emphasis on processes of social construction of knowledge, the development of a critical vision of realities, and involvement in projects for improving interpersonal and social relationships as well as the quality of the environment, as a shared living place.

THE LEARNING COMMUNITY: A PEDAGOGICAL STRATEGY[4]

The Concept of the Learning Community

The idea of the learning community draws on social and educational practices that have a long history[5] and are, as H. Reeves (1990) states, related to the construction of "spaces of freedom" (Orellana, 2002b). These spaces are shared in order to better apprehend the reality of the living place, learn to transform that which poses a problem, and conceive collective projects aimed at enhancing the conditions of the shared milieu and at living better together. It essentially involves structuring a working group and creating conditions for learning together around a common project that has significance for the participants and relevance for the context and which is aimed at change: changes among the participants and/or in the living place (Orellana, 2001, 2002a, b). The learning community involves implementing meaningful and stimulating processes that take into account the individual and collective needs and interests of the participants and that are adapted to the characteristics of each specific context. It promotes the development of a capacity for critical reflection and leads to a new reading of reality in all its complexity in order to rethink ways of being and acting. The shared experience within such a community may foster individual and collective maturity and increases what J. Rappaport (1981) calls the "empowerment" of the participants. Finally, the learning community is an appropriate strategy in any situation in which people want to learn together in order to carry out a common project that aims at transforming realities they want to change. Because it leads to dialog and involvement among various parties who are attempting to address socioenvironmental issues in their living place, the learning community provides a context within which to educate towards a culture of peace and environmental responsibility.

Learning communities consist of three main dimensions: a structural dimension, a pedagogical-process dimension (Gregoire, 1997) and a learning-dynamics dimension (Orellana, 2002a, b). The *structural dimension* refers to a structure or unit formed by a group of people who choose to join their forces in order to learn together. The point here is to recreate a community in which a sense of identity and belonging may develop and within which a common culture may gradually emerge regarding the proposed project. The *pedagogical-process dimension* is characterized by the integrated implementation of complementary approaches: cooperative, interdisciplinary, praxis-based, experiential, problem-solving oriented, holistic, systemic, and critical. The aim is to learn with and from each other complementarily within a praxis rooted in a concrete reality, taking into account its specific cultural, social and environmental aspects (Orellana, 2002a, b). Learning is here viewed as a dialogical and dialectical process of continuous construction, deconstruction and reconstruction of the understanding and meaning of realities (Freire, 1998). Such a process occurs *in, with,* and *for* the milieu in which the learning community is implemented, that is, the local community, community of interest, community of professional practice . . . (Orellana, 2002b).

The third dimension, the *dynamics* of the learning community, fosters the development of a web of interpersonal relations based on cooperation, mutual aid and sharing, collaboration, synergy, complementarity, reciprocity, respect, solidarity, closeness, mutual commitment, and a commitment to the living place (Orellana, 2002b). The emphasis is on developing a network of social, affective, cognitive, emotional, and moral relations based on dialog between the members in order to produce changes among the participants and in the living place where the learning community operates. Thus, the learning community, where one learns to live in, with, and for this shared world, becomes the crucible in which identity grows and a culture of exchange, confrontation, negotiation, and democratic life takes shape (Orellana, 2002b).

The Learning Community as a Pedagogical Strategy

The three dimensions described above are integrated in the learning community, which can be considered a *pedagogical strategy* (Orellana, 2001, 2002a, b) as shown in figure 4.3. It redefines the role of the actors, that is, of teachers and students, for example; gives comprehensive meaning to the learning process, and guides it's different phases, that is, the emergence of a project, organization of work structure, establishment of strategies of cooperation, management, appropriation, maturation, consolidation, and development of partnerships.

The following projects, which took place in the course of EDAMAZ, are examples of community-based projects centred on the pedagogical strategy of the learning community. Brazil's Santo Antonio bioregion was the scene of a rediscovery and development project that focused on medicinal flora and involved primary school pupils in partnership with their parents and other members of the community. In Bolivia, the My Clean Street project was also carried out by primary school pupils in cooperation with the neighborhood. In Colombia's Caquetá region, an ecological trail designed as a context and resource for community environmental education activities was developed by a protection and re-education center for troubled youth in partnership with the

FIGURE 4.3

A Conceptual Schema for the Learning Community Strategy (Orellana, 2002)

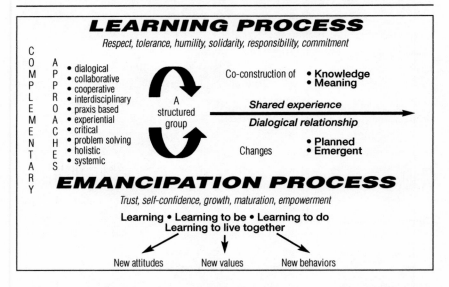

Source: Orellana, I. (2002b). *La cojmmunauté d'apprentissage en éducation relative à l'environnement: signification, dynamique, enjeux.* Thèse de doctorat. Université du Québec à Montréal.

university. Also in Colombia, a project for municipal refuse management was piloted by a nongovernmental organization in partnership with members of the community and the university.

The educational vision that is foundational to the learning community as pedagogical strategy is one in which educational responsibility is to be shared by the various actors in an "educational society." Education is no longer to be perceived as the sole responsibility of educational institutions but also to involve the society's other organizations and institutions (Antikainen, Houtsonen, Huotelin, & Kauppala, 1996; Ranson, 1994; Faure, 1972; Schön, 1971), including, among others, government agencies, businesses, associations, museums, non governmental organizations and medias, all putting together their complementary resources in a coherent global educational project aiming at social development. From such a perspective, the educational institution opens up to the living place so as to involve as partners the various actors from the "educational community," the one of proximity, and, more broadly, from the whole "educational society" (Orellana, 2002b). This openness leads various actors with shared interests to join together around concrete common projects and to pool their talents and resources. The educational institution thus comes to stand at the center of a community dynamic for the development of socioenvironmental or ecodevelopmental projects.

As noted above, social dynamics is a key factor in the process by which knowledge emerges in the learning community. P. Freire (1970) points out that the process stems from the complex reciprocal relations that human beings develop with the world, that is, their relations with others and with the living place, in which social practice is a crucial factor. Dialog, an essential component of the learning community, is seen as a creative act that, according to P. McLaren (1997), fosters the pursuit of change. Creativity within the learning community is stimulated by a process of integrating different types of knowledge—scientific knowledge, traditional knowledge, common-sense knowledge, experiential knowledge—that confront and fertilise each other (Orellana, 1997). It may also be stimulated by the challenge posed by the need to resolve conflicts within the learning community or in the surrounding milieu: such challenges are seen as a motor for problem resolution.[6]

The learning community as pedagogical strategy is also characterized by the importance attributed to the connection between educational and social concerns: the quality of being is closely related to the quality of being together in a shared living place (Orellana, 2001; Schnüttgen, 1997; MacCaleb, 1994; Clark, 1996). Indeed, as various authors (including Wenger, 1999; Schnüttgen, 1997; Clark, 1996; Potapchuk & Polk, 1994; Sergiovanni, 1994) point out, the development of people is related to the development of their community. It is at the heart of this development process that peace is built, linked intimately to the construction of a harmonious relationship with the environment.

Finally, the learning community invites people to learn "in," "about," and "for" the living place (Orellana, 2002b). It creates the conditions for collectively developing attitudes, values, and conduct that help counter degradation of the environment and deterioration of the quality of life of people and social groups. It can also help re-establish the sense of belonging to Nature and repair the ruptures between humans and between humans and Nature. It fosters bonds of belonging and identity (Wenger, 1999) and promotes respect, solidarity, responsibility, and commitment to help attain a lucid perception of reality so as to better apprehend, understand, objectify, and transform it responsibly (Orellana, 2002; Wenger, 1999). Figure 4.4 presents a synthesis of the various elements and characteristics of the learning community which contribute to environmental education, as these have emerged from our reflections and experiments, specifically in the framework of the EDAMAZ project.

Establishing a learning community is certainly not easy. The collaborative work that is required is a very complex one, littered with traps and obstacles and often leading to moments of chaos and wandering. It nonetheless remains a very

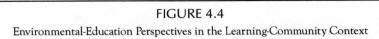

FIGURE 4.4

Environmental-Education Perspectives in the Learning-Community Context

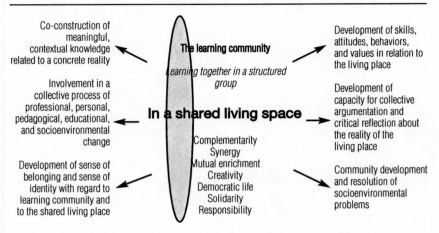

Co-construction of meaningful, contextual knowledge related to a concrete reality

The learning community

Learning together in a structured group

In a shared living space

Complementarity
Synergy
Mutual enrichment
Creativity
Democratic life
Solidarity
Responsibility

Involvement in a collective process of professional, personal, pedagogical, educational, and socioenvironmental change

Development of sense of belonging and sense of identity with regard to learning community and to the shared living place

Development of skills, attitudes, behaviors, and values in relation to the living place

Development of capacity for collective argumentation and critical reflection about the reality of the living place

Community development and resolution of socioenvironmental problems

Source: Orellana, I. (2002a). Buscando enfrentar los desafíos educativos contemporáneos: la estrategia pedagógica de la comunidad de aprendizaje en educación ambiental. In L. Sauvé, Orellana, I., & Sato, M. (Eds.), *Sujets choisis en éducation relative à l'environnement. D'une Amérique à autre. Textos escogidos en educación ambiental. De una América a otra. Textos escolhidos em edução ambiental. De uma América à outra* (pp. 221–231). Montréal: Les Publications de la Chaire de recherche du Canada en éducation relative à l'environnement.

Orellana, I. (2002b). *La communauté d'apprentissage en éducation relative à l'environnement: Signification dynamique, enjeux.* Thèse de doctorat. Université du Québec à Montréal.

promising strategy for encouraging educational processes that will lead to the questioning of traditional conditions of teaching and learning, and contribute to the improvement of education itself, to make it more meaningful, relevant and responsible.

ENVIRONMENTAL EDUCATION FOR PEACE: REFLECTING ON DEVELOPMENT

In this chapter, we have presented the elements of the theory of environmental education underlying our research and educational interventions. Specifically, our projects are undertaken from a critical perspective with a view to transforming realities and improving conditions in the living place. Such a perspective leads us to consider the close links between social and ecological realities, including the relationship between conflict situations and environmental problems. The EDAMAZ Project was particularly significant in this regard: it raised questions and led us to identify elements of a response. Among these elements, the learning community appears as an appropriate strategy: it fosters the development of projects for improving socioenvironmental conditions in the living place, and for constructing or re-constructing harmonious social relations.

The reflections that emerge from our work include considerations about the close relationship between the ways our contemporary societies develop and the interrelated issues of the environment, human rights, and peace. Societal choices nowadays actually lead to inequity and conflict; they usurp human rights, damage the environment and are detrimental not only to other living beings, but to the fabric of life itself. It is, therefore, important to promote and support the exploration of alternatives modes of development founded on a culture of peace and the ethics of environmental responsibility. It might be tempting to adopt the proposal for "sustainable development" that has received so much promotional publicity and media attention as a way of dealing with social and environmental issues. In fact, this notion is becoming the predominant framework for thought and action concerning the relations between people, between societies, and between humans and the environment. We must, however, remain vigilant in the face of such a proposition based on a so-called international consensus[7] and recognize its economicist tendencies. It regards the environment as a resource reservoir for human consumption and legitimates an economy that is exogenous to the social sphere and that determines relations between society and the environment. Sustainable development has become not merely a "buzzword" but a "watchword" (Traoré, 2002) for our societies, as evidenced by the recent Johannesburg Summit, where heads of state found a new context for their essentially economically driven debates. However, critical appraisal of the sustainable development prescription, which is put forward as the all-purpose solution to the problems of society and the environment, is far from over (Jickling, 1999; Sauvé, 1999).

Education stands at the forefront in the search for new "modes of development," for new directions and meanings for the human experience. We must develop an emancipatory education focused on the human being-as a living and social being-who questions the commonplace as well as society's hegemonic propositions and who can envisage creative and courageous new ways of living together with other humans and with the rest of Nature and of realizing our human potential in a responsible way. The complementary and synergistic fields of environmental education and peace education can contribute to this finality.

NOTES

1. The main trends may be identified as naturalist, conservationist, problem-solving, systemic, holistic, socially critical, bioregional, and feminist (Sauvé, 2002a). Each of these approaches provides a different perspective on the multidimensional object of environmental education. Each of them gives rise to integrated and contextually relevant educational choices.

2. The EDAMAZ project was developed as part of the Association of Universities and Colleges of Canada's (AUCC) Program for University Partnership for Cooperation and Development, funded by the Canadian International Development Agency (CIDA). This project has won two awards for excellence: from the AUCC and Scotia Bank and from CIDA http://www.unites.uqam.ca/EDAMAZ/

3. This information comes from *Le Monde diplomatique*, January 2001.

4. The learning community is the object of the doctoral thesis of Isabel Orellana (2002b), who devised an original theoretical framework which she used to study the dynamics of learning communities in the EDAMAZ Project.

5. We may cite, among others, John Dewey's *School as a social center* project, initiated in1896 in Chicago, Meiklejohn's *Experimental College* at the University of Wisconsin in 1927 (Wenger, 1999), the "academies" put forward by Gramsci that drew on the basic structures of nonformal education, and the popular-education and community-education movements (Orellana, 2002b).

6. EDAMAZ gave us a unique opportunity to explore the notion of conflict and envisage the development of a "pedagogy of conflict." According to such a pedagogy, there is a need not to obscure tensions but to recognize and if necessary legitimize them and exploit their transformative potential. It is also important to discuss the different possible avenues for solving problems: dialogical solutions, strategic solutions, and, in some cases, violent solutions, when the exacerbation of conflict becomes the only way to combat injustice. We must recognize the potential pitfall posed by "pacifism" when "favoring peace at the expense of justice, real improvements in livelihoods, and the conservation of nature" (Chevalier & Buckles, 1999).

7. Seeking consensus at any price, sometimes constructing false consensus, is essentially problematic. N. Rescher (1993) develops a rigorous argument to this effect to demonstrate that "consensus is not a criterion of truth, is not a standard of value, is not an index of moral or ethical appropriateness, is not a requisite for cooperation, is not a communal imperative for just social order, is not, in itself, an appropriate ideal" (p. 199). Moreover dogmatic adherence to consensus does not take into account the diversity of visions, desires, meanings, and potentialities. The search for consensus should not overshadow pluralism and dissension which can become significant creative forces in society.

REFERENCES

Alzate Patiño, A., Castillo Lara, L. A., Garavito, B. A., and Muñoz, P. (1993). *Propuesta pedagógica para el desarrollo local ambiental. Una estrategia en construction.* Colombia: Planeta Rica, Grafisinú.

Antikainen, A., Houtsonen, J., Huotelin, H., & Kauppila, J. (1996). *Living in a learning society: Life-stories, identities & education.* London: The Falmer Press.

Beck, U. (1992). *Risk society: Towards a new modernity.* London: Sage Publications Inc.

Buckles, D. (Ed.). (1999). *Cultivating peace: Conflict and collaboration in natural resource management.* Ottawa, Canada: IDRC/World Bank.

Buckles, D., & Rusnack, R. (1999). Conflict and collaboration in natural resource management. In D. Buckles (Ed.), *Cultivating peace: Conflict and collaboration in natural resource management* (pp. 1–12). Ottawa, Canada: IDRC/World Bank.

Carr, W., & Kemmis, S. (1986). *Becoming critical.* Geelong: Deakin University Press.

Chevalier J. M., & Buckle, D. (1999). Conflict management: A heterocultural perspective. In D. Buckles (Ed.), *Cultivating peace. Conflict and collaboration in natural resource management* (pp. 15–47). Ottawa, Canada: IDRC/World Bank.

Clark, D. (1996). *Schools as learning communities. Transforming education.* New York: Cassell.

Faure, E. (1972). *Apprendre à être?* Rapport de la Commission internationale sur le développement de l'éducation. Paris: A. Fayard, UNESCO.

Freire, P. (1970). *Sobre la acción cultural.* Santiago, Chile: ICIRA.

Freire, P. (1998). *¿Extensión o comunicación? La concientización en el medio rural* (21e éd.) México: Siglo veintiuno editores.

Grégoire, R. (1997). *Communauté d'apprentissage. Attitudes fondamentales.* Productions Tact, Université Laval. Retrieved October 1999 from http://www. fse.ulaval.ca/fac/tact/fr/html/prj-7.1/commune3.html

Jacquart, A. (1999). *L'homme est l'avenir de l'homme.* Liège: Alice Éditions.

Jares, X. (1999). *Educación para la paz. Su teoría y su práctica.* Madrid, España: Editorial Popular.

Jickling, B. (1999). Beyond sustainability: Should we expect more from education? *Southern African Journal of Environmental Education, 19,* 60–67.

Leff, E. (Ed). (2000). *La complejidad ambiental.* Mexique: Siglo veintuno editores.

Lucas, A. M. (1980-81). The role of science education in education for the environment. *Journal of Environmental Education, 12* (2), 32-37.

McCaleb, S. P. (1994). *Building communities of learners. A collaboration among teachers, students, families and community.* New York: St. Martin's Press.

Mclaren, P. (1997). A *vida nas escolas. Uma introdução à pedagogia crítica nos fundamentos da educação.* (2ᵉ éd.) Porto Alegre: Artes médicas.

Miguelez, R. (1997). L'éducation au dialogue: Éducation pour la paix—Une approche philosophique. *Revue des Sciences de l'Education, 27* (1), 101-112.

Nozick, M. (1999). No place like home: Building sustainable communities. Ottawa, Canada: CCSD Publications.

Orellana, I. (1997). La creatividad como un proceso metodológico de resolución de problemas. *Actas del seminario internacional de investigación-formación EDAMAZ—Educación ambiental en Amazonia* (p. 217-222). CIRADE, Université du Québec à Montréal, 30 septembre–11 octobre 1996.

Orellana, I. (2001). La comunidad de aprendizaje en educación ambiental, un nuevo enfoque estratégico dentro de un proceso de cambios educacionales. Revista *Tópicos en Educación Ambiental.* Guadalajara,Mexico: *SEMANARP, 3* (7), 43-51.

Orellana, I. (2002a). Buscando enfrentar los desafíos educativos contemporáneos: la estrategia pedagógica de la comunidad de aprendizaje en educación ambiental. *In* L. Sauvé, Orellana, I., & Sato, M. (Eds.), *Sujets choisis en éducation relative à l'environnement. D'une Amérique à autre. Textos escogidos en educación ambiental. De una América a otra. Textos escolhidos em educação ambiental. De uma América à outra,* (pp. 221-231). Montréal: Les Publications de la Chaire de recherche du Canada en éducation relative à l'environnement.

Orellana, I. (2002b). *La communauté d'apprentissage en éducation relative à l'environnement: Signification, dynamique, enjeux.* Thèse de doctorat. Université du Québec à Montréal.

Potapchuk, R. W., & Polk, C. (1994). *Building collaborative community.* Washington, DC: National Institute for Dispute Resolution, National Civic League, Program for Community Problem Solving.

Ranson, S. (1994). *Towards the learning society.* London: Cassell.

Rappaport, J. (1981). In praise of paradox: A social policy of empowerment over prevention. *American Journal of Community Psychology, 9,* 1-25.

Rassekh, S. (1996). *Éducation et culture de la paix: Sélection bibliographique mondiale.* Paris: UNESCO.

Reeves, H. (1990). *L'heure de s'énivrer: L'univers at-il un sens?* Paris: Éditions du Seuil.

Rescher, N. (1993). *Pluralism—Against the demand for consensus.* New York: Clarendon Press—Oxford).

Rist, G. (1996). *Le développement—Histoire d'une croyance occidentale.* Paris: Sciences Po.

Robottom, I., & Hart, P. (1993). *Research in environmental education—Engaging the debate.* Deakin: Deakin University Press.

Robottom, I., & Sauvé, L. (2003). Reflecting on participatory research in environmental education: Some issues for methodology. *Canadian Journal of Environmental Education, 8* (in press).

Sauvé, L. (1997). *L'éducation relative à l'environnement à l'école secondaire Québécoise—Éléments de diagnostic,* Montréal, Canada: CIRADE. 1998.

Sauvé, L. (1999). Environmental education, between modernity and post-modernity—Searching for an integrative framework. *Canadian Journal of Environmental Education, 4,* 9-35.

Sauvé, L. (2001). L'éducation relative à l'environnement. Une dimension essentielle de l'éducation fondamentale. In G. Goyer & S. Laurin (Eds.), *Entre culture, compétence et contenu: la formation fondamentale, un espace à redéfinir* (pp. 293-381). Montréal, Canada: Logique.

Sauvé, L. (2002a). *Courants d'intervention en éducation relative à l'environnement.* Module 5. Programme international d'études supérieures—Formation de formateurs en éducation relative à l'environnement. Canada Research Chair in Environmental Education, Université of Québec à Montréal.

Sauvé, L. (2002b). Environmental education: possibilities and constraints. *Connect, La Revue d'Education Scientifique, Technologique et Environnementale de l'UNESCO, 27* (1/2), 1-4.

Sauvé, L., & Orellana, I. (2001a). *EDAMAZ—Education relative à l'environnement en Amazonie. Rapport final.* Montréal, Canada: Chaire de recherche du Canada en éducation relative à l'environnement—Université du Québec à Montréal.

Sauvé, L., & Orellana, I. (2001b). La formación continua de profesores en educación ambiental: la propuesta de EDAMAZ. In J. E. dos Santos et M. Sato. (Ed.), *A contribução da educação ambiental à esperança de Pandora* (pp. 273-287). São Paulo, Brésil: RiMa Editora.

Sauvé, L., Berryman, T., & Villemagne, C. (2002). *L'éducation relative à l'environnement: une diversité de perspectives.* Module 1. Programme international d'études supérieures—Formation de formateurs en éducation relative à l'environnement. Montréal, Canada: Chaire de recherche du Canada en éducation relative à l'environnement—Université du Québec à Montréal.

Schnüttgen, S. (1997). Open learning communities under construction—are NGO's contributing to the process? Communication CIES *Conference on Education, Democracy, and Development at the Turn of the Century,* (March, 1997), 18–23.

Schön, D. (1971). *Beyond the stable state: Public and private learning in a changing society.* New York: W. W. Norton and Co.

Sergiovanni, T. J. (1994). *Building community in schools.* San Francisco: Jossey-Bass.

Traoré, A. D. (2002). L'oppression du développement. *Le monde diplomatique,* (Septembre, 2002), p. 28.

UNESCO. (1974). Recommandation sur l'éducation pour la compréhension, la coopération et la paix internationale. *Conférence générale de l'UNESCO 1974.* Paris: UNESCO.

UNESCO. (1976). La charte de Belgrade. *Connexion.* Bulletin sur l'éducation relative à l'environnement, No. 1, 1–3.

Weil, P. (1994). *L'art de vire en paix.* Paris: UNESCO.

Wenger, E. (1999). *Communities of practice. Learning, meaning, and identity.* New York: Cambridge University Press.

CHAPTER 5

Learning on the Edge

Exploring the Change Potential of Conflict in Social Learning for Sustainable Living

Arjen E. J. Wals and Fanny Heymann

There is no single outlook on what sustainable living entails nor on how to achieve it. We do know, however, that working towards sustainable living involves raising questions with regard to values, ethics, justice, and equity. Pathways towards sustainable living are unlikely to develop without friction, controversy, and conflict. After all, as is illustrated in figure 5.1 (p. 124), we live in a pluralistic society, characterized by multiple actors with diverging interests, values, perspectives, and constructions of reality. Moreover, the ill-defined and uncertain nature of working towards sustainable living does not allow for universally applicable recipes for sustainable development. Governments cannot rely on the exclusive use of economic instruments and legislation to enforce sustainable living. At the same time, reliance on the *instrumental* use of education, training, and communication to promote or even force one particular view of "sustainable living" is problematic as well.

In this chapter, the dialectic between the divergence of interests, values, and world views, on the one hand, and the need for a shared resolution of issues that arise in working towards sustainable living, on the other, will be explored. The main idea underlying our position is that the conflicts that emerge in the exploration of sustainability are prerequisites, rather than barriers, to reaching solutions that can be sustained for longer periods of time. In other words, conflict can be a driving force for reaching solutions to sustainability issues that are rooted in the everyday lives of people. Social learning will be introduced as a transformative (re)framing process which is considered essential in moving towards these solutions. Central to our position is the need for facilitated cultivation of pluralism and conflict in order to create more space for social learning in nonformal and informal educational settings.

FIGURE 5.1

Creating a Sustainable Community in The Netherlands

The Dutch Ministry of Environment, Housing, and Spatial Planning developed legislation that encourages municipalities and individual citizens to promote sustainable housing. Citizens can get all kinds of subsidies to move towards energy efficiency, for instance. Municipalities can get subsidies when they allocate municipal land to housing development that meets certain sustainability criteria.

In 1999 a few sustainability-minded citizens became interested in developing an entire neighborhood (over 200 households) on principles of sustainable living as outlined by themselves (i.e. a community garden owned, designed and maintained by all members) and by the government (i.e. with regards to the building materials used, double water system, solar energy, triple pane glass, etc.). By placing advertisements in magazines and on web-sites aimed at people who had an interest in nature, environment and sustainable living, the initiators of this sustainable neighborhood were able to create a group of potential buyers large enough to persuade a municipality to allocate land for this innovative neighborhood. They presented their plan to several municipalities and contractors and eventually one municipality, the town of Culemborg, and one developer signed a contract with the group.

From this point on, the core group of citizens entered into a dialogue with both the contractor (about the design of the houses) and the municipality (about the design of the community garden). They were given seed money by the town of Culemborg to organize themselves and to hire a process facilitator. Their tasks included generating sufficient interest in the 200 homes to be built, developing a contract to be signed by all buyers, and developing a plan for the municipal garden. The contract had to reflect the sustainable nature of the neighborhood and to outline the role of the inhabitants in making the experiment a success. The municipal gardens were to honor some of the principles of perma-culture, but also needed to be child-friendly and a natural extension of people's own private yards. The process of reaching an agreement about the design of the gardens and its contents required a lot of dialogue since people's ideas of what a garden should look like varied greatly. Furthermore there was quite some variance in the extent to which involvement in designing, developing, and maintaining the garden was desired.

In order to reach a common understanding regarding the design, implementation, and maintenance of the community garden, many meetings were held as well as so-called "Sustainability Masterclasses" and workshops with several experts on, for instance, perma-culture, landscape architecture, and biodiversity. During these meetings people were allowed to express their desires, views and expectations. In mediated confrontation with sometimes diametrically opposed desires, views and expectations, they arrived at a design and maintenance system that received the support of all involved. The process did not involve all potential inhabitants since not all were interested in the garden, but they were frequently informed through the neighborhood's web-site and newsletter about the process outcomes and agreed early on that they would support these outcomes. For those more passive inhabitants a set of guidelines (code of ethics & code of behavior) was provided to make sure their gardening activities did not clash with the carefully thought out community garden.

Today the community gardens and the housing designs serve as an inspiring example for many other municipalities, home owners, architects, landscapers and urban planners from around the world.

The process of determining how to live sustainably undertaken by a group is viewed as a particular manifestation of social learning, that is, of deriving insights on what sustainable living will entail in a specific situation. In other words, sustainable living is viewed both as an evolving product and as an engaging process. In the research literature in environmental education, working towards sustainable living as a social learning *process* has until now received less attention than concepts of sustainability as expert *predetermined teachable products* (Wals & Jickling, 2002). This chapter, therefore, focuses primarily on informal and non-formal learning contexts (i.e. learning as a part of everyday semistructured events that may or may not touch explicitly upon issues of sustainable living). It does not focus on institutional or school-based learning which tends to focus on a product (i.e., a set of "right" attitudes and behaviors) that is to be understood and reproduced. This is not to say that the process-oriented approach we advocate here has no place in the school community. On the contrary, process-based approaches also have a place in formal education as has been advocated elsewhere (Wals & Jickling, 2002; Sterling, 2001).

SUSTAINABLE LIVING AND SELF-DETERMINATION

If the premise that there is no single outlook either on what sustainable living entails or on how to achieve it is accepted, then it follows that determining the meaning of sustainability will be a process involving all kinds of citizens in all kinds of contexts who might not always agree with one another. There will be different degrees of self-determination, self-responsibility, and autonomy people can exercise while engaged in such disputes. That is, the amount of space people have for making their own choices, developing their own possibilities to act, and for taking responsibility for their own thinking and acting will vary (Wals & Jickling, 2002*)*. We will argue that it is precisely *enhanced* space for alternative thinking, valuing, and acting that lies at the root of more enduring sustainable solutions. Conflicts, as we will show later, play an important role in creating such space.

The extent of citizen involvement in the decision-making processes oriented towards sustainable living depends not only on the degree of self-determination they can exercise but also on the amount of openness and the extent to which outcomes and processes are prescribed to citizens. As indicated in figure 5.2, a continuum can be used to indicate different degrees of self-determination and autonomy in decision making (Margadant & Wals, 1998) and a second one to express the amount of openness and the extent to which outcomes and processes are prescribed.

The resulting force field shows four different conceptualizations of sustainable living and the role citizens play in moving towards sustainable living, to the extent that this is possible (Wals & Jickling, 2002).

In the upper left quadrant of the force field there is "big brother" sustainability, which refers to sustainability that has been authoritatively determined and defined by experts and prescribed to obedient and passive citizens (see also Orwell, 1989). Such sustainability could be part of a kind of eco-totalitarian regime which very well might sustain the Earth for a very long time from an ecological and natural resource management point of view. It is questionable, however, whether (all) people will be happy in such a regime as such an approach is likely to violate some basic human rights and values. In the cell in the lower right quadrant we find so-called grassroots sustainability, characterized by the active and critical involvement of competent and action-oriented citizens with high degrees of self-determination in finding pathways towards "sustainable living as agreed upon by all" and with high degrees of empowerment and self-actualization. Whether the resulting society will be sustainable for long from an ecological point of view is questionable, but the people living in it might be happier at least for a while. Sustainability education in its most educative form and critical pedagogical interpretation would fit well in this quadrant.

FIGURE 5.2
Sustainability and Citizen Involvement

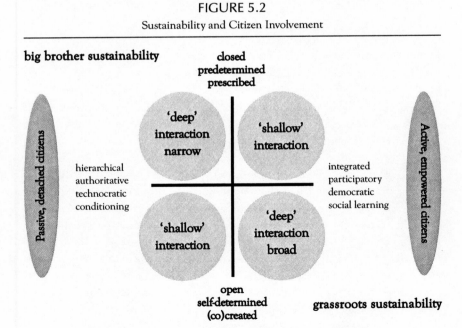

Source: Based on A. E. J. Wals and B. Jickling, Sustainability in higher education, *Higher Education Policy* 15: 121–131.

The other two cells represent forms of sustainable living and involvement characterized by a limited openness and/or citizen involvement. This can be seen, for instance, when groups are encouraged to actively participate in the execution of a sustainability action that has been predetermined with minimal or no involvement. Limited and even false or shallow participation often is the result. Think, for instance, of school children involved in a corporately sponsored recycling program which might provide children with some space to think of ways to recycle and to develop a recycling action plan but does not critically examine the possibility of reducing consumption. From a sustainable living point of view an emphasis on the "R" of "reduce" might be far more effective than an emphasis on the "R" of "recycle," but the children are not engaged in this discussion. On the contrary, controversy is avoided and a deeper engagement with the issues blocked. The result often is "feel good sustainability": the corporate sponsor takes pride in supporting community recycling and improves its sustainability image. At the same time, the company doesn't have to worry about a serious challenge to its need to grow year after year, quarter after quarter. After all, the more we consume, the more we can recycle. Meanwhile the children and schools involved feel good about having done something positive for the environment and, possibly, having raised some money for the school in the process.

It should be stressed that figure 5.2 is quite normative with a strong bias towards openness and participatory democracy. The language, for example, "shallow" and the "big brother" metaphor, reveals this bias, which is shown to be somewhat contrived when looking, for instance, at the role of expertise. In the upper left quadrant, there is a tendency to downplay the people's voices and to stress expert knowledge ("the experts know what's right, the people know nothing"), while in the lower right quadrant there's a tendency to downplay expert knowledge and to stress the people's voices ("leave it to the people and there own local knowledge, don't let outside experts interfere . . ."). A more fruitful perspective perhaps would be to consider each quadrant as a likely starting point in moving towards sustainable living and to recognize that all quadrants are likely to be visited and needed at some point in the process. As presented here, it (figure 5.2) should be seen as a heuristic that can help analyze one's own positions within the force-field and the direction in which one might wish to move to in the future.

CONFLICT IN SUSTAINABILITY

Many attempts have been made to classify both the contents (elements and dimensions) and the process (dynamics and phases) of conflict (cf. Glasl,

1980; van Dongen et al., 1996). These classifications and reductions tend to de-contextualize conflict and under-emphasize, if not deny, the existence of multiple realities and the role of conflict itself in their social construction. On the other hand, it is also acknowledged by some that conflict can, when carefully introduced and guided, play a fundamental role in meaningful learning and in bringing about personal change. H. J. Van Dongen, W. A. M. de Laat, & A. J. J. A. Maas (1996) speak of conflict or sociocognitive conflict as the motor for constructions of reality with interdependent social and cognitive components (van Dongen et al., 1996, p. 123). In cognitive psychology (i.e., Festinger's *cognitive dissonance*, 1957), developmental psychology (i.e., Piaget's *disequilibrium*, 1964) and educational psychology (i.e., Berlyne's *conceptual conflict*, 1965), the virtue of conflict in conceptual, developmental, and personal change had already surfaced by the mid-twentieth century. "No change or development without conflict," and "No change or development with too much conflict" put simply represent the main conclusions of studies in the above fields. Another phrase often used in this context is "resistance to change." Kurt Lewin referred to this resistance as a potentially positive source and "motor of change" (Lewin, 1946).

With the renaissance of (social) constructivism and (social) constructionism, there has been a renewed interest in the role of conflict in change which no longer limits it to conceptual and cognitive conflict. Rather emphasis is placed on the role of conflicting constructions of reality in social and organizational change processes (cf. Kolb & Bartunek, 1992; van Dongen et al., 1996; Pearce & Little-john, 1997); in addition, new domains of application are being considered, for instance, environmental management (Glasbergen, 1995) and peacebuilding (Harris & Forcey, 1999; Wals, 1999). However, although recognized in other contexts, the constructive role of the conflict that results when divergence converges is hardly explored in the context of sustainable living.

Nonetheless, when considering, for example, the varied degree of self-determination outlined in figure 5.2, one can imagine the different types of conflict that can emerge in citizens' attempts to move towards sustainable living. Let us, for the sake of debate and argument, look at two extremes: the big brother version and the grassroots version of sustainable living and citizen involvement. In big brother sustainability, conflict is avoided by using "objective," scientifically determined standards or norms. Examples of such standards and norms are plentiful these days. Think, for instance, of outcome-based national standards for environmental education or of ISO 14001-like norms for business and industry. After determination of such norms and standards, a whole range of instruments to implement or enforce them is often used: laws, legislation, regulation, reward and punishment schemes, (mandatory) training and instruction. These instruments tend to have in common that they leave people little choice but to subscribe to a particular outlook or behavior whether they believe in it or not. Conflict might occur in the setting of the standards and during the selection of the instruments but once agreed upon and transplanted to the public arena, ambivalence is avoided as much as possible to show confidence in the schemes developed. However, it should be noted that when rules are broken, or when standards are not met, met superficially, or critiqued by certain groups, conflict does emerge amongst those affected by the rules, regulations, and standards.

On the other hand, in grassroots sustainability different perspectives, kinds of expertise, values, and interests converge in a consensus-seeking process that inevitably will not take place without conflict. Cultivating these conflicts and making them forces for conceptual change and creative problem-solving is a prerequisite for arriving at solutions that people can identify with and act upon as they will be their *own* solutions. Sustainable living, here, is rooted in a context and takes on many forms and shapes as contexts differ both in space and time. It develops on the edges of the carefully facilitated and sometimes mediated encounters between different interests, values, and world views. In an ideal social learning process all participants involved jointly arrive at a temporary vision of sustainable living which they share and with which they identify—a vision that is not prescribed from the outside but that is derived from the life-world of the participants. There may not be consensus about everything but there might be a renewed sense of community and interdependency and even a respect for differences or a respectful dissension about the things with which people strongly differ (Lijmbach, Margadant-van Arcken, Koppen, & Wals, 2002). It should be recognized that this quadrant, too, has its flip side. After all there will always be differences in knowledge base, access to resources and networks and, therefore, inequities, which will also lead to conflict and even a demand for instrumental guidance and outside expertise. Once again, both perspectives are extremes, but they do emerge frequently in education for sustainability (Hesselink, van Kempen, & Wals, 2000).

While the situations suggested in figure 5.2 are hypothetical, when considering that in the coming decades, dramatic changes in lifestyles are anticipated if we are to cope with changing environmental conditions, the resolution of issues both leading up to and resulting from these shifts is unlikely to occur without friction, controversy, and conflict. For they represent complex social, political, economic, ecological, aesthetic, and ethical concerns and clearly dictate the need for a more sustainable approach to development (Wals & Bawden, 2000). Dealing with this complexity and uncertainty, with conflicting norms, values, and interests in a world characterized by ever-expanding globalization requires a re-conceptualization of the role of conflict in transformative learning processes.

SOCIAL LEARNING

Solving conflicts that arise in working towards sustainable living is a process that can be meaningfully interpreted from a social learning perspective. Social learning, understood as a collaborative reframing process involving multiple interest groups or stakeholders, is located in the multitude of actions, experiences, interactions, and social situations of everyday life (Vandenabeele & Wildemeersch, 1998). Through discursive dialogue and cooperation between people positioned within different configurations or frames (i.e., interests, values, reality constructions, and contexts) such learning can be intensified and can lead to change. Social learning theory recognizes the existence of collective learning goals and the need for creating the right conditions for stimulating the learning of individuals. In other words, social and individual learning are intricately linked. Hence, social learning can be viewed as an intentionally created purposeful learning process that hinges on the presence of the "other" or others. Social learning can, however, also take place in everyday life where intention and purpose may be less clear. The life-world of those involved in a social learning process can be both prohibitive of and conducive to the learning that takes place. Life-world, here, refers to the conglomerate of experiences, contexts, and interpretations people live by, of which they are part, and to which they contribute (Wals, 1994).

In social learning the interactions between people are viewed as possibilities or opportunities for meaningful learning. The motivation to participate in a social learning process is not always naturally present but does play a critical role. Much depends on the collective goals shared by those engaged in the process. Whether such collective goals can actually be achieved depends on the amount of space available in the learning process for possible conflicts, oppositions, and contradictions. A main thesis underlying this contribution is that any learning process that seeks to address issues related to sustainable living, for example, diverging norms, values, interests, and constructions of reality, should be designed so that these differences are explicated rather than concealed. By explicating and deconstructing these diverse norms, values, interests, and constructions of reality, it becomes possible to analyze the nature and flexibility of the perceived differences. From this perspective, learning can be viewed as a change process, resulting from a critical analysis of ones own norms, values, interests, and constructions of reality (deconstruction), exposure to alternative ones, and the construction of new ones (reconstruction). Such a change process is greatly enhanced when the learner is mindful and respectful of other perspectives. In addition there needs to be room for new views that broaden the realm of possibilities, in other words, space for dialogue rather than the mere transmission or exchange of viewpoints. For, after all, sustainable living requires more than consensus on a present situation and condition. Sustainable living requires a dialogue to continuously shape and reshape ever changing situations and conditions.

Dialogue, as it is intended here, requires that stakeholders involved *can* and *want* to negotiate as *equals* in an *open* communication process which *celebrates diversity* and *conflict* as the driving forces for development and social learning (Kunneman, 1996; Wals & Bawden, 2000). Such dialogue rarely emerges spontaneously but rather requires careful designing and planning since differences in interests and possibilities can be significant, especially when there are major power imbalances. Through dialogue participants can develop an understanding and appreciation of social learning, the role of conflict and diversity, and an awareness of different norms, values, interests, and constructions of reality, their underlying assumptions and their history. Viewed as such, dialogue provides the basis for purposeful action.

Although concepts of social learning are noticeably absent in the literature on environmental education or education for sustainability, they do surface frequently in literature on interactive policymaking and conflict management. Terms and phrases, such as coproductions, multiple actor perspectives, participatory methods, alternative dispute resolution, community problem solving, interactive policymaking, stakeholder analysis, joint decision making, all hint at a collaborative social learning process, notwithstanding their different roots and underpinnings.

FRAMING AND REFRAMING SUSTAINABILITY

The crucial role frames play in collaborative social learning processes is a topic that recurs in social psychology and in management and policy research. How an issue is initially framed can greatly affect the problem-solving perspectives and extent of conflict between those involved in the process (Smutko & Garber, 1998). It is no surprise therefore that frames and (re)framing are central concepts in environmental and social psychological change processes (see for instance Gray, 1997). E. Goffman (1974) defines frames as "principles of organization which govern events—at least social ones—and our subjective involvement in them." Whereas framing represents an individual's or a group's attempt to control how a particular view will be perceived by others, reframing consists of a deliberate attempt to alter someone else's perspective or point of view (Kaufman & Smith, 1999).

D. A. Schön and M. Rein (1994, p. 28) note that people use metaphors stuffed with normative dualisms as frames (i.e., artificial-natural, integral-piecemeal, quick fix-sustainable, healthy-sick) to lead others to a desired solution to the issue at stake. According to S. Kaufman and J. Smith (1999) some frames are characterized by a shared meaning that can spur the public's engagement. They offer the Not In My Back Yard or NIMBY label as an example. NIMBY, originally associated with high-risk land uses (e.g. nuclear plants, hazardous waste sites), now extends to any unwanted land use, including shopping malls. S. Kaufman and J. Smith (1999) argue that NIMBY has acquired frame status because when it gets attached to a change proposal it can trigger communitywide opposition.

B. Gray (1997) has developed a typology to describe frames that can be utilized in conflict related to environmental change: substantive, loss-gain, characterization, process, outcome, and aspiration. Of particular interest to the purposes of this chapter are the characterization, process, and outcome frames. We will add yet another, based on the work of Kaufman and Smith (1999), called the "complexity frame." *Characterization* has to do with the stereotypical or prejudiced nature of perceptions of the other or of other groups based on either personal experience, exposure to media or both. Such a characterization can hinder communication between groups and often causes interpersonal or intergroup conflict. Kaufman and Smith (1999) list a number of examples of conflict-laden characterization frames: "industry is only looking for short term profits or has deep pockets," "environmentalists are extremists always opposing economic development and pursuing the return of all land to its prior state," "poor neighborhoods are mostly African American in the case of the United States of America or immigrant neighborhoods in the case of western Europe." People also develop self-characterization frames which help them determine their chances of reaching an outcome which they view as positive.

Frames people hold with regard to the decision making and/or planning process, its rules, its transparency, its accessibility, its phases . . . , are called *"process frames."* These frames are colored not only by people's own prior participation or nonparticipation in similar processes, but also by the way the media and the process initiators present the process to the stakeholders involved. Kaufman and Smith (1999) note, for instance, that a *done deal* frame leading to the belief that negotiations are futile might have a chilling effect on public participation. At the same time an *open ended* frame may lead people to believe that their input is valued and crucial.

Outcome frames, expressed as preferred solutions, portray conflicts in terms of people's or parties' positions (Fisher & Ury, 1991). As Kaufman and Smith (1999) state, "Parties come into a change dispute favoring a particular outcome that can become their frame for the dispute" (p. 171). As an example they refer to the zero risk frame held by people who in specific cases will only accept a new project (i.e., new power lines in the neighborhood) when there is zero risk involved (i.e., zero magnetic radiation) even though their own personal lifestyles involve far greater risks (i.e., cigarette smoking or driving a car).

Another type of frame that affects the way people respond to sustainable living has to do with *complexity*. Complexity refers to the frames people hold about the value or status of information. According to Kaufman and Smith (1999), a complexity frame leads parties either to treat information with undue respect or to unduly discount it. They distinguish between a *science-as-truth* frame (upper left quadrant in figure 5.1) and a *science-as-deception* (lower right quadrant in figure 5.1) frame. Those holding on to the former frame have high regard for scientific data, reports, statistics, particularly when generated and presented in a high-tech form. Those holding on to the latter frame are skeptical of scientific information and believe it is normative, essentially political, and manipulable.

Whatever the type of frame, however, frames, at least individual frames, are not static but rather dynamic. "Individuals may adopt frames when needed, and shift to other frames in time. In fact, some reach for a handy frame only when queried about their views . . ." (Kaufman & Smith, 1999, pp. 173–174).

Frame awareness, frame deconstruction, and reframing can be viewed as central steps in the transformative social learning process referred to earlier. For instance, when people are engaged in the redesigning of the commons (i.e., the public space in between housing blocks) in a multi-ethnic neighborhood, it may not only be enough to find out what they find important, but also to find out what frames they use in defining both the commons and what they find important to have in the commons if one is to facilitate the decision-making process. A "commons as playground" frame may be far more child-centered and safety-oriented and lead to quite a different design of the commons as opposed to a "commons as public parking space," or "commons as city nature frame" as was one of the frames illustrated in figure 5.1 at the beginning of this chapter. People can become so stuck in their own frames that they may fail to see how those frames color their judgment and interaction.

The essence of social learning for sustainability, one could argue, is the transcending by the various groups and actors involved in a conflict of their own idiosyncratic frames and the frames of the interest group of which they are members in order to be able to view others in an open manner and to create enough "chemistry" amongst themselves to feel sufficiently empowered to work jointly at the challenges that they face. For this to happen, people must make their frames and the assumptions underlying these frames explicit so as to better position themselves to see their shortcomings or one-sidedness. This will require skill (reflection, introspection, and expression) and willingness to share with others (and thereby making oneself potentially vulnerable). However, once frames have been made explicit, this is when what we will call, de-framing begins (sometimes referred to as deconstruction). *De-framing*, in its essence, is a process of untangling relationships, becoming aware of one's hidden assumptions, ideological underpinnings and blinding insights, and confronting these with those of others not "seen" before.

In addition to frame awareness and de-framing, *reframing* is an essential component of transformative social learning. Through reframing people can develop shared frames that offer mutually acceptable solutions to multiple interest issues. Collaborative reframing is more likely to be successful when all parties involved have deconstructed their own frames and come to understand and perhaps even appreciate those held by others.

DIALOGICAL DECONSTRUCTION

Earlier we introduced social learning as a transformative (re)framing process which is considered essential in designing, implementing, monitoring, and evaluating plans for sustainable living. It is now necessary to address the question of how such social learning can be organized. F. V. Heymann (1999; 2001) describes *dialogical deconstruction*, a method for framing, de-framing, and reframing, as central to facilitating the process of transformative social learning. As suggested earlier, individual learners construct their own frames based on often persistent meanings which are of a cognitive (i.e., knowledge), affective (i.e., emotions), and social (i.e., relational) nature. Dialogical deconstruction is a stepwise process characterized by the unraveling and untangling of these divergent frames as they become manifest in an interactive process revolving around (semi-) controversial issues.

Steps in the Process of Dialogical Deconstruction

Dialogical deconstruction consists of the following steps, which resemble the conceptual change process as described by R. Driver and V. A. Oldham (1986): orientation, frame awareness, de-framing, reframing, application, evaluation. It should be noted that though these steps can be distinguished for purposes of description, they are hard to separate in reality as they interrelate and overlap. They are presented in a linear fashion here but in dialogical deconstruction they form an ongoing cyclical learning process.

Orientation. Participants identify key issues of concern or challenges which they wish to address, connecting them to their own prior experiences and background. In this way their motivation to participate in the learning process increases as does their sense of purpose.

Frame Awareness. Frames which participants hold regarding the collective issues or challenges identified in the orientation phase are elicited. Narratives can be useful in bringing these presuppositions to the forefront. (Mishler, 1991; Kohler Riessman, 1993).[1] Participants then confront the way they ascribe meaning to their ideas, interests, values, and knowledge. Rather than focusing on their often persistent frames of reality, attention is immediately shifted to their prior perceptions and process of sense making. This guided self-confrontation usually leads to an increased understanding of the different frames that can be found within the group of involved stakeholders. Participants become aware that people's frames are rooted in different contexts of sense and meaning making. Finally this frame analysis provides the input for deconstruction, the step that follows.

Deframing. Participants deconstruct their own frames and those of the other stakeholders in the group. This requires the softening and untying of construed meanings, which can be accomplished by helping participants gain a clearer understanding of their own frames and their potential influence on social action and by exposing participants to conflicting or alternative frames. This may be done, for example, by (1) projecting (frames are extrapolated to the future and the potential consequences for the individual and for others of acting on the basis of this frame is considered); (2) using metaphors (carefully chosen metaphors or analogies that encourage a better understanding of one's own frame and its potential shortcomings are analyzed); and (3) mirroring (people with contradicting frames present or explain the frame of the other party). Only when individual frames are thus deconstructed is space created for the reconstruction of alternative frames that will allow for the resolution of the conflict/problem at hand.

Reframing. Prompted by discomfort with their de-constructed frames and the need for a new more consistent frame understood by all involved, participants jointly begin to reconstruct or create alternative frames which they will hold in common. This creation of collective frames is central to the process of dialogical deconstruction. For it to be successful, participants must, through a process of exchange, interaction, and even confrontation, create recognizable images of possible situations that transcend reality as members of the group currently perceive it. By focusing on desired future outcomes, confrontation provoked by the divergence in frames within the group will take place in a positive and less threatening environment. As a result, more collective frames will gradually emerge and a (renewed) sense of community and shared responsibility for the solutions generated jointly will develop ("we are all in this process together and as a group we will make things happen even though it is not exactly what I had in mind in the beginning"). This will make the softening of individual demands easier though, of course, in the end, individual frames may remain in conflict with collective frames. However, as a result of the deconstruction process, these individual frames may no longer be dominated by inaccurate assumptions and implicit knowledge that impede communication and block future learning. In sum, at the heart of dialogical deconstruction is an ongoing process of deconstruction of individual frames and a reconstruction which creates frames participants hold in common, thus allowing a more open, more sensitive, and better-informed discussion of diverging frames that are present within the group and the gradual transformation of a negotiation into a dialogue. This process may well prove to be a central feature of more sustainable lifestyles and structures.

Application. The newly constructed frames are translated into a joint plan of action which helps move the group towards a solution to the issues(s) identified.

Evaluation. Participants—individually and as a group—reflect upon and assess the degree to which the issues or challenges identified at the beginning of the process have been addressed. They also review the changes that have occurred in the way the issue was framed originally to determine whether they have reached convergence towards collective frames with which they all can identify at least to a degree. This evaluation of the commonality of newly formed frames is an important step within dialogical deconstruction. Awareness of their individual and group changes will give participants a better sense of progress. As for those issues about which there appears to be continuing dissent, at least some understanding and respect will have emerged which may have been lacking at the beginning of the process.

Facilitating Dialogical Deconstruction

The following conditions need to be taken into account for dialogical deconstruction to be successful:

Role of the Facilitator. Organizing and guiding dialogical deconstruction requires the presence of facilitators who must be equipped with the skills to meet the challenging demands of the task. First of all, they must be professional in approaching and involving the various stakeholders. They have to be sensitive towards all involved and be willing and able to put themselves into the construction of their world. Only then will they gain their much needed confidence and trust. Facilitators also need to separate themselves from each of the groups involved in the process in order to be able to make explicit their different assumptions and positions. D. A. Schön (1983) notes that problems are not just "out there" but construed out of problematic situations. Hence, facilitators must also make sense of an uncertain situation that initially seems to make no sense at all. At the same time, while engaged in the process of problem framing and re-framing, a necessary prerequisite for the ability to think in terms of possible solutions, facilitators must be mindful of their own constructions and interpretations since they will inevitably have their own frames on the issues at stake. They must be capable of bracketing these interpretations in order to avoid a biased framing of the discussion.

One potentially critical aspect of dialogical deconstruction is working within people's "zone of proximal development" or their comfort zones (based on Vytgotsky, 1978). Facilitators of social learning need to be mindful of these zones both in helping people confront the normative underpinnings and limitations of their own frames and in helping them reconstruct alternative frames. They will need to assess them (the comfort zones) by obtaining sufficient insights in the life-world of those involved in the change process and by combining these insights with knowledge of the local context. Thus, they can avoid confronting people with ideas that are radically different from their own, ideas which, no matter how good they may be, can be threatening and rather, more fruitfully, introduce mildly dissonant ideas that are strong enough to lead the participants to question their thoughts and actions.

Motivating Participants. Participant motivation is considered a determining factor in social learning for sustainable living. How are people to be kept engaged in the process? One strategy is to investigate cases of successful transformative social learning processes carried out elsewhere. Careful investigation of such cases can reveal that moving towards sustainable living requires an amalgamation of a variety of smaller actions and a number of critical decisions (Monroe, 1990). As social psychologist, Karl Weick (1984) notes, since smaller problems are more easily solved, framing an issue in smaller pieces may provide enormous psychological benefit. Frequent feedback on how the issues at stake have been framed and re-framed, on how the group is moving towards a better mutual understanding and towards a shared frame in reaching a solution is also crucial to keep motivation levels high.

Cultivating Diversity. As noted above, the multiple groups and actors involved in the exploration of sustainable living bring divergent frames to the task of describing and interpreting reality. In attempts to relate diverging frames and to reconstruct common frames that can serve as a basis for dealing with issues that are problematic to the group, it is essential that "singularism" be avoided, that is, an approach for dealing with divergent views whereby, through the (ab)use of power, particular frames are selectively elevated to be the basis for decision making and planning while others are discounted. This may lead to a distributive outcome when, for instance, ecological frames are privileged over economic frames, or, as is more common, when economic frames are privileged over ecological ones. In such cases, we often see a hardening of positions dividing the group in two—those who have won and those who have lost. Singularism can also lead to a false consensus, when a neutral third party tries to mold the different frames into one universal reality in order to arrive at a solution that appears to be satisfactory to all involved but fails to address the underlying issues at stake. Clearly, singularism rarely leads to satisfying long-lasting results. In contrast, dialogical deconstruction advocates pluralism. This approach is based on the premise that conflict is inherent to the interaction between dissimilar and diverse societal groups. It is founded on respect and openness for difference, in other words, for sensitivity to frames that differ from one's own. In this regard, the language used in dialogical deconstruction is crucial. Efforts must be made to use language that is inclusive and inviting as opposed to exclusive and alienating.

Drivers of the (re) Framing Process

The (re)framing process is driven by a mix of continuous encounters that occur within the two force fields described in figure 5.2. These force fields point to tensions between prescriptive and closed frames handed down authoritatively by policymakers and scientific experts *and* self-determined and open frames co-created in a participatory process. These encounters serve as drivers of the (re)framing processes. The dialectic between top-down and bottom-up governance and between open and closed learning processes is considered essential in improving the quality of learning for a more sustainable future. Figure 5.3 provides a somewhat less normative presentation of the two force fields from figure 5.2.

As illustrated by the case presented at the beginning of the chapter (figure 5.1), the (re)framing process that leads toward sustainable living requires *both* emancipatory and instrumental change. Figure 5.3 provides an overview of what this entails. The shaded circles illustrate the different degrees of involvement and autonomy that are possible, that is, from closed and prescribed to open and self-determined. Both universal expert knowledge (i.e., hierarchical technocratic) and local contextual knowledge (i.e., participatory democratic) are needed to realize more sustainable solutions to issues that potentially have strong political, moral, and ideological underpinnings. Figure 5.3 also suggests that citizens do not have to be active and empowered in every issue but can move from more passive detachment to active involvement at different times and vice versa. Triggered by mediated

FIGURE 5.3
Continuous Framing and Reframing towards Sustainability (ies)

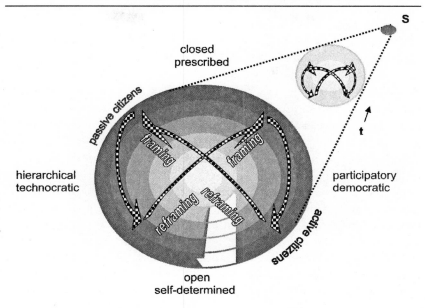

confrontation and through the dialectic of framing, de-framing and re-framing, improved understanding of the issues at stake and of the frames different groups in society use to interpret these issues is likely to emerge. The arrows and the circles illustrate this dynamic. They are to be seen as confrontation between frames leading to simultaneous de-framing and reframing. Whether these confrontations indeed lead to reframing depends on peoples' comfort zones. Some people are better able to deal with radically different perspectives (i.e., more comfortable with the other end of the continuum) and are actually challenged by them while others are challenged by positions that only slightly differ from their own. Figure 5.3 also shows that sustainability is an emerging product—the product of a social learning process which evolves over time towards an ever-advancing horizon.

CONCLUSION

This chapter has introduced the notion of social learning as a transformative (re)framing process which is considered essential in moving towards contextual sustainability. It has argued that conflict about sustainability issues rooted in the everyday lives of people, when resolved constructively, can be a force which drives this process and proposed dialogical deconstruction as a method for facilitating it. In this concluding section, some of the implications of these ideas for sustainability education will be outlined.

Many sustainable living conflicts arise from the differences in ways of looking at the world and become problematic when these differences manifest themselves in all kinds of prejudices and false stereotypes (see, for example, the characterization frames introduced earlier). One key aim of sustainability education should be to help people recognize the nature and relativity of their own frames and of those of others, and to engage people in a reframing process that moves them to mutually acceptable solutions to the issues they themselves have identified. The process of dialogical deconstruction outlined in the chapter intends to facilitate the reframing process. It provides an opportunity for the joint contextualization and exploration of meaning. Through dialogue, discourse, negotiation, joint fact-finding, mediation, people can arrive at their own interpretation of sustainable living as contextual and relevant to their own situation within a broader context of ecological responsibility and ethical defensibility (see also Wals & Bawden, 2000). In other words, given that we do not know what comprises the right or best "sustainable lifestyle" in a particular context, it is argued that it would not be correct for "technical experts," or the government to prescribe to citizens how they should behave. This is not to say that policymakers or scientific experts have nothing to contribute. On the contrary their input will often be needed as citizens will find that not all information is available in their own context and that alternative ways of knowing, acting, and valuing, not present at the local level, can provide the necessary imagery to develop new solutions. However, in the last analysis, final decisions and plans should be made within the local context by those who live there.

Sustainability education should also take into account that educating *for* something (peace, biodiversity, sustainability), unlike educating *about* something, is essentially political and has to do with democracy and participation in the broadest and deepest sense. Preconditions for education *for* sustainability, then, should include a focus on transparency of power relations, communicative competence of the participants, diversity of perspectives, values and interests entering the learning process, equal opportunity and access for all learners, and room for creativity and space for alternative, deviant, and nonconforming outcomes (Wals & Jickling, 2000). These notions about democracy and participation can also be applied to processes for making decisions about the content and direction of the learning to take place. They suggest questions that need to be addressed if learners are to be fully involved in their learning process. That is, to what extent are learners and facilitators of learning involved in such decisions? Does education for sustainability respond to the challenges identified by the community? Is the learning process and its content sensitive to the ideas, values, interests, and concepts embodied by the learners themselves? Are the goals and objectives of the learning process itself also subject to permanent discussion and negotiation ?

One other serious issue to consider if sustainability education is to aim for democracy and participation is that of power relations. It is important that groups with weak voices receive extra attention and support so that they can operate on an equal level with more powerful groups. In reality, it can be difficult to change procedures in order to remove barriers for the "unorganized." The formal language used, formal discussion techniques applied, and the way sessions are organized often represent barriers to equal participation in the process. Therefore, time and energy will be needed to develop an appealing learning process which is accessible for all. The use of everyday narratives, photographs, videos, exhibits, joint site visits, for example, can help to achieve this. Without such attention to structural conditions, it is likely that certain groups will withdraw from the process altogether.

Furthermore, it must be recognized that people learn in many contexts and that traditional environmental educators have only worked within a small subset of potential learning contexts. Where people meet to discuss their needs, desires, future, their being and their environment, there is potential for transformative social learning as long as this potential is recognized and carefully tapped by skilled facilitators. The proposed methodology of dialogical deconstruction, while still subject to continuous discussion and improvement, represents an attempt to facilitate this process, that is, to provide support for educators, community leaders, and interactive policymakers who recognize the central place of the life-world of the various stakeholders and the crucial role of conflict and dissonance in bringing about social and environmental change.

Finally, as educators with broad concerns about the future of the Earth and concerns about the multiple aspects of human relationships within society and the relationship between humans and Nature, we must seek more, not less diversity of thought (Wals & Jickling, 2002). Sustainability education should, therefore, provide people an opportunity to confront their core values, their practices, and their entrenched lifestyles. This observation has far reaching implications for the goals, content, and process of education and of sustainable living as a topic of education. That is, education for sustainable living should, above all, mean the creation of space for social learning that will allow for more diversity of thought. This should include space for alternative paths of development and new ways of thinking, valuing, and doing; space for participation minimally distorted by power relations and for pluralism, diversity, and minority perspectives; space for deep consensus but also for respectful *dissensus* (Lijmbach et al., 2002); space for autonomous and deviant thinking, for self-determination, and, finally, space for contextual differences.

NOTE

1. Narratives also prove useful to facilitators in assessing the change potential of each individual actor involved in the process and can be checked against both the possibilities and limitations for change embedded in local contexts.

REFERENCES

Berlyne, D. E. (1965). Curiosity and education. In J. D. Krumboltz (Ed.), *Learning in the educational process* (pp. 67-84). Chicago: Rand MacNally & Co.

Driver, R., & Oldham, V. A. (1986). Constructivist approach to curriculum development in science education. *Studies in Science Education, 13,* 105-122.

Festinger, L. (1957). *A theory of cognitive dissonance.* New York: Harper & Row.

Fisher, R., and Ury, W. (1991). *Getting to yes: Negotiating agreements without giving in.* 2nd. Edition. Boston: Houghton Mifflin Co.

Glasbergen, P. (Ed.). (1995). *Managing environmental disputes: Network management as an alternative.* Dordrecht: Kluwer Academic Publishers.

Glasl, F. (1980). *Konfliktmanagement: Diagnose und behandlung von konflicten in organisationen.* Bern: Haupt Verlag.

Goffman, E. (1974), *Frame analysis: An essay on the organization of experience.* Cambridge, MA: Harvard University Press.

Gray, B. (1997). Framing and reframing of intractable environmental disputes. In B. Lewicki, R. Bies, & B. Sheppard (Eds.), *Research on negotiation in organisations.* Vol. 6. Greenwich, CT: JAI Publishing.

Harris, I., & Forcey, L. (Eds.). (1999). *Peacebuilding strategies for teachers and community leaders.* New York: Peter Lang Publishers.

Hesselink, F., van Kempen, P. P., & Wals, A. E. J. (2000). *ESDebate: International on-line debate on education for sustainable development.* Gland, Switzerland: IUCN.

Heymann, F. V. (1999). *Denken en doen in dialoog.* Ph.D. diss., Wageningen: Wageningen University.

Heymann, F. V. (2001). *Denken en doen in dialoog.* Utrecht: Lemma.

Kaufman, S., & Smith, J. (1999). Framing and reframing in land use conflicts. *Journal of Architecture, Planning and Research,* Special Issue on Managing Conflict in Planning and Design 16 (2), 164-180.

Kohler Riessman, C. (1993). *Narrative analysis.* London: Sage Publications Inc.

Kolb, D. M., & Bartunek, J. M. (Eds.). (1992). *Hidden conflicts in organizations: Uncovering behind-the-scenes disputes.* Newbury Park, CA: Sage Publications Inc.

Kunneman, H. (1996). *Van theemutscultuur naar walkman-ego. Contouren van postmoderne individualiteit.* Amsterdam: Boom.

Lewin, K. (1946), Action research and minority problems. *Journal of Social Issues, 26,* 3–23.

Lijmbach, S., Margadant-van Arcken, M., Koppen, C. S. A., & Wals A. E. J. (2002). 'Your view of Nature is not mine!' Learning about pluralism in the classroom. *Environmental Education Research, 8* (2), 121–135.

Margadant-van Arcken, M., & Wals, A. E. J. (1998). *Pedagogical dimensions of environmental education.* Paper submitted for discussion during the conference "Das Kind als 'sozialer Akteur'? Soziologische Kindheitsforschung—in kritischer pädagogisch-phänomenologischer Sicht" Giessen, Germany: 17–20 February 1998.

Mishler, E. G. (1991). *Research interviewing. Context and narrative.* Cambridge, MA: Harvard University Press.

Monroe, M. C. (1990). Converting "It's no use" into "Hey, there's a lot I can do:" A matrix for environmental action taking. In D. A. Simmons, C. Knapp, & C. Young (Eds.), *Setting the EE agenda for the '90's: 1990 conference proceedings.* Troy, OH: NAAEE.

Orwell, G. (1989). *Nineteen Eighty-four.* 1949. Reprint, London: Penguin Books.

Pearce, B. W., & Littlejohn, S. W. (1997). *Moral conflict: When social worlds collide.* Thousand Oaks, CA: Sage Publishing Inc.

Piaget, J. (1964). Development and learning. *Journal of Research in Science Teaching, 2,* 176–186.

Schön, D. (1983). *The reflective practitioner: How professionals think in action.* New York: Basic Books.

Schön, D. A., & Rein, M. (1994). *Frame reflection: Towards the resolution of intractable policy controversies.* New York: Basic Books.

Smutko, S., & Garber, S. (1998). *Public dispute resolution and participatory decision-making.* Faculty In-service Training, University of Wisconsin-Extension Service, Madison, WI: University of Wisconsin.

Sterling, S. (2001). *Sustainable education: Re-visioning learning and change.* Schumacher Society Briefing no. 6. Dartington: Green Books.

van Dongen, H. J., Laat, W. A. M. de, & Maas, A. J. J. A. (1996). *Een kwestie van verschil: Conflicthantering en onderhandeling in een configuratieve integratie theorie.* Delft: Eburon.

Vandenabeele, J., & Wildemeersch, D. (1998). Learning for sustainable development: examining life-world transformation among farmers. In D. Wildemeersch, M. Finger & T. Jansen (Eds.), *Adult education and social responsibility* (pp. 115-132). Frankfurt am Main.: Peter Lang Verlag.

Vygotsky, L. S. (1978). *Mind in society: The development of the higher psychological processes.* Cambridge, MA: Harvard University Press.

Wals, A. E. J. (1994). *Pollution stinks! Young adolescents' perceptions of nature and environmental issues with implications for education in urban settings.* De Lier, Netherlands: Academic Book Center.

Wals, A. E. J. (Ed.). (1999). *Environmental education and biodiversity.* Wageningen: National Reference Centre for Nature Management.

Wals, A. E. J., & Bawden, R. (2000). *Integrating sustainability into agricultural education: Dealing with complexity, uncertainty and diverging worldviews.* Gent: ICA.

Wals, A. E. J., & Jickling, B. (2002). "Sustainability" in higher education: From doublethink and newspeak to critical thinking and meaningful learning. *Higher Education Policy, 15,* 121-131.

Weick, K. E. (1984). Small wins: Redefining the scale of social problems. *American Psychologist, 19* (1), 40-49.

CHAPTER 6

Value-Based Perspective Development

Anita L. Wenden

We are all familiar with the Sufi folk tale about the blind men, from an Indian city near Ghor, who tried to determine the form and shape of an elephant. Each of them gathered information about the animal by touching a different part of it. The man who had felt the ear said the elephant was "a large, rough thing, wide and broad like a rug" while the one who had felt the trunk said it was like "a straight and hollow pipe, awful and destructive" and the one who had felt its feet and legs described it as "mighty and firm, like a pillar" (Shah, 1969, p. 25). Their distinct understandings were shaped and limited by where they stood to feel the animal and the frame of reference they used to interpret what they had perceived, thus suggesting the influence of perspectives from which we view and through which we interpret experience. Implicitly agreeing with the folk tale about the importance of perspectives, results of a casual sampling of the ERIC data base using the keywords "critical perspective" and "perspective development," which yielded about three dozen titles, point to the fact that perspectives also provide the basis for critical understanding and that they need to be learned. The theoretical writings of adult educators who propose that perspective development be a key goal in adult education clearly underlines this latter concern (Brookfield, 1985; Cranton, 1994; Mezirow, 1997).

Indeed, the need to make perspective development an educational priority cannot be ignored if one considers the manner in which many younger and even more mature adults perceive and respond to personal encounters with or media reports about social conditions, practices and events antithetical to a culture of peace. Their views often evidence an understanding that remains on a factual level. As P. Cranton (1994) notes, they respond with trite or superficial statements, or to borrow from T. Kisiel's definition of a perspective (cited in Mezirow,

1991), they look *at* the world rather than *through* it. At the same time, views they may hold and communicate on such matters often reveal the dominant perspectives through which the media frames political realities (Brookfield, 1990; Howson & Cleasby, 1996). Therefore, if these social and ecological realities are to be evaluated critically and autonomously and if acquired perspectives on these realities that are antithetical to a culture of peace are to be challenged, perspective development is necessary.

However, thus far perspective *development* has received scant attention from either peace or environmental educators.[1] In the literature one finds references to specific perspectives that should be included as goals in educational curricula. B. Reardon (1988a) puts forth the development of a planetary perspective as a goal of peace education, while A. Bjerdstedt (1990) includes a value perspective in his schematic presentation of components relevant to peace education. One of the four level goals for curriculum development in environmental education listed by Hungerford, Peyton, and Wilke (cited in Braus & Wood, 1993) is the ability to analyze environmental issues and their associated value perspectives, while the statement of entitlement proposed by the National Curriculum Council of the United Kingdom includes among its aims the notion that pupils must be encouraged to examine and interpret the environment from a variety of perspectives, for example, physical, historical, aesthetic, ethical (Palmer, 1998). F. C. Verhagen (1999; 2001) proposes the development of an Earth and Peace Literacy perspective as one of the goals of the Earth Community School. Finally and more generally, S. Greig, S. Pike, and D. Selby (1987) include perspectives (unspecified) among the aims of an education which takes into account the needs of person and planet, and D. Pike (2000) lists perspectivity, that is, the recognition that one's perspectives are partial and that one needs to seek other perspectives, as a goal of contemporary global education.

The content and/or manner of developing *specific* perspectives has also been outlined. For example, D. King (1973) provides sample lessons for teaching global perspectives in the fourth and fifth year of elementary school. P. Stillman (1978) and R. Hanvey (1982) outline the content or dimensions of a global perspective which young people should be helped to acquire. L. T. McCabe (1994) reports on the results of a study which showed that study abroad programs can lead to a refinement and expansion of a global perspective. C. Hopkins & R. McKeown (2002) list the assumptions that underly an international perspective on sustainability. Referring to the work of M. Kearney (cited in Ahearn, 1994), S. Ahearn (1994) outlines seven categories that will define the content of a perspective of partnership towards Nature.

However, except for S. Ahearn (1994) and F. Verhagen (1999; 2001) the need for perspective development is not *explicitly* referred to in the writings of the other peace and environmental educators cited above. One must infer th'at this may be what is intended from the fact that perspectives are included as learning objectives in curricula. Moreover, the need for a critical perspective for understanding and evaluating both social and ecological realities that inhibit the achievement of a culture of peace has not been acknowledged. F. Verhagen (1999; 2001) appears to be the exception. Nor have the contents of such a critical perspective been specified or the manner of developing it addressed.

This chapter aims to respond to this educational need. It first defines the nature and function of a perspective and presents a rationale for making values the components of perspective development. A description of the value components for a perspective for evaluating media reports and/or personal experiences of social conditions, practices, and events that may either inhibit or facilitate the achievement of a culture of social and ecological peace follows. Finally, the chapter outlines a process for facilitating the development of such a value-based perspective.

DEFINITION AND FUNCTION OF A PERSPECTIVE

The term *perspective* is rarely defined in the literature in general education. One infers from the way it is used that it is a point of view or a way of looking. However, it is central to views on adult learning, and for an expanded and more precise understanding of its nature and function one can turn to this body of literature, specifically J. Mezirow's (1991) definition of *meaning perspective* and his explanation of terms from various disciplines that also refer to this concept (see figure 6.1).

The meaning of the term, *perspective*, as it is used in this chapter, is based on a synthesis of the definitions in Figure 6.1. It is understood to be an organized set of assumptions and values about a social reality which is acquired and can be applied to selected situations as a matter of habit.

The functions of a perspective highlight the relevance of perspective development for a curriculum that educates for a culture of social and ecological peace. As implied by the definitions, it provides a frame for making sense of given situations and events and shapes the boundaries of our expectations, perceptions, and comprehension, including the understanding of new data. Thus, a perspective orients the perceiver to familiar and unfamiliar aspects of what is perceived. As a result, it can limit future learning and diminish our awareness of reality especially when the unfamiliar may appear threatening (Mezirow, 1995). Other than providing a conceptual apparatus for making sense of experience, perspectives provide criteria for evaluating what is construed. Moreover, by predisposing our intentions and purposes, they influence our actions.

FIGURE 6.1
Definitions of a Perspective

Meaning perspective: the structure of assumptions that constitutes a frame of reference for interpreting the meaning of an experience (Mezirow et al., 1990, p. xvi); a habitual set of expectations that constitutes an orienting frame of reference that we use in projecting our symbolic models and that serves as a (usually tacit) belief system for interpreting and evaluating the meaning of experience (Mezirow, 1991, p. 42) ADULT EDUCATION

Frames of reference: pre-existing structures in the mind of the perceiver (Nisbet and Ross cited in Mezirow, 1991, p. 42); structures of assumptions through which we understand experience (Mezirow, 1997, p. 5.) PSYCHOLOGY

Metascientific concept: a conceptual apparatus with the help of which one defines, describes and explains certain problematic matters* (P. Sztompa cited in Mezirow, 1991, p. 42); a frame—shared definition of a situation that organizes and governs social interaction—a frame that tells us the context of a social situation and how to understand and behave in it. (E. Goffman cited in Mezirow, 1991, p. 46). SOCIOLOGY
*33 terms were found signifying this notion.

Paradigm: a collection of ways of seeing, methods of inquiry, beliefs, ideas, values and attitudes that influence the conduct of a scientific inquiry. (T. S. Kuhn cited in Mezirow, 1991, p. 46.) SCIENCE

VALUES AS THE BASIS FOR PERSPECTIVE DEVELOPMENT

The influence of values on human thought and action is both pervasive and profound. They constitute the core of human cultures and are central to an individual's belief system. Values have been shown to predict behavior and are listed as goals in the curricula of both peace and environmental education.

Values as Building Blocks of Culture

Values are the building blocks of culture, shaping and justifying a society's norms and providing the ultimate measure for determining the appropriateness of accepted social practices and suggested alternatives when change is proposed (Scupin, 1992). Linguistically expressed in the form of goals, they are a culture's response to three universal requirements with which all individuals and societies must cope, that is:

- the needs of individuals as biological organisms-their basic human needs
- the requisites of coordinated social interaction, and
- the requirements for the smooth functioning and survival of groups (Schwartz, 1994).

Values can be held by individuals as well as groups; they are abstract, global ideals that are not tied to any situation or object, but, rather, are employed transcendentally across objects and situations (Schwartz, 1994):

. . . . to guide action; to guide us to the positions that we take on various social, ideological, political and religious issues; . . . to evaluate and judge ourselves and others by; . . . to guide the process of conscious and unconscious justification and rationalization of action, thought, and judgment (Rokeach, 1979, p. 48).

In sum, values have direction (Hofstede, 1984): they provide a measure for identifying certain outcomes as good or bad, desirable or undesirable, holy or unholy, beautiful or ugly (Scupin, 1992); they shape our thoughts and guide our actions. They have intensity: they confer relevance to a particular issue, action, object, situation (Hofstede, 1984) merging affect and concept and appearing in various admixtures with knowledge and beliefs.

Values as Central to Personal Belief Systems

Acquired through formal schooling and the process of informal socialization, which continues throughout life, social and cultural values are central to an individual's belief system. In his seminal work on values, M. Rokeach (1973) outlines the following assumptions about the hierarchical arrangements of these interconnected values and beliefs. An individual's self-conception, he notes, is central to her belief system. The next most central element consists of two types of hierarchically arranged values: terminal values and instrumental values. Closer to the center of an individual's belief system, terminal values refer to desirable end states, such as a nonviolent world. There are many fewer terminal values than instrumental values, which refer to how one should act, for example, with courage, justice, and honesty. It is assumed that the instrumental values are a means of achieving terminal values: to achieve ethnic harmony, one strives to be tolerant. In contrast to attitudes that are located at the outer core of the complex and which focus on one object or situation, values, as noted earlier, are applied across specific situations and objects.

Values as Predictors of Behavior

Values can be valid predictors of behaviors and attitudes, including those that are facilitative of achieving a culture of peace. Theories regarding the development of values through learning in early life state that the link between values and overt behavior becomes tighter with increasing age, a link that has been established empirically by both experimental and nonexperimental studies which have shown that human values are significantly related to both attitudes and behavior (cf. Williams, 1979 and Mayton & Furnham, 1994 for a review of some of these studies). Especially relevant to the purposes of this chapter, D. M. Mayton & A. Furnham (1994) refer to studies that have shown human values to be linked to political activist behaviors and to attitudes towards nuclear issues. They further report on their own study, which has shown that people who hold the value of universalism, that is, understanding, appreciation, tolerance, and protection for the welfare of people and for nature (as defined by Schwartz & Bilsky, 1987; 1990) appear motivated to engage in antinuclear activism, in other words, political actions that will achieve a stable peace. In a later study, D. M. Mayton & F. A. Lerandeau (1996) showed a similar link between universalism and the global consciousness inherent in the concept of world-mindedness.

Values as Goals in Peace Education and Environmental Education

Peace education has long recognized values as a key to promoting a culture of peace. It is considered a normative field, with an explicit value base (Thorpe & Reardon, 1971; Wahlstrom, 1991). Referring to developments in the field in the 1980s, B. Reardon (1988) noted that value concepts were at the core of education for positive peace, a statement that was confirmed in the results of a survey of K–12 teacher-designed curricula for peace education, which showed value concepts to be central to the selection of curriculum content, design, and the choice of issues to be studied. (Reardon, 1988a, p. xi). Value perspectives appear as one of the three dimensions about which learners must be instructed if the interacting goals of A. Bjerdstedt's (1990) schema of peace education are to be achieved. More recently, the immense power of values has been acknowledged by peace educators who see cultural value change and/or the teaching of values as a requisite for peacebuilding (Forcey & Harris, 1999; Rousseau & Rousseau, 1999; Pace & Podesta, 1999; Castro, 2001); universal values as the key for unifying the human species (Mitina, 1994); values as the basis for promoting lifestyle changes necessary to reduce environmental degradation (Nordland, 1994); selected attitudes and values as part of the core of education *for* peace (Rosandic, 2000; Castro, 2001).

Like peace education, environmental education is a normative field; it is "not neutral but is value based" (NGO Forum, 1992), steeped in the politics of justice and equality (Fagan, 1996; Sterling, 1996; and Huckle, 1996). Environmental educators view value systems as an important factor in determining the kind and extent of a society's impact on ecosystems (Engleson cited in Braus & Wood, 1993) and value change as a requisite to changing attitudes and behaviors that harm the environment (Braus & Wood, 1993). Therefore, D. W. Orr (1992) points to the need to complement objectivity with a strong value orientation in educating for sustainable living in a finite world. In fact, dating back to 1975, value learning is explicitly included as constitutive of the goals of environmental education in a series of basic texts on this topic issued by international conferences organized or sponsored by the United Nations (figure 6.2).[2]

FIGURE 6.2
Documents which Include Values as Content in Environmental Education

Place & Date	Title of Document
Belgrade, 1975	The Belgrade Charter: A Global Framework of Environmental Education
Tblisi, 1977	The report of the Intergovernmental Conference on Environmental Education
Moscow, 1987	International Agenda Strategy for Environmental Education and Training for the 90's
Rio, 1992	United Nations Commission for the Environment and Development, Chapter 36 of Agenda 21
1996	Learning: The Treasure Within. Report to the UNESCO International Commission Education for the 21st Century
Montreal 1997	Montreal Declaration on Environmental Education at the Planet'ERE Forum

Source: Based on Orellana & Fauteux, 2000.

VALUES FOR A PERSPECTIVE ON SOCIAL AND ECOLOGICAL REALITIES

Central to either peace education or environmental education or to both fields, the following value concepts are proposed as the core components of a perspective for analyzing and evaluating the social and ecological realities of our time, that is, *nonviolence, social justice, ecological sustainability, intergenerational equity,* and *civic participation.* Included in the Earth Charter's statement of universal values, they may be considered to reflect what cultures and societies of our planetary community view as social ideals.[3]

Nonviolence

Nonviolence is a measure for assessing the manner in which interpersonal and intergroup conflict is resolved and by which power imbalances are changed and oppression overcome. In a nonviolent society, the use of physical force and aggression would be opposed as would attitudes, language, and individual actions that demean and brutalize another psychologically. As a value base for human actions, nonviolence advocates the peaceful and nonaggressive resolution of conflict through negotiation and mediation. When faced with unyielding power imbalances, discrimination, and oppression, it offers the practices of nonviolent *resistance* as an alternative to violence. These include demonstrations, sit-ins, strikes, and other forms of civil disobedience. The lives and work of both Gandhi and Martin Luther King provide clear examples of the success of these practices. However, nonviolent resistance need not depend on a charismatic leader to be organized. It can be the response of individual groups within a society, for example, students and workers who contributed to the overthrow of the Milosevic regime in Yugoslavia; the refusal of some reservists in the Israeli army to participate in military actions that would bring harm to the civilian population in Palestinian towns during the 2001–2002 uprising generally referred to as the second Intifada.

In sum, then, nonviolence is a value concept that is not only intended to shape individual attitudes and behavior, but also to organize group efforts to bring about, through peaceful means, a change in social conditions and practices that violate human rights. It is a core and defining value in peace education, foundational to the content of antinuclear education and disarmament education and, more recently, to instruction in the skills for conflict resolution. A nonviolent society is the context essential to the achievement of ecological sustainability.

Social Justice

Social justice provides a measure for assessing how power, wealth, and resources in a society are distributed and used. In a just society, power and wealth are used *for* the benefit of all groups; they are not used by any particular group *to control* other groups. Thus, social justice is a value concept which opposes and aims to undo the violence on the quality of life that is inflicted by unjust and inequitable social structures, in other words, *structural violence*. The Universal Declaration of Human Rights (1948) and subsequent extensions of this document (e.g., The Covenant on Social and Political Rights 1966; the Covenant on Economic, Social and Cultural Rights, 1966; the Convention to Eliminate Racial Discrimination 1965; the Convention to Eliminate all Forms of Discrimination against Women; 1979; and the Rights of the Child, 1989) provide a blueprint for achieving a just society, and a society's progress toward that goal would be measured by the extent to which what these human rights allow are made accessible to all. On the other hand, when social justice fails to inform social institutions and dictate social norms, when social conditions and practices condone social injustice, the context is set for conflict that may lead to physical violence between groups and individuals. In other words, social injustice breeds social violence and through the impact of this violence on Earth's life-supporting processes, it indirectly contributes to environmental degradation.

Social justice was acknowledged as a value goal in peace education with the realization that not only the absence of war, but also changes in social and economic systems were a prerequisite for world peace (Reardon, 1988). Recognizing the link between injustice and environmental degradation, global educators (e.g. Greig, Pike & Selby, 1987) and some environmental educators (e.g. Orr, 1992; Verhagen, 2001) have also included social justice as a value goal in their curricula.

Ecological Sustainability

Ecological sustainability is a value concept that is focused on Earth rights, making the Earth Community the focus of our ethical considerations (Naess, 1989; Rasmussen, 1996). It measures the appropriateness of the relationship between humans and the Earth, specifically the practices which determine how we use and exploit the Earth's resources and affect her life-supporting processes. For these practices to be sustainable, they must not exhaust these natural resources, nor should they cause serious, or even irreversible harm to these processes. Rather they should ensure their maintenance so that all living beings, human, plant, and animal, may survive and thrive in the present and in the future.

More specifically, an ecologically sustainable society would be characterized, for example, by its choice of climate benign energy sources and its policies to decrease population growth (Brown, Flavin & Postel, 1990; Orr, 1992; Brown, 2000), poverty, material consumption, and waste (Green Cross International, 2002). In the longer term it would aim for developing a world economy which is more equitable and secure (Brown, Flavin & Postel, 1990). In its attempts to ensure sustainability, it would take into account traditional knowledge and folkways that focus on the needs of local communities and cultures. The building and design of housing, cities, neighborhoods, farms, regional economies would aim to heal the planet, not degrade it. Human limits to comprehend and care for complex systems would be taken into account in determining the size and complexity of its cities, corporations, technologies. Finally, recognizing the link between ecological degradation and social violence, an ecologically sustainable society would not allow conflict to dictate the relationship between diverse groups but rather goodness, mercy, justice (Orr, 1992).

Ecological sustainability is a value goal that is antithetical to ecological violence and may be seen as yet another dimension of nonviolence with a particular focus on Earth-human relations. It is a core value goal in education for sustainability and is also central to the tradition of stewardship and related educational activities endorsed by religious communities (Sitarz, 1998).

Intergenerational Equity

Intergenerational equity is a notion implicit in the definition of a sustainable society, that is, as one that provides for its needs while ensuring that future generations will be able to do so as well (Bruntland Commission, 1987; Brown, Flavin, & Postel, 1990; Sitarz, 1998). However, since skills to facilitate thinking about long-term consequences are not typically included in educational curricula, this value is presented as distinct from ecological sustainability to emphasize the need for thinking about how human actions that degrade the environment in the present will affect citizens of future generations; it is proposed as the value foundational to such thinking. Intergenerational equity, a theory proposed by E. B. Weiss (1989; 1990), views the human community as a partnership among all generations. It postulates that humans hold the Earth's natural and cultural legacy in common with members of the present, past, and future generations. Therefore, on the one hand, each generation has the right to inherit the same diversity in natural and cultural resources enjoyed by previous generations and to equitable access to the use and benefits of these resources. In other words, each generation should be the beneficiary of a previous generations' stewardship. On the other hand, it is also a custodian of the planet for future generations. Each generation is obliged to conserve this legacy so that future generations may also enjoy these same rights.

Three principles of intergenerational equity have been suggested as a measure for determining to what extent a contemporary society meets these obligations (Weiss, 1990). They would guide the making of government policies and be used to develop curricula for educating its citizenry about the long-term future impact of an unsustainable economy and life style.

Conservation of Options. The diversity of the Earth's cultural and natural resource base must be conserved so that future generations are not restricted in the options available to them to solve their problems and satisfy their own values.

Conservation of Quality. The quality of life on the planet must be maintained so that it is handed over to future generations in no worse conditions than when it was received.

Conservation of Access. Equitable access to the legacy of the planet should be ensured for future generations.

By thus emphasizing the human rights of future generations, intergenerational equity extends the scope of social justice into the future. A component of ecological sustainability, it is a value concept that is central to education for sustainability and is foundational to its emphasis on teaching skills for understanding short term and long term consequences of human decisions and actions (Sitarz, 1998).

Civic Participation

Civic participation is a value concept with a twofold emphasis: participatory decision making and social responsibility. On the one hand, it measures whether the right of individuals and groups to be consulted in matters that will affect their lives is honored and, on the other, the extent to which individuals and groups engage in social action that promotes the common good locally, nationally, and globally. In a society that values civic participation, authentic opportunities are provided and structures devised to seek the input of citizens in matters pertaining to the social and ecological good. That is, this input is taken into account in the final decision making. At the same time, civic participation is reflected in citizens' engagement in these opportunities and in the initiatives they take to organize social action to protest violent, unjust, ecologically unsustainable practices and to effect changes in these conditions. It is a value concept that motivates action through which policies and practices that are nonviolent, ecologically sustainable and just for the present and future generations of the Earth community, both human and other living species, are developed and the society envisioned by these value goals striven for and achieved. Therefore, it stands in a means-end relationship to nonviolence, social justice, ecological sustainability, and intergenerational equity.

Citizens are given a key role by both environmental education and peace education. An active and competent citizenry is seen as the foundation of a sustainable society (e.g. NGO Forum, 1992; Wilke, 1993; Orr, 1992; Sitarz, 1998; O'Sullivan, 1999; Barraza, 2000) and the preparation of citizens for global responsibility as one main purpose of comprehensive peace education (e.g. Bjerdstedt, 1990; Wahlstrom, 1991; Reardon, 1999).

PEDAGOGY FOR DEVELOPING A VALUE BASED PERSPECTIVE

A key goal in adult learning, autonomy of thought is viewed as a requisite for responsible civic action. J. Mezirow (1997) writes: "Thinking as an autonomous and responsible agent is essential for full citizenship in democracy and for moral decision making in situations of rapid change (p. 7)." Indeed, as this chapter argues, a value-based perspective is the basis for autonomy of thought and action. However, if autonomy is to be the intended outcome, the process whereby the perspective is learned and acquired should address the cognitive and affective factors that may inhibit its exercise. Therefore, learning activities which are intended to help learners understand the value concepts and what they entail should also promote the development of critical reflectiveness and of analytical and imaging skills.

Critical Reflectiveness

Autonomy of thought is constrained if one is not aware of the existence and power of one's values and assumptions. Naturalized beneath consciousness, they shape and limit a person's existing perspectives on social reality, and as a result, anomalies which bring their validity into question are ignored. Critical reflectiveness is a process whereby learners can be led to uncover, reflect upon, critically evaluate and, if necessary, reconstitute assumptions they hold about what is desirable, good, moral, relevant, that is, their values. It is considered central to adult learning (Brookfield, 1987; Mezirow, 1991; Cranton, 1994) and is characterized by the following four-stage process (based on Brookfield, 1987):

Learners Become Aware of Their Assumptions and Values. Values are not easily articulated, nor is their existence readily acknowledged. Therefore, when asked
to provide a reason for a choice of action or a strongly held opinion, individuals
are apt to say that it is just "common sense." In real life, the personal discomfort
resulting from an encounter with opposing values, that is "trigger events," which
suggest the irrelevance of thoughts and actions based on one's acquired values is,
in fact, an emerging awareness within the individual consciousness of their existence though at this point they may not be articulated or even acknowledged as
values. Culture shock is a classic example of such a trigger event. The discomfort
felt by individuals who find themselves living in a new culture is not just a manifestation of homesickness or a reaction to strange and new ways of doing things.
Basically, it is the response to an encounter with a different set of values that appear to be effective in the new culture and, which therefore, implicitly call their
own into question.

Within an educational setting, when the goal is the acquisition of new values, it is necessary to organize activities that will bring acquired values to awareness. S. Brookfield (1987) describes how he uses critical incidents for this purpose:

- Learners are asked to write a brief description of significant events
  in their lives that are related to the area/topic, the values of which
  are to be examined.

- In small groups, each one reads his/her incident and group members infer what the assumptions and related values underlying the
  account may be.

- The writer of the incident decides if these inferences are accurate.

- Once each individual incident has been assessed in this way, group
  members may look for common and divergent assumptions/values
  in their accounts and discuss what this implies.

- Group members can also ask for more information about the circumstances described, and inferences of values underlying these
  questions can be another source of insight into the values of the
  group members.

A similar approach could be used to elicit values and related assumptions
through which learners view social events, practices, and conditions related to
the achievement of social and ecological peace.[4]

*Alternative Values Are Examined and Compared with One's Existing Assumptions
and Related Values.* Values and the ways of thinking and acting they support are

basic to one's self-concept and to one's worldview. They will not be changed so easily. Therefore, an opportunity should be provided for learners to compare the values that have emerged through the analysis of their critical incidents to the value concepts that form the perspective, that is, nonviolence, social justice, ecological sustainability, intergenerational equity, and civic participation. They can be asked to determine whether any of their own values are similar to any one of these five values. This comparison will require that the value concepts be explained, thus providing learners with an introduction to their meaning and relevance.

Learners' Uncovered Assumptions and Related Values Are Questioned. Some values a learner holds may prove to be either incompatible with the value concepts or irrelevant to assessing social and ecological realities. They must be challenged or questioned. Seminal research on value change and on adult perspective transformation suggests two factors that can be taken into account in developing learning activities to facilitate the process of self-questioning.

M. Rokeach (1979a) reviews studies which have shown that becoming aware of contradictions within one's value system, for example, supporting civil rights for blacks but considering equality unimportant, can effectively challenge an individual's values. This has led to enduring value change, he notes, because the inconsistency offends one's self esteem, that is, one's conception of oneself as a moral or competent person. On the other hand, the research on adult perspective transformation, which examines the process whereby adults reconstitute or reject a long held set of assumptions and related values, has shown that an individual's values are challenged when they are shown to no longer be effective or relevant to one's situation and needs, therefore prompting a person to search for alternatives (Mezirow & Associates, 1990). The process of self- questioning or challenging learners' existing values will lead to the need to examine alternative values, thus providing a cognitive and affective base from which to provide further explanations about what the five value concepts that constitute the perspective entail and how they relate to one another.

New Value Concepts Are Tested and Assessed. Having developed a general understanding of the five value concepts, opportunities must be provided for learners to experience how the perspective works. They will need to develop facility in using it to assess social and ecological events, practices, and conditions that may inhibit or facilitate the achievement of peace if it is to become a stable frame of reference to be readily and appropriately applied. Such an application of the perspective to authentic situations in learners' social environment would provide an opportunity to clarify questions learners have about particular values and further serve to reinforce their understanding of each one. At the same time, in applying the perspective, learners must question its relevance and its ability to enhance insight. It must not be accepted uncritically.

Analytical Skills

Autonomy of thought is also constrained if an individual does not fully comprehend social events, conditions, and practices that inhibit the acquisition of a culture of peace. Such an understanding is a prerequisite to the use of the value-based perspective to assess these social realities. To facilitate comprehension, therefore, an analysis must be undertaken, the quality of the outcome being dependent upon an individual's ability to ask the right questions. Take the case of media reports of the 9/11 attack on the World Trade Towers (a social event), deforestation in the Amazonian region of Brazil (social practice), or poverty in Calcutta (a social condition). The questions by which experts analyze these social realities will be complex and wide ranging, evidencing their knowledge of what is relevant to understanding the problem. On the other hand, those of younger and older adults who have not been instructed about these matters will be limited and naive. They will not have this quality of background knowledge, nor will educational interventions to make up for this lack always be possible and, when provided, adequate. In fact, however, according to J. Bruner (1973), expanding learners' knowledge *about* a topic may not necessarily provide them with the most effective educational tool for comprehending social or physical realties. Referring to the teaching of physics, he suggests an alternative approach:

> For the basic assumption is that physics is not so much a *topic* as it is the mode of thought, an apparatus for processing knowledge about nature rather than a collection of facts that can be got out of a handbook. (p.109)

In other words, the core learning to be derived from the subjects that constitute a school or college curriculum should not be a mere collection of facts but rather frameworks for thinking about different aspects of social and physical reality. And as suggested above, modes of thinking can be operationalized as questions. As implied by Bruner (1973), modes of thinking are derived from specialized knowledge of the field, but in the case of nonexpert learners who are trying to understand the dynamics of a social or ecological event, for example, it can be argued that their analytic abilities will be enhanced if they learn to think about these events in terms of a framework of questions such as those listed in figure 6.3.

Implicit in the framework is a mode of thinking about these events which should lead to an insightful analysis of a situation, and in some cases, perhaps most, beyond what learners' existent knowledge would allow them to consider. Of

FIGURE 6.3

Questions for Analyzing Social and Ecological Problems

Classifying the problem

What is the nature of the problem? For example, is it a matter of child abuse? a wasteful use of resources? the resolution of a conflict?

Identifying systemic causes

What is the cause of the problem? is it a person? an institution? a cultural norm? Is their only one? or more than one? Are there any hidden causes?

Identifying consequences of the problem

How does the problem and the situation it creates affect people? the economy? the culture? Earth systems? other? Are these consequences intended and planned?

Highlighting the link between impacts on human society and Earth systems

Is there a link between the consequences experienced by people and by the Earth?

Determining the scope of the problem

Does this problem affect only people in the immediate situation?
Or does/will it also influence people in other parts of the country?
In other countries on the planet? that is, what is the scope of the problem? is it local, national and global?

---

course, an individual may lack the background knowledge required for a comprehensive response to each of these questions. However, the collective knowledge of a group may serve to complement the knowledge of each individual and if not, the questions will alert learners to what needs to be further investigated. Thus, the framework should provide them with a conceptual tool for taking control of their process of analyzing and comprehending.

Imaging Alternative Futures

Another constraint to autonomy of thought and action is the inability to think in alternative and creative ways about the future. In the case of those social and ecological realities that inhibit the achievement of a culture of peace, while it is agreed that violence is abhorred, our imaginations often appear to be prisoners of the present, apparently incapable either of visualizing the consequences of continued violence, be it physical, structural, or ecological, in the long term future or of creating positive alternatives. Reasons put forth to explain this paralysis include the belief that things cannot change or fear and, therefore, the unwillingness to face what present realities portend. It is also true that the educational system does not usually try to change such beliefs and attitudes or help students acquire skills related to thinking in terms of the distant future.

Imaging alternative futures, that is, "the capacity to visualize the present in fresh ways and to visualize the not-yet in positive ways . . ." (Boulding, 1988, p. 116) is an educational methodology for freeing the social imagination from the tyranny of present perspectives and so of further extending a learner's intellectual autonomy. Working from the social event, condition or practice that has been selected as the focus of analysis, learners can be led through the following steps which constitute the process of imaging (adapted from Boulding, 1988).[5]

Writing a Goal Statement. Individuals are asked to write a goal statement about the social achievements they hope or wish will have taken place three decades from now as a response to the social situation they have analyzed. They are asked to set aside concerns about what is "practical," or "realistic" and to dream even if it appears impossible. They are also reminded that this is not a personal goal statement but a social one; they may consider it locally, nationally, or globally. The statements are shared with members of their group.

Imaging Their Preferred Future. Learners are now asked to move into the future they have just referred to in their goal statement to record and observe what they see. This is done in three stages. First they are led through an exercise which intends to allow them to discover and free up their ability to imagine. For example, they are asked to step into a memorable incident in their past and to describe it to members of their group in vivid detail. Next, learners are led through an exploratory trip that will enable them to experience moving through the barrier separating the present-present from the future-present. Referring to the social achievements described in their goal statement, they are asked to observe how things are working. They return to the present-present briefly to share what they have seen with their group. The final stage consists of a 20–30 minute stay in the future, during which time they observe and record what they see in detail.

Clarification and Synthesis. What has been imagined will become clearer if shared with others. Therefore, having returned from their trip into the future, learners explain what they have seen to members of their group. Questions for

clarification should lead to an expanded picture as each one checks forward mentally to find an answer to a group member's question. At this point, if there are
enough similarities among their individual preferred worlds, groups may be asked
to synthesize their individual models into one.

Evaluating Preferred Worlds. Groups should, then, apply the value-based
perspective to their preferred world. Do the value concepts shape the actions and
workings of the institutions they have observed and how? If no or if only in a limited way, how could what they have seen be changed so that they are in line with
the norms implied by the value concepts? Using the value perspective to evaluate
and shape what is imagined will demonstrate its utility not only as an instrument
to evaluate the present, but also to prescribe for a preferred future.

CONCLUSION

While the pedagogy described in the previous section should facilitate
the development of a value-based perspective, this should not obscure the fact
that it is essentially a complex and difficult process. As noted earlier, acquired
perspectives and related values may not be easily changed. Nor will learners always have all the background knowledge needed to apply the perspective appropriately. Moreover, social and ecological realities with dire consequences to
people and planet in world regions outside local and national borders are often
not viewed as relevant. In most cases, the capacity for personal empathy essential to citizenship in a culturally diverse world and an appreciation of global interdependence may be limited or totally absent. Therefore, the need to assess
these realities and to act upon what one has assessed may not be compelling.
Additionally, given the discrete approach to the organization of curricula both
in secondary and post-secondary education, the utility of a value-based perspective that is to be applied across disciplines may not be immediately appreciated. In sum, it should be recognized that perspective development is a clear
educational challenge.

Nonetheless, the difficulties inherent in this challenge should not deflect
from its importance. It has already been noted that citizens who think and act autonomously is one intended educational outcome of perspective development.
Others further add to its social relevance. For example, while the development of
critical thinkers has been considered a national priority as far back as the early
1980s (Brookfield, 1987), the literature describing critical thinking skills and the
manner of acquiring them does not take into account the need for learners to

develop a frame of reference that will serve as a measure for their critique. Value-based perspective development would make up for this lack. Additionally, by acquiring a perspective consisting of value concepts basic to a culture of social and ecological peace, learners will be provided with an integrated way of thinking about and assessing obstacles to its achievement. This should lead to an understanding of the dynamic relationship between injustice, war, ecological degradation, and an apathetic citizenry. It should, further, provide citizens with a shared vision of a social and ecological order, towards which they should strive, that is, one that is ecologically sustainable, nonviolent, and just and in which citizens take responsibility for the well-being of all life in the present and the future.

NOTES

1. Approaches to environmental education are very diverse advocating the need to (1) develop respect and care for the Earth, and/or (2) ensure that ecological degradation does not continue and that the Earth's life systems are not irrevocably harmed; and/or (3) work towards an ethic of sustainability within the context of social justice. The first two themes are ordinarily included in what is known as "environmental education" whereas sustainability education also includes the third. In this chapter, the term environmental education will be used in a broad sense to include all three themes, and education for sustainability when the literature has made it clear that what is being discussed is specific only to sustainability education.

2. See I. Orellana & S. Fauteux (2000) for a description of the contents of these documents, which for the greater part have been published by UNESCO/UNEP.

3. These value concepts are also either explicit or implicit in *universalism*, that is, broadmindedness, social justice, equality, protecting the environment, a value type which values research has shown to be recognized by many people across contemporary societies when they think about their values (Schwartz & Bilsky, 1987; 1990, & Schwartz, 1992).

4. For other approaches to eliciting assumptions and values, see J. Mezirow (1990) and P. Cranton (1994).

5. See E. Boulding (1988) for the action stages in the process and F. Hutchinson (1996) for futures workshops which also aim to help students learn to image alternative futures. Fountain (1995)'s list of concepts which outline what education for the future should make children aware of would also contribute to freeing imagination for autonomous thinking.

REFERENCES

Ahearn, S. (1994). Educational planning for an ecological future. In B. Reardon & E. Nordland (Eds.), *Learning peace: The promises of ecological and cooperative education* (pp. 121–148). Albany: State University of New York Press.

Barraza, L. (2000). Promoting environmental learning at school. In A. Jarnet, B. Jickling, L. Sauvé, A. Wals, & P. Clarkin (Eds.), *A colloquium on the future of environmental education in a postmodern world?* (pp. 188-193). Available from *Canadian Journal of Environmental Education*, Yukon College, Whitehorse, Yukon, Canada.

Bjerdstedt, A. (1990). Towards a rationale and a didactics of peace education. In A. Bjerdstedt, (Ed.), *Education for peace in the nineties: A conference report*. Peace Education Reports No. 1. (pp. 45-72). Malmo, Sweden: Lund University.

Boulding, E. (1988). *Building a global civic culture*. New York: Teachers' College Press.

Braus, J., & Wood, D. (1994). *Environmental education in the schools: Creating a Program that works!* Rock Spring, GA: North American Association of Environmental Education.

Brookfield, S. (1985). *Self-directed learning: From theory to practice*. New Directions for Continuing Education, No. 25. San Francisco: Jossey Bass.

Brookfield, S. (1987). *Developing critical thinkers*. San Francisco: Jossey Bass.

Brookfield, S. (1990). Analyzing the influence of media on learners' perspectives. In J. Mezirow and Associates (Eds.), *Fostering critical reflection in adulthood: A guide to transformative and emancipatory learning* (pp. 235-250). San Francisco: Jossey Bass.

Brown, L., Flavin, C., & Postel, S. (1990). Picturing a sustainable society. In *State of the world*, chapter 1: 173-190. The Worldwatch Institute. New York: W. W. Norton & Co.

Brown, L. (2000). Challenges of the new century, chapter 1: 3-20. In *State of the world*. The Worldwatch Institute. New York: W. W. Norton & Co.

Bruner, J. (1973). *The relevance of education*. New York: The Norton Library.

Bruntland Commission. (1987). *Our common future*. Oxford: Oxford University Press.

Castro, L. (2001). Peace Education: A teacher training manual. Paper presented at the International Institute in Peace Education, Byblos, Lebanon.

Cranton, P. (1994). *Understanding and promoting transformative learning: A guide for educators and adults*. San Francisco: Jossey Bass.

Fagan, G. (1996). Community-based learning. In J. Huckle & S. Sterling (Eds.), *Education for sustainability* (pp. 136-148). London: Earthscan Publications Ltd.

Fountain, S. (1995). *Education for development: A teacher's resource for global learning.* Portsmouth, NH: Heinemann.

Forcey, L., & Harris, I. (Eds.). (1999). *Peacebuilding for adolescents: Strategies for educators and community leaders.* New York: Peter Lang Publishing, Inc.

Greig, S., Pike, G., & Selby, D. (1987). *Earthrights: Education as if the planet really mattered.* London: Co-published by the World Wildlife Fund and Kogan Page Ltd.

Green Cross International. (2002). *Battle for the planet: Johannesburg Declaration.* Retrieved December 6, 2003 from http://www.gci.ch/communication/DigitalForum/digiforum/ARTICLES/articles2002/gorbachevmenchu.html

Hanvey, R. (1982). An attainable global perspective. *Theory into Practice, 21,* 162-167.

Hofstede, G. (198 4). *Cultures consequences: International differences in work-related values.* Newbury Park, CA: Sage Publications Inc.

Hopkins, C., & Mckeown, R. (2002). Education for sustainable development: An international perspective. In D. Tillbury, R. Stevenson, J. Fien, D. Schreuder (Eds.), *Education and sustainability: Responding to the global challenge* (pp. 13-24). Gland, Swtizerland and Cambridge, UK: IUCN.

Howson, J., & Gleasby, A. (1996). Towards a critical media. In J. Huckle & S. Sterling (Eds.), *Education for sustainability* (pp. 149-164). London: Earthscan Publications, Ltd.

Huckle, J. (1996). Realizing sustainability in changing times. In J. Huckle & S. Sterling (Eds.), *Education for sustainability* (pp. 3-17). London: Earthscan Publications Ltd.

Hutchinson, F. (1996). *Educating beyond violent futures.* London: Routledge and Kegan Paul.

King, D. (1973). Teaching towards global perspectives. *Intercom, 7,* 73-79.

Mayton, D. M. II, & Furnham, A. (1994). Value underpinnings of antinuclear political activism: A cross-national study. *Journal of Social Issues, 50* (4), 117-128.

Mayton, D. M. II, & Lerandeau, E. A. (1996). *Values as predictors of global consciousness.* ERIC Document ED415143.

McCabe, L. T. (1994). The development of a global perspective while participating in a semester at sea: A comparative global education program. *Educational Review, 46* (3), 275-286.

Mezirow, J. (1991). *Transformative dimensions of adult learning.* San Francisco: Jossey Bass.

Mezirow, J. (1995). Transformation theory of adult learning. In M. R. Welton, (Ed..), *In defense of the lifeworld* (pp. 39-70). Albany: State University of New York Press.

Mezirow, J. (1997). Transformative learning: Theory to practice. In P. Cranton (Ed.), *Transformative learning in action: Insights from practice. New directions for adult and continuing education 74* (pp. 5-13). San Francisco: Jossey Bass.

Mezirow, J., & Associates (Eds.). (1990). *Fostering critical reflection in adulthood: A guide to transformative and emancipatory learning.* San Francisco: Jossey Bass.

Mitina, V. (1994). New thinking: Its application for a new learning. In B. Reardon & E. Nordland (Eds.), *Learning peace: The promises of ecological and cooperative education* (pp. 45-66). Albany: State University of New York Press.

Naess, A. (1989). *Ecology, community and lifestyle.* New York: Cambridge University Press.

Nordland, E. (1994). Steps to a renewal of education: Concluding words. In B. Reardon & E. Nordland (Eds.), *Learning peace: The promises of ecological and cooperative education* (pp. 211-214). Albany: State University of New York Press.

NGO Forum. (1992). *Treaty on environmental education for sustainable societies and global responsibility.* ICAE Tel: 551162-7053; Fax: 5511623457.

Orellana, I., & Fauteux, S. (2000). Environmental education: Tracing the high points of its history. In A. Jarnet, B. Jickling, L. Sauve, A. Wals, & P. Clarkin (Eds.), *A colloquium on the future of environmental education in a postmodern world?* (pp. 13-24). Available from *Canadian Journal of Environmental Education,* Yukon College, Whitehorse, Yukon, Canada.

Orr, D. W. (1992). *Ecological literacy: Education and the transition to a postmodern world.* Albany: State University of New York Press.

O' Sullivan, E. (1999). *Transformative learning: Educational vision for the 21st century.* London: Zed Books.

Pace, R., & Podesta, A. (1999). Teaching peace with Dr. Seuss. *Kappa Delta Pi Record, 35* (3), 118-121.

Palmer, J. (1998). *Environmental education in the 21ˢᵗ century.* London: Routledge and Kegan Paul.

Pike, D. (2000). A tapestry in the making: The strands of global education. In T. Goldstein & D. Selby (Eds.), *Weaving connections: Educating for peace, social & environmental justice* (pp. 218–241). Toronto: Sumach.

Rasmussen, L. (1996). *Earth community, earth ethics.* Maryknoll, NY: Maryknoll.

Reardon, B. (1988). *Comprehensive peace education: Educating for global responsibility.* New York: Teachers College Press.

Reardon, B. (Ed.). (1988a). *Educating for global responsibility: Teacher-designed curricula for peace education, K–12.* New York: Teachers College Press.

Reardon, B. (1999). *Peace education: A review and projection. Peace Education Reports No. 17.* School of Education. Malmo, Sweden: Lund University.

Rokeach, M. (1973). *The nature of human values.* New York: Free Press.

Rokeach, M. (1979). From individual to institutional values: With special reference to the values of science. Chapter 3. In M. Rokeach (Ed.), *Understanding human values* (pp. 47–70). New York: Free Press.

Rokeach, M. (1979a). Long-term value change initiated by computer feedback. Chapter 13. In M. Rokeach (Ed.), *Understanding human values* (pp. 210–225). New York: Free Press.

Rosandic, R. 2000. Grappling with peace education in Serbia. *Peaceworks 33.* United States Institute of Peace. 1200 17ᵗʰ Street NW, Washington, DC.

Rousseau, N., & Rousseau, S. (1999). Dr. King's giant triplets: Racism, materialism and militarism. In L. Forcey & I. Harris (Eds.), *Peacebuilding for adolescents: Strategies for educators and community leaders* (pp. 17–33). New York: Peter Lang.

Schwartz, S. H. (1994). Are there universal aspects in the structure and contents of human values? *Journal of Social Issues, 50* (4), 19–45.

Schwartz, S. H., & Bilsky, W. (1987). Toward a universal structure of human values. *Journal of Personality and Social Psychology, 53,* 550–562.

Schwartz, S. H., & Bilsky, W. (1990). Toward a theory of the universal content and structure of values: Extensions and cross cultural replications. *Journal of Personality and social psychology, 58,* 878–891

Scupin, R. (1992). *Cultural anthropology: A global perspective.* New Jersey: Prentice-Hall.

Shah, I. (1969). *Tales of the Dervishes.* New York: E. P. Dutton & Co.

Sitarz, D. (Ed.). (1998). *Sustainable America: America's environment, economy and society in the 21ˢᵗ century.* Carbondale, IL: Earth Press.

Sterling, S. (1996). Education in change. In J. Huckle & S. Sterling (Eds.), *Education for sustainability* (pp. 18–39). London: Earthscan Publications Ltd.

Stillman, P. 1978. Global perspectives: Bridging social studies. *Intercom, 88,* 2–4.

Thorpe, G., & Reardon, B. (1971). Simulation and world order. *High School Journal, 55* (2), 53–62.

Verhagen, F. C. (Fall, 1999). The Earth Community School: A back-to-basics model of secondary education. *Green Teacher, 59,* 28–31.

Verhagen, F. C. (2001). The Earth Community School (ECS) model of secondary education: Contributing to sustainable societies and thriving civilizations. *Journal of Social Alternatives, 21,* 11–16.

Wahlstrom, R. (1991). Growth towards peace and environmental responsibility. *Theory into practice, 67,* 1–78.

Weiss, E. B. (1989). *In fairness to future generations: International law, common patrimony and intergenerational equity.* New York: Transnational Publishers and the United Nations University.

Weiss, E. B. (1990). In fairness to future generations. *Environment, 32* (2), 7–31.

Wilke, R.J. (1993). *Environmental education teacher resource handbook: A practical guide for K–12 environmental education.* Millwood, New York: Kraus International Publications in cooperation with the *National Science Teachers Association.*

Williams, R. M. (1979). Change and stability in values and value systems: A sociological perspective. In M. Rokeach (Ed.), *Understanding human values: Individual and societal* (pp. 15–46). New York: The Free Press.

CHAPTER 7

Environmental Peacemaking, Peacekeeping, and Peacebuilding

Integrating Education for Ecological Balance and a Sustainable Peace

Ian Harris and Patricia M. Mische

The French philosopher, Blaise Pascal, observed that human beings are "running carelessly towards a precipice" (cited in Nastase, 1982, p. 185). This metaphor applies accurately to environmental crises that are the outcome of excessive human consumption, toxic pollutants, and other unsustainable human practices. Such practices ultimately kill human beings as well as exterminate thousands of species on this planet. The metaphor also applies to increasing human violence ranging from child abuse and domestic violence to street violence, civil strife and interethnic violence, terrorism and international warfare. Environmental education and peace education try to make students aware of this abyss and offer skills to avoid such destructive behaviors. In doing so they fall within the tradition of education for social responsibility whereby teachers help students learn about pressing problems and search for solutions.

Both peace and environmental educators proceed from the premise that world views and systems rooted in a will to conquest, dominance, and power over the other is inimical to true security and well-being. They strive to enable students to supplant these world views, values, and practices which support violence with those that will support ecological balance and a sustainable peace. Underlying the violence by humans against both Nature and other humans is an allegiance to a myth of human domination and conquest. Peace education and environmental education also aim to deconstruct this myth and replace it with a vision of and competencies for humans as nurturers cooperating to preserve the natural world and human communities. They share UNESCO's view that since war and violence begin in the minds of people, it is in the minds of people that peace needs to be sowed and nurtured. This axiom also applies to human relationships with Nature. As Patricia M. Mische (1986) has observed:

> Human destruction of the Earth begins first in the mind, when we objectify it (see it as object rather than subject of creative life processes) and, psychologically distancing ourselves from these processes, gradually devalue, deny or succumb to collective amnesia concerning our integral relationship and participation in those processes. A similar mental process is undergone as prelude and psychological preparation for war. The "other" is first seen as distinctly "other," as alien, "enemy," then as subhuman and monstrous and "deserving" destruction. (p. 2)

On the other hand, peace and environmental education differ in the focus of their educational interventions. Peace education has tended to focus on conflict in human interactions. It is concerned about violence and seeks alternatives to violence (e.g. Smith & Carson, 1998; Reardon, 2001). It includes the study of conflict, conflict prevention, and conflict resolution between individuals, groups, and nations.[1] Ian Harris (1988) has stated that the ten goals of peace education should be to appreciate the richness of the concept "peace;" to address fears; to provide information about security systems; to understand violent behavior; to develop intercultural understanding; to provide for a future orientation; to teach peace as a process; to promote a concept of peace accompanied by social justice; to stimulate a respect for life; and to end violence (p. 17). He also emphasizes that a peaceful pedagogy must be part of any attempt to teach about peace. The key ingredients of such a pedagogy are cooperative learning, democratic community, moral and environmental sensitivity, and critical thinking.

In contrast, environmental education is concerned about human relationships with the natural world. It has focused on human exploitation of the Earth and the damaging effects of human activities in the biosphere—how one group of humans exploits natural resources to the detriment of both Nature and other humans.[2] In teaching ways to live more sustainably on the planet, environmental education aims to:

- provide opportunities to acquire the knowledge, values, attitudes, commitment, and skills needed to protect and improve the environment.

- encourage pupils to examine and interpret the environment from a variety of perspectives—physical, geographical, biological, sociological, economic, political, technological, historical, aesthetic, ethical, and spiritual.

- awaken student curiosity about the environment and encourage active participation in resolving environmental problems (Palmer, 1998, p. 20).

In their efforts to address the complex forms of violence in human communities, peace educators often overlook the devastating impact of human violence upon the Earth, its ecosystems, and the various species that inhabit it.[3] Likewise, environmental educators often overlook the importance of peace to environmental sustainability. This chapter will address this shortcoming. It will propose how insights about natural systems can enhance concepts of peace and how peace strategies can be applied to environmental crises.

ENVIRONMENTAL LEARNING ENHANCES CONCEPTS OF PEACE

Peace theory distinguishes between negative and positive peace (Galtung, 1969). Negative peace is the absence of *physical* violence such as war. Positive peace is the absence of *structural* violence or systemic injustice. Recently these concepts have been expanded to include the absence of direct and indirect human violence against Nature. Expressed as a *presence* rather than an absence, negative peace can be defined as the presence of norms, policies, structures, and practices that prevent or end physical violence, which undermines human life and Earth's functioning integrity. Positive peace can be defined as the presence of norms, policies, systems, and practices that respect human dignity, meet human needs, uphold standards of social and environmental justice, and sustain human and natural communities. Both negative and positive peace imply a commitment to nonviolence in interhuman relations and human relationships with Nature. However, peace educators can further refine and deepen their understanding of peace by studying natural systems.

Conflict in the Natural World

A study of Nature shows that just as there are inevitable conflicts in interhuman relations, conflicts exist in Nature. But conflict in Nature, as well as in interhuman relationships, needs to be distinguished from violence. In interhuman affairs, violence is only one way some humans may employ to resolve conflict. In fact, most human conflicts are resolved creatively, without recourse to violence.

And in Nature, some Earth processes may seem violent to human observers, for example, volcanoes, earthquakes, tornadoes, fires caused by lightning, and predators hunting and eating their prey. But these processes are more properly understood as part of Earth's tremendous evolutionary creativity. Through such processes have come the conditions in which life has emerged and proceeded toward increasing diversity. The overall direction of these Earth processes is toward greater life.

Such understandings of the natural world can open peace educators to new understandings of "peace." Like the Earth's evolutionary processes, peace is not a passive, static, or finished state. It is an active process in which tremendous creativity is expended in an effort to balance conflicting forces and find equilibrium. It is also a process of mutual nurturance of conditions that will help sustain humans and other members of the community of life.

Earth as an Interdependent Community of Life

A study of Earth processes further shows that natural systems are interdependent communities of life. While some consider the "eating" of members of one species by those of another as a form of violence, those who view the Earth as a community of life see it as a form of mutual nurturance. This view was held by conservationist Aldo Leopold in his ground breaking, 1949 essay on a "Land Ethic." More recently it is supported by the work of biologist, Elisabet Sahtouris in *Gaia: Living Systems in Evolution* (1989). In this communal view of Nature, soil, water, sun, and microbial life nurture plants that in turn nurture animals who nurture one another. All go back to the soil contributing to an ongoing process of regeneration and self-renewal. Predators help prevent other species from overpopulating and thus contribute to a healthy planet. They do not destroy their food supplies and are themselves held in check by other predators. This system of checks and balances preserves the precious balance of Nature. Each species and element plays a part in the life and health of the whole community, and complex interactions between the individual members serve to preserve and enhance its diversity.

Understanding the Earth as an interdependent and mutually nurturing community of life can also help peace educators deepen their understandings of the communal aspects of peace. First of all, it can help them extend their concept of community beyond the human social realm to include the whole biotic community. The spiritual/religious concept, "I am my brother's keeper," also applies to animals and plants. In such a view, humans are not apart from or over Nature, but part of Earth's larger community of life. The Earth is like a single cell in the universe, and all—humans and all other species—are part of the cell. They will live or die as this single cell lives or dies (Berry, 1979). It should be understood, therefore, that a culture of peace has both social and ecological dimensions.

Second, while peace educators often discuss human violence in ways that ignore its impact on Nature, the expanded concept of community derived from an understanding of the Earth as an interdependent and mutually nurturing community of life suggests that the study of peace should consider the impact of human violence upon natural systems. For example, recent violent conflicts in Southeast Asia and Africa have created millions of refugees whose movement into concentrated settler communities has harmed the natural habitat of those areas, which, as a consequence, can threaten the food source of these communities. Thus, what harms humans also harms the land, and, in turn, when the land is harmed, humans will suffer. Greedy materialism, which is often described as an aspect of structural violence in peace studies (because of the poverty it produces), also has a negative impact upon the environment. Therefore, when teaching the different forms of violence that threaten human communities, peace educators should include the environmental impacts of those forms of violence upon natural systems. Their study of the impact of human violence upon individuals and social communities is incomplete without also describing the devastation of violent human behavior upon the natural order. Conversely it should be understood that peace implies the well-being of all living organisms. In fact, the goals of peace education should be to nurture all forms of life.

Finally, the study of natural systems, which teaches us about the interdependence and preciousness of life, further encourages a holistic approach to peace education. Peace educators can teach humans how to live as responsible members of the larger life community, extending our sense of ethics to the whole. Human violence that destroys natural systems, for example, a wetland to build a resort or a desert or an ocean to test weapons—should be viewed as the antithesis of Earth's creative, self-renewing and healing processes. Peace theory and peace education can provide insights into how to transform such human behavior that might lead to ecocide into behavior that promotes environmental sustainability. Peace educators who share concerns with environmental educators about the threats to human existence caused by degradation of the environment should teach ways to minimize human harm to natural systems. Their goal should be "to have humans live in peace with Nature," appreciating that their own survival and health depends upon the health of water, air, plants, animals. They can teach humans how to use natural resources in ways that do not degrade or destroy them. That is, we can eat from the whole, but we also have to help nurture and give back to it. They can also help them develop an appreciation for natural processes and for the human interconnectedness to all beings in the life community. In sum, they should prepare students to live responsibly within the life community, nurturing and preserving its rich diversity and not exceeding the limits of its self-renewing capacities.

APPLYING PEACE STRATEGIES TO ENVIRONMENTAL CRISES

Peace theory examines a variety of approaches to peace, including preventive diplomacy, peacemaking, peacekeeping, and peacebuilding (Boutros-Ghali, 1992). Peace educators (for example, Berlowitz, 1994; Forcey & Harris, 1999) teach about how these different strategies can be taught both to children and adults. They can expand their teachings by showing how these peace strategies can be applied to environmental crises in a process of making peace with the Earth. Environmental educators can also use insights gained from a study of these peace strategies to expand their teachings of ways to preserve ecosystems.

Preventive Diplomacy

As defined by the United Nations, prevention is "action to prevent disputes from arising between parties, to prevent existing disputes from escalating into conflicts, and to limit the spread of the latter when they occur." The goal is to "ease tensions before they result in conflict—or, if conflict breaks out, to act swiftly to contain it and resolve its underlying causes" (Boutros-Ghali, 1992, p. 11). Measures include confidence-building (e.g., arrangements for the free flow of information, exchanges of military missions, monitoring of arms agreements); information gathering and formal and informal fact finding; early warning systems (e.g. concerning environmental threats, nuclear accidents, natural disasters, mass movements of populations, the threat of famine, and the spread of disease); and demilitarized zones to separate potential belligerents. Preventive diplomacy has counterparts in everyday lives in family, community, workplace, and other settings.

Preventing Environmental Harm

The maxim, "an ounce of prevention is worth a pound of cure," applies to both safeguarding peace and environmental protection. If preventing war is the best way to safeguard peace, preventing environmental harm is the best way to ensure a healthy planet. Where harm has already occurred, prevention of further harm is needed. Preventing violence to the Earth costs much less than cleaning up after environmental disasters. It spares the suffering, death, and social, economic, and health problems that result from environmental destruction. The same measures used to prevent war can be used to prevent environmental harm.

Peacemaking

As defined by the UN, peacemaking is "action to bring hostile parties to agreement by peaceful means" (Boutros-Ghali, 1992, p.11). There are a wide variety of peacemaking methods, including negotiation, mediation, arbitration, and the use of the World Court, or regional courts. Such means of resolving conflicts appeal to agreed-on standards of fairness and justice and accepted authorities. When parties to a conflict feel that their concerns are heard and that they are treated equitably and fairly by legitimate authorities rather than being forced to submit, the resulting peace is likely to be more stable and enduring.

Peacemaking is akin to preventive diplomacy in that it brings together opposing forces to resolve conflicts but usually after they break out, or when hostilities are at a crisis point. In its broadest sense, peacemaking begins with the commitment to talk about tensions and relies upon the tools of creative problem-solving—genuine communication, effective listening, step-by-step problem solving, and shared decisions about actions. Peacemakers are *facilitators*—ones who help conflicting parties negotiate a peaceful resolution of differences. *Peacemaking* is also used by ordinary people in every day life—in families, communities, and the workplace.

Environmental Peacemaking

The same peacemaking skills can be applied to environmental crises. How is this to be done? First, the world community needs to agree on a clear definition of what constitutes an environmental crime. The United Nations is currently facilitating international dialogue and negotiations to arrive at an accepted definition. If successful, it will be a step toward more effective international environmental protection. Second, just as an International Criminal Court and war crimes tribunals were instituted to hold individuals accountable for crimes against humanity and other gross violations of human rights, so some are proposing that an International Environmental Court be established to hold individuals and corporations accountable for crimes against the environment. Governments alone have not caused environmental damage and alone they cannot stop it (Mische, 1989). The private sector and individuals also need to be accountable. Third, citizens can be called upon to act as environmental peacemakers, that is, to use their rational, ethical, and legal skills to develop norms, treaties, and legislation to protect Nature from human-caused degradation. Such activities, for example, led to the Clean Air Act in the United States and to the Earth Charter, a statement of ethical principles for sustainability developed as a follow-up to the 1992 United Nations Conference on Environment and Development (UNCED) in Rio de Janiero, where governments agreed on several major intergovernmental treaties, which aimed to promote sustainable economic development.

If effectively developed and supported by the world community, the existence of such ethical, legal, and judicial measures can serve as both a deterrent and remedy for environmental crimes. When they are applied, they usually do help to diminish environmental harm, just as effective laws, courts, and police help diminish violence between nations and groups within nations. Of course, the question of enforcement is a challenge. While most international agreements provide that compliance will primarily be the responsibility of national governments who are party to the agreement, many developing countries lack the means to train and support the personnel needed to monitor the implementation of these measures. Moreover, some violence will elude even the most vigilant and conscientious authorities, and authorities who should enforce compliance can be corrupted. Thus, measures aimed at environmental peacemaking, while making a potential difference, cannot be expected to totally eliminate the problem of ecological harm.

Nonetheless, through these measures and other environmental peacemaking initiatives, which need to be undertaken in tandem, humans can gradually move toward norms that respect Earth's functioning integrity and agree to regulate their behavior to stay within the limits of environmental sustainability.

Peacekeeping

As used by the United Nations, peacekeeping refers to the deployment of a United Nations presence in the field to help prevent or stop violence between hostile parties. UN peacekeepers traditionally could be deployed only with the consent of all concerned parties and were prohibited from taking sides or using deadly force except if they were personally attacked. The purpose of peacekeepers is generally to serve as a buffer between conflicting parties so as to prevent armed combat and assure that preventive diplomacy, peacemaking and peacebuilding processes can effectively proceed. In recent years UN peacekeepers have sometimes been deployed to prevent one country from attacking another, or for humanitarian intervention (e.g. to assure that food gets through to refugees or to stop genocide within a country).

Environmental Peacekeeping

Along lines similar to the way blue berets are deployed to areas requesting UN peacekeeping services, environmental peacekeepers could be deployed to areas in environmental crisis. Such forces could be comprised of women and men with the needed environmental, health, public safety, and other forms of expertise to assess the environmental threat. They could propose ways of containing the threat, either by developing capacities within the community necessary for doing so and/or organizing local representatives of the broad based environmental movement of international NGO's and local community based organizations, including political parties (e.g. Green parties), formal organizations (e.g. the Sierra Club, Audubon Society), and spontaneous groupings for purposes of advocacy. Their newsletters and protests can inform populations about threats to the natural community. Environmental peacekeepers could also assess the extent of the environmental damage if it has already occurred. They could propose short-term remedies for containing the damage and preventing further harm. They could monitor public health and safety and work with the local residents in developing ways to prevent further harm and to restore environmental health.

Peacebuilding

Peacebuilding is employed by the UN in post-conflict situations once violent hostilities have ceased. It is a comprehensive strategy to prevent a recurrence of violence and to sustain peaceful relationships among and between different sectors of society at local, national, and regional levels. Methods employed may range from "disarming previously warring parties, repatriating refugees, monitoring elections, advancing human rights, reforming or strengthening governmental institutions, and promoting a vibrant civil society and formal and informal processes of political participation" (Boutros-Ghali, 1992, p. 32). Whereas peacekeeping and peacemaking are reactive, seeking to end and resolve conflicts once they have flared up, peacebuilding seeks to prevent this recurrence by redressing the causes of conflict.

Peacebuilding is related to both negative and positive peace in that it aims to prevent the recurrence of physical violence and warfare, but does so in a way that addresses underlying conditions of structural violence and social injustice that cause conflict. To that end, peace educators teach peacebuilding strategies for resisting and overcoming norms and institutions that would otherwise lead to violence and war. Through these strategies, repressive laws, norms, and institutions are replaced with attitudes, policies, institutions, and laws that will advance social justice and make peace sustainable. Conditions whereby human needs and human rights are realized and human dignity is respected are developed. This involves the development of participatory government and a strong and vibrant civil society able and willing to participate in governance. Thus, peacebuilding promotes political discourse and standards of social justice that guarantee that all people have their rights protected, as set forth in the Universal Declaration of Human Rights as adopted by the United Nations General Assembly (1948).

The old dictum of *real politic* was "if you want peace, prepare for war; peace-building proposes the new realism that "if you want peace, prepare for peace." Preparing for peace includes developing social, economic, cultural, and environmental conditions that will sustain a stable peace. The aim of peacebuilding is to advance nonviolent and sustainable communities. Like the other peace strategies described above, it has applications in homes, communities, and workplaces as well as within and between states.

Environmental Peacebuilding

Applying peacebuilding to environmental crises would include developing an understanding of eco-justice and promoting its advancement. Racial or ethnic minorities and poor people often see their neighborhoods become dumping grounds for toxic waste or sites selected for polluting industries. Eco-justice would prevent such environmental apartheid. Eco-justice also points to the enormous disparities between consumption and waste levels in wealthy industrialized countries of the North, who use a disproportionate share of ecological capital and resources, and those in poorer sectors of many countries in the South. It is concerned about equitable distribution of Earth's resources within sustainable limits of natural systems.

A universal declaration setting forth a set of principles that would provide some beginning standards of eco-justice is the Earth Charter.[4] This charter urges human beings to think of the Earth as their home. It encourages signatories to, "Strengthen democratic institutions at all levels, and provide transparency and accountability in governance, inclusive participation in decision making, and access to justice" (Principle 13). It urges the application of standards of justice to human interactions with Nature, providing norms for fairness and equity so that all are treated with full human rights and dignity. Concepts of eco-justice envision and seek to achieve a sustainable community where all humans have equal access to the world's resources within sustainable limits, and the needs of the natural world are considered in making decisions about human activities. Achieving ecological justice requires that humans accept personal responsibility to preserve resources for future generations.

CONCLUSION

Just as peace educators saw the growth in conflict–resolution education in the 1990s as a response to increased levels of violence in schools, so environmental educators have seen the emergence of education for ecological responsibility as a response to human violence against the Earth. Massive deforestation, desertification, global warming, acid rain, the depletion of fishing stock, the extermination of an average of one hundred species a day, shortages in clean water, population growth, soil erosion, and wide spread pollution—all these interactive and compounding environmental problems have social and economic impacts that in turn lead to conflicts and civil strife that may grow into low intensity warfare or even international strife. Peace and environmental educators alike need to recognize this interconnectedness between the degradation of Earth processes and destructive human activities.

Both peace and environmental educators have a common goal—of stopping violence. The challenge both face is learning and teaching ways to resolve conflicts nonviolently, to share limited resources equitably, and to live within the limits of sustainability. This will become increasingly important as the twenty-first century unfolds with increasing human populations all seeking a better life. Peace will require environmental sustainability and environmental sustainability will require peace.

NOTES

1. Other types of peace education include: "international education," "human rights education", and "development education." Each has a form of violence it is addressing and different strategies for achieving peace (Harris, 2002).

2. Like peace education there are different types of environmental education. In teaching about the damaging effects of human activities in the biosphere, environmental educators have helped to create a new branch of education for social responsibility, education for sustainability (or sustainability education). According to Frans Verhagen (2002), "Ecological sustainability refers to the continued health of interdependent local and global ecosystems as they are impacted upon by activities of humans and other organisms. Thus, ecologically sustainable societies are those that live within the ecological limits and opportunities of the Earth's carrying capacity" (p. 12). Here the concept of education for social responsibility is expanded to include ennvironmental responsibility.

Environmental education is also sometimes referred to as "ecological education:" Rather than seeing Nature as other—a set of phenomena capable of being manipulated like parts of a machine—the practice of ecological education requires viewing human beings as one part of the natural world and human cultures as an outgrowth of interactions between our species and particular places (Smith & Williams, 1999, p. 3). Ecological education tends to rely more on the hard sciences and explores relationships between species and the Earth's strata. Sustainability education rests more on the study of human behavior and how it can develop precious resources in ways that do not degrade the environment. It includes insights from anthropology, economics, history, sociology as well as the study of the hard sciences. Whereas the hard sciences pretend to be value neutral, sustainability education and environmental education promote the value of decreasing the impact of humans upon natural systems and of using resources in a way that preserves natural diversity. In this chapter, the term "environmental education" will be used in a broad sense to include education for sustainability and ecological education though it is recognized that there are technical differences between them.

3. A recent contribution to the field of peace education, *Peace Education: The Concept, Principles, and Practices around the World* (Salomon and Nevo, Eds., 2002), and one to the field of peace studies, *Peace, Conflict, and Violence: Peace Psychology for the 21ˢᵗ Century* (Christie, Wagner, and DuNann Winter, 2002) make no mention of the environmental crisis. On the other hand, P. Mische (1998/91; 1992), B. Reardon, E. Nordland, and R. Zuber (1994), and B, Reardon (2001), all discuss the educational implications of the relationship between environmental sustainability and peace.

4. For a discussion of the history of the Earth Charter and its educational uses, see chapter 8 and for more information see http://www.earthcharter.org

REFERENCES

Berlowitz, M. (1994). Urban educational reform: Focusing on peace education. *Education and Urban Society, 27* (1), 82–95.

Berry, T. (1979). The Ecological Age. *The Whole Earth Papers* No. 12. Global Education Associates.

Boutros-Ghali, B. (1992). *An Agenda for Peace: Preventive diplomacy, peacemaking, and peace-keeping.* Report of the Secretary-General. New York: United Nations.

Christie, D., Wagner, R., & DuNann Winter, D. (Eds.). (2002). *Peace, conflict, and violence: Peace psychology for the 21ˢᵗ century.* Upper Saddle River, NJ: Prentice Hall.

Forcey, L., & Harris, I. (Eds.). (1999). Introduction. In L. Forcey & I. Harris (Eds.), *Peacebuilding for adolescents: Strategies for educators and community leaders* (pp. 1–14). New York: Peter Lang.

Galtung, J. (1969). Violence, peace, and peace research. *Journal of Peace Research, 6* (3), 167–191.

Harris, I. (1988). *Peace education.* Jefferson, NC: McFarland & Co.

Harris, I. (2002). Peace Education theory. Paper presented at American Educational Research Association conference, New Orleans, LA, April 3, 2002.

Leopold, A. (1949). Land Ethic. In *A Sand County Almanac*. New York: Oxford University Press.

Mische, P. M. (1992). Toward a pedagogy of ecological responsibility. *Convergence, 25* (2) 9–25. Also in *Peace, Environment and Education, 3* (3) 37–56.

Mische, P. M. (1989). Ecological security in an interdependent world. *Break-through* (Summer/Fall), 7–17. Reprinted in modified form in four other journals from 1989–1990.

Mische, P. M. (1988/1991). The Earth as peace teacher. In E. Boulding, C. Brigagao & K. Clements (Eds.), *Peace culture & society: Transnational research and dialogue* (pp. 139–146). Boulder, CO: Westview Press. Adaptation of a paper originally presented at the International Institute on Peace Education in Manila, the Philippines, November 22–28, 1987 and also presented, in adapted form, at the International Peace Research Association conference in Rio de Janeiro, August 14–19, 1988. Published by Phoenix Publishing in Manila in 1988.

Mische, P. M. (1986). The psychology of destruction: The challenge to creativity: Some tentative and outrageous thoughts on the linkages between peace and environmental movements." Paper presented at the Meadowcreek Conference, Fox, Arkansas. October 16–19, 1986. Excerpts published in *Meadowcreek Notes.*

Nastase, A. (1982). Education for disarmament: A topical necessity. *Teacher's College Record, 84* (1), 184–191.

Palmer, J. (1998). *Environmental education in the 21st century: theory, practice, progress, and promise.* London: Routledge and Kegan Paul.

Reardon, B. (2001). *Education for a culture of peace in a gender perspective.* Paris: UNESCO.

Reardon, B., Nordland, E., & Zuber, R. (1994). *Learning peace: the promise of ecological and cooperative education.* Albany, NY: State University of New York Press.

Sahtouris, E. (1989). *Gaia: The human journey from chaos to cosmos.* New York: Pocket Books.

Salomon, G., & Nevo, B. (Eds.). (2002). *Peace education: The concept, principles, and practices around the world.* Mahwah, NJ: Lawrence Erlbaum.

Smith, G., & Williams, D. (1999). *Ecological education in action: On weaving education, culture, and the environment.* Albany, NY: State University of New York Press.

Smith, D., & Carson, T. (1998). *Educating for a peaceful future*. Toronto: Kagen and Woo, Ltd.

United Nations General Assembly. (1948). *Universal declaration of human rights*. General Assembly Resolution 71, UN Doc A/810.

Verhagen, F. (2002) The Earth Community school (ECS) model of secondary education: Contributing to sustainable societies and thriving civilizations. In I. Harris and J. Synott (Eds.), *Social Alternatives: Peace Education for a New Century*, 21, 11–17.

CHAPTER 8

The Earth Charter as an Integrative Force for Peace Education and Environmental Education

Peter Blaze Corcoran

Inspirational documents have changed the course of events and impacted on human societies: the Magna Carta, the American Declaration of Independence, the French Declaration of the Rights of Man and of the Citizen, and the Universal Declaration of Human Rights: all stirred human imagination and changed the quality of life of peoples all over the globe.

—Hassan, 2002, p. 24

It was not until 1972 at the Stockholm Conference on the Human Environment that the United Nations recognized the environmental impact of human activity on the health of the systems that sustain life. Destruction of habitat, pollution, and loss of natural beauty had not been considered as part of the United Nations agenda for world security from its formation in 1945. However, the work of people's movements and the actions of nongovernmental organizations (NGOs) gradually brought the environmental problems caused by industrialization and overdevelopment to the agenda of nations and of the United Nations. According to Steven Rockefeller (2002):

Beginning with the Stockholm Declaration, the nations of the world have adopted over seventy declarations, charters, and treaties that seek to build a global partnership that protects the environment and integrates conservation and development. In addition, a variety of nongovernmental organizations have drafted and circulated at least two hundred of their own declarations and people's treaties that address issues of environment, development, and social justice (p.16).

From the perspective of values, the most significant among these was the "World Charter for Nature," adopted in 1982 by the United Nations General Assembly. It was the first intergovernmental declaration to frame an ethic of respect for Nature as critical for protecting the human environment.

In 1987, under the enlightened leadership of Gro Harlem Brundtland, a former Prime Minister of Norway and now Secretary General of the World Health Organization, the World Commission on Environment and Development (WCED) made several significant contributions to the understanding of our responsibilities to future generations. *Our Common Future* introduced the vocabulary of sustainable development to a broad audience. Brundtland (WCED, 1987) defined sustainable development as development which "ensure[s] that it meets the needs of the present without compromising the ability of future generations to meet their own needs " (p. 8) and addressed in no uncertain terms the question of intergenerational responsibility: "We borrow environmental capital from future generations with no intention or prospect of repaying. . . . The results of the present profligacy are rapidly closing the options for future generations" (p. 8). The WCED also called for "a new charter" to consolidate and extend relevant legal principles creating "new norms . . . needed to maintain livelihoods and life on our shared planet" and to "guide state behavior in the transition to sustainable development" (p. 332). Thus, the challenge of sustainable development was thrust upon the community of nations.

The Earth Summit in Rio de Janeiro in 1992 began to respond to calls from the WCED, NGOs and governments, and the religious and spiritual community to draft an Earth Charter. However, while consensus had gradually begun to emerge as to the content and structure of an Earth Charter as a statement of fundamental ethical principles widely "shared by people of all races, cultures, religions, and ideological traditions" (Rockefeller, 2002, p. 23), many governments disagreed with the idea of an ethical commitment, and efforts within the United Nations structure were ended. The consensus among participants was that the Earth Charter was "ahead of its time"[1] even in the enthusiastic environment of the Earth Summit.

Therefore in 1994, a civil society initiative was launched to advance the development of a people's charter of ethical principles for sustainability. Under the leadership of Canadian Maurice Strong, who had chaired both the Stockholm and Rio conferences, and Mikhail Gorbachev, the Earth Council was established. The Earth Charter Commission with worldwide membership was formed in 1997, an International Secretariat was established, and a formal drafting process took place from 1997 to 2000.[2] Under the umbrella of the Earth Council, the activities of the Earth Charter Commission and of the staff of the Earth Charter International Secretariat in San José, Costa Rica comprise what is called the "Earth Charter Initiative."[3]

This chapter first discusses the activities of the Earth Charter Initiative. It describes the sources of the values that constitute the Charter and the process by which they were incorporated into the document. Then, it considers two key educational uses of the Earth Charter. Finally, it provides illustrative examples of how the Earth Charter has been used for educational purposes in diverse settings and a list of existing educational resources for teaching about the Charter. The thesis of the chapter is that the Earth Charter is a valuable educational resource for both peace education and environmental education with integrative power to teach the connectedness, interdependence, and, even, unseverability of environmental challenges, human rights, and peacemaking.

THE EARTH CHARTER INITIATIVE

> The Earth Charter initiative has involved the most open and participatory consultation process ever conducted in connection with the drafting of an international document. Thousands of individuals and hundreds of organizations from all regions of the world, different cultures, and diverse sectors of society have participated. The Charter has been shaped by both experts and representatives of grassroots communities.
>
> —Earth Charter International Secretariat, 2000a, p. 1

The major unfinished business of Rio was the further development of the Earth Charter. To that end, in 1994 the Earth Council was created by Maurice Strong, Secretary General of UNCED and Mikhail Gorbachev to conduct consultations "throughout the world in an effort to promote the global dialogue on common values and to clarify the emerging worldwide consensus regarding principles of environmental protection and sustainable living" (Earth Charter International Secretariat, 2000b, p. 22). The first consultation, held in 1995 in the Peace Palace in The Hague, involved over 70 organizations from 30 countries. A study of over 50 international law instruments, entitled *Principles of Environmental Conservation and Sustainable Development: Summary and Survey* (Rockefeller, 1996), was prepared and circulated as a resource for those contributing to the consultation process. The outcome was a set of criteria for the proposed Earth Charter. Regarding the content, it was agreed that it should be a set of ethical principles for environmental conservation and sustainable development. The principles should be of enduring significance and held in common by people of all races, cultures, religions, and ideological traditions. The document should present a holistic perspective and a spiritual and ethical vision adding to what had already been presented in related and relevant documents (Earth Charter USA, n.d.).

Early in 1997, the Earth Charter commission was formed to give oversight to the drafting process and an international drafting committee was created. In 1997, a benchmark draft emerged from the Rio +5 forum, a meeting organized as part of a worldwide review of the progress that had been made towards sustainable development since the Rio Earth Summit in 1992. From 1997 to early 1999 many conferences, held on several continents, led to the development of Benchmark Draft II. During the consultation process, which followed this second draft and which led to the issuance of the final version in March 2000, the views of experts from various fields, including a team of international lawyers, specializing in environmental law and representatives from grass roots communities were sought. Online conferences, multistakeholder fora, presentations, and workshops were organized to discuss the text and make recommendations, bringing together members of 45 Earth Charter Committees and representatives of all world regions and from all sectors of society. (See Earth Charter USA, n.d. for specific details about these events.) Thus, the text emerged from a process of extensive consultation.

Moreover, the contributions to the substantive content of the Earth Charter were derived from a prodigious array of sources. These ranged from the global ethics movement to sacred texts of the world's major religions, from international law documents to new thinking in the sciences of physics, cosmology, and evolutionary biology. Extensive research was conducted in these fields as preparation for the drafting of the Earth Charter. The Earth Charter Initiative has also worked especially closely, and continues to work, with a number of indigenous peoples groups, including the Indigenous Peoples' Program at the Earth Council, the Indigenous Peoples Consultative Council, the Inuit Circumpolar Conference, and the Russian Association of the Indigenous Peoples of the North. (*Earth Charter Initiative Handbook*, 2002, p. 16) As a result, the worldviews of the first peoples infuse the document with traditional wisdom.

The *Earth Charter Briefing Book* (Earth Charter International Secretariat, 2000a) lists *the following* eight of the most important influences on the substantive content:

1. Contemporary science, including especially physics, cosmology, ecology, and biology;

2. International law, especially declarations and treaties pertaining to environmental conservation and sustainable development adopted over the past three decades;

3. The agreements and reports of the seven UN summit conferences held during the 1990s on children (New York, 1991), the environment (Rio de Janeiro, 1992), human rights (Vienna, 1993),

population (Cairo, 1994), social development (Copenhagen, 1994), women (Beijing, 1995) and the city (Istanbul, 1996);

4. The wisdom of the world's great religions and philosophical traditions;

5. The global ethics movement and the worldwide dialogue on common goals and shared values;

6. The growing literature on the ethics of environmental conservation and sustainable development;

7. Nongovernmental declarations and people's treaties relevant to environment, development, human rights, democracy, and peace, of which over 200 have been issued in the last thirty years;

8. Best practices for building sustainable communities (p. 8).[4]

These built on the birthright content and structure discussions which preceded Rio.

The Earth Charter Initiative supports and coordinates with programs, national Earth Charter committees, and organizations worldwide. It promotes endorsements of the Earth Charter by individuals, organizations, businesses, and governments at all levels. It coordinates translations of the Earth Charter into the world's languages. It supports and documents education activities in many cultures. It raises funds and coordinates the organizational activities of the Earth Charter Commission—a prestigious group of activists and public figures from all continents and many diverse fields of endeavor.[5] Work is divided into several areas of activity—youth, civil society and business, media, government, and multistakeholder collaboration for a culture of peace.

Perhaps the area of greatest activity and significance is education. The primacy of education in the Earth Charter Initiative was reconfirmed at meetings of the Earth Charter activist community and the Steering Committee of the Earth Charter Commission at the World Summit for Sustainable Development in August 2002. The aim of a major fundraising effort, as of 2002, is to support diverse educational uses of the Earth Charter.

EDUCATIONAL USES OF THE EARTH CHARTER

The Earth Charter is a valuable educational resource. . . . It can be used to generate in individuals and communities the kind of internal reflection that leads to a change in attitudes, values, and behavior.

—Earth Charter International Secretariat, 2000a, p. 18

From the beginning the Earth Charter has provided both theme and content for educational endeavors in formal and nonformal sectors which would aim to:

1. raise awareness of the fundamental challenges and choices that face humanity

2. help people to learn to think globally and holistically

3. serve as a catalyst for cross-cultural and interfaith dialogue on shared values and global ethics

4. focus attention on fundamental ethical issues and their interconnectedness

5. generate in individuals and communities the kind of internal reflection that leads to a change in attitudes, values, and behavior. (Earth Charter International Secretariat, 2000a, p. 18)

It is the Charter's potential as a basis for an integrated approach to teaching ethical values foundational to a culture of social and ecological peace, alluded to in the last two of the above purposes, that make it an integrative force for peace education and environmental education.

Integrated Teaching

The Earth Charter in its entirety can be used to teach the interdependence among environmental challenges, human rights, and peacemaking. Indeed, as has been acknowledged, "its integrated perspective circumscribes the necessary pedagogy for a "culture of peace" (Earth Charter Education Advisory Committee, in press, p. 14) The need for such a perspective in education is first made explicit in the Preamble to the Earth Charter. Describing the cosmological and ecological context within which human activities take place and highlighting the challenges and opportunities before us, the Preamble urges that we join together "to bring forth a sustainable global society founded on respect for Nature, universal human rights, economic justice, and a culture of peace" (Earth Charter Commission, 2000). Following the Preamble, the interdependent nature of the social, economic, and environmental challenges that confront us is reflected in the four parts into which the Earth Charter principles are organized, that is, respect and care for the community of life (Section 1), ecological integrity (Section 2), social and economic justice (Section 3), democracy, nonviolence and peace (Section 4). As B. Mackey (2001) writes: "together these (challenges) define the domains of responsibility that must be *jointly* (emphasis in original) considered when assessing the critical problems we face and their possible solutions" (p. 9).

Advocating respect and care for the community of life, the first principle establishes the interconnectedness between humans and nature—we are one community. Ecological integrity refers to the environmental challenges; it is a value that is antithetical to the violence that has led to the degradation of the Earth's living systems. Social and economic justice and democracy, nonviolence, and peace, values that stand in opposition to structural and physical violence, point to essential human rights which are both the context within which a sustainable peace can be achieved and the means for doing so.

Each part of the Earth Charter consists of four main principles, which, in turn, are elaborated by supporting principles (p. 191). The four principles in the first section provide an integrated overview of the Earth Charter vision. The first of these principles, *respect for Earth and life in all its diversity*, is the foundation for the other three as well as for the principles in the other three sections of the Charter. A sense of ethical responsibility flows from an attitude of respect. The Earth Charter challenges us to expand our moral awareness and to respect and value all living things, including ourselves, other persons, other cultures, other life forms, and Nature as a whole. The second, third, and fourth principles deal with the three major spheres of *our* human relationships and ethical responsibility—relations between human beings and the greater community of life, relations among human beings in society, and the relations between present and future generations. The second principle refers to caring for the community of life "with understanding, compassion and love." It recognizes that the best thought and action flow from the integration of the head and the heart, knowledge and compassion, science and a sense of the sacred. However, respect and care for the community of life cannot be exercised if a violent social context militates against it. Therefore, principle three calls for a democratic society whose norms and practices are just, participatory, sustainable and peaceful, thus preventing or reducing structural and physical violence. The fourth principle affirms that fundamental to the new global ethics is intergenerational responsibility, which includes two fundamental concepts. First is the idea of integenerational equity—that each generation ought to take into account the needs of future generations for access to the beauty and bounty of the Earth. Second is the notion that each generation also must create institutions and traditions that transmit values of respect and care for the community of life to succeeding generations (Clugston, Calder, Corcoran, 2002).

A similar integration characterizes the entire text. The four principles that define ecological integrity focus on the Earth's ecological systems, emphasizing protection, restoration, and prevention. At the same time, principle 7 recognizes the need for economic practices to safeguard not only the Earth's ability to renew itself, but also human rights and community well-being. As regards social and economic justice (part 3), all four principles define it in social and environmental terms. The consequences of poverty are social and environmental. Human development must be promoted in a manner that is both equitable and sustainable. Gender equality and equity are prerequisites to sustainable development, and all humans have the right to both a natural and social environment that ensures an acceptable quality of life. While focusing on social values and the characteristics of democratic institutions, the principles that constitute the fourth part also point to the need to promote a way of life that ensures the integrity of the environment (principle 14); to be respectful and considerate of all living beings, a notion that appeared in earlier sections (principle 15). In sum, the Earth Charter allows for an integrated approach to the teaching of human rights and peacemaking, on the one hand, and environmental challenges, on the other, because of the proximate nature of the related principles in the document itself. Social peace is defined by a series of right relationships with oneself, one's community, both past and present, and one's *biosphere*. Ecological integrity, the principles acknowledge, cannot be achieved if the social context is not just and participatory, nonviolent and peaceful.

Values Education

Foundational to the ethical principles that constitute the Earth Charter is a set of universal human values. It is the values that define the ethical principles. Therefore, at all levels of education, formal and informal, primary, secondary, and postsecondary, the Earth Charter can be used to awaken values, most of which are also central in peace education or environmental education curricula. However, values education is controversial in many cultures, raising questions of "what values?" and "whose values?" and "how will they be used?." Its normative nature has made it problematic for many educators, in particular in American public education in which the teaching of values has increasingly been politicized by a clash between religious and secular values, and in a pedagogical debate on how to find methods to educate, rather than to proselytize. In the academy, there is a long-standing critique of the universality of cultural values.

Brendan Mackey (2001), Education Director of the Earth Charter Initiative, *responds to these* concerns. Values education can be accommodated, he says, so long as the values represent core values that are life-affirming, promote human dignity, advance environmental protection and social and economic justice, and respect cultural and ecological diversity and integrity. Mackey believes the Earth Charter can validly lay claim to represent such a core set of values, particularly given the participatory and multicultural process that underpinned the drafting of the document. The Earth Charter, therefore, provides a critical content for the

THE EARTH CHARTER

RESPECT AND CARE FOR THE COMMUNITY OF LIFE

1. *Respect Earth and life in all its diversity.*

2. *Care for the community of life with understanding, compassion, and love.*

3. *Build democratic societies that are just, participatory, sustainable, and peaceful.*

4. *Secure Earth's bounty and beauty for present and future generations.*

ECOLOGICAL INTEGRITY

5. *Protect and restore the integrity of Earth's ecological systems, with special concern for biological diversity and the natural processes that sustain life.*

6. *Prevent harm as the best method of environmental protection and, when knowledge is limited, apply a precautionary approach.*

7. *Adopt patterns of production, consumption, and reproduction that safeguard Earth's regenerative capacities, human rights, and community well-being.*

8. *Advance the study of ecological sustainability and promote the open exchange and wide application of the knowledge acquired.*

SOCIAL AND ECONOMIC JUSTICE

9. *Eradicate poverty as an ethical, social, and environmental imperative.*

10. *Ensure that economic activities and institutions at all levels promote human development in an equitable and sustainable manner.*

11. *Affirm gender equality and equity as prerequisites to sustainable development and ensure universal access to education, health care, and economic opportunity.*

12. *Uphold the right of all, without discrimination, to a natural and social environment supportive of human dignity, bodily health, and spiritual well-being, with special attention to the rights of indigenous peoples and minorities.*

DEMOCRACY, NONVIOLENCE, AND PEACE

13. *Strengthen democratic institutions at all levels, and provide transparency and accountability in governance, inclusive participation in decision making, and access to justice.*

14. *Integrate into formal education and life-long learning the knowledge, values, and skills needed for a sustainable way of life.*

15. *Treat all living beings with respect and consideration.*

16. *Promote a culture of tolerance, nonviolence, and peace.*

development of curricula with the educational aim of teaching values that can be acceptable and appropriate for all cultures.

Outlined by the Earth Charter Education Advisory Committee, three main outcomes of education based on the Charter suggest how the document can be used to awaken values, that is, through "Consciousness raising . . . application of values and principles . . . [and] call for action . . ." (Mackey, 2001, p. 9) In other words, as Mackey (2001) explains, it is necessary to:

1. create *awareness and* understanding of the interrelatedness of environmental and social problems and the need to educate and behave in light of this reality;

2. then, put into action specific *values and* principles as a guide to more sustainable ways of living;

3. and finally, to collaborate in promoting *the values of* justice, sustainability, and peace.

Thus, values education moves from an understanding of the relevance of values to their application and, then, to action to promote them. Such an approach ensures that the values contribute to forming a culture of social and ecological peace.

A philosophy of education, based on the spirit and philosophy embedded in the Earth Charter itself, has also been developed by the Earth Charter Advisory Committee. Consisting of the four following tenets, it outlines a methodology that could be used for implementing values education:

1. *Action research.* Material should be developed in collaboration with a network of educators representative of the target audience.

2. *Experiential learning.* Wherever possible, use should be made of learning activities that involve action-orientated learning or "learning by doing."

3. *Transdisciplinarity.* The integrated ethical perspective presented by the Earth Charter requires inquiry unconstrained by conventional disciplinary boundaries.

4. *Collaboration.* It is essential that we find collaborative ways to join efforts with educators in all fields (Mackey, 2001, p. 9),

Educational Programs Based on the Earth Charter

The Earth Charter has been utilized in diverse cultural and geographic settings for a multiplicity of educational purposes. The examples described below illustrate how the Earth Charter can be used to integrate education for social and ecological peace and how social or ecological peace might follow from education endeavors drawing on the Earth Charter.

Higher Education. Terry Link, Director of the University Office of Campus Sustainability teaches a course at Michigan State University entitled "Earth Charter: Pathway to a Sustainable Future?" The course utilized the Earth Charter "as a vehicle for *personal, institutional, community, national* and *global transformation*" (emphasis in original) (Link, 2002).

The course is based on the assumption that much education perpetuates unsustainability. It seeks to use principles from transformative education to shape a pedagogy for Earth. The syllabus states:

> We believe that you cannot talk about global sustainability without including our current system of education as part of the equation. The present patterns of distanced, abstract, and objectified teaching and learning only serve to perpetuate a way of knowing and being that is detrimental to planet Earth and her inhabitants. This course has been purposefully designed as an alternative model for students, teachers, and the subject to come together in a meaningful way. In developing this course we have designed opportunities for:
>
> 1. thoughtfulness and deep reflection rather than rote memorization of information
>
> 2. action and engagement rather than passive receptivity
>
> 3. creative self-expression rather than one-size-fits-all assignments
>
> 4. individualized self-assessment rather than multiple guess tests with one right answer
>
> 5. collaborative construction of meaning through dialogue rather than lobbying for position with debate and discussion. (Link, 2002)

The instructors wanted the course to empower students. Their goal was to use the sixteen main principles of the Earth Charter—and all were examined in detail, mostly one each week by an expert in the topical area of the principle—to inspire students to see the integration in the ethical principles. In reflective course review, Link writes: "The power of the principles is in their wholeness." He also writes: ". . . there were clear differences among student values. . . . Environmental activists learned to consider and balance the social and economic factors, while the social justice activists began to look at environmental and economic elements with more openness" (Link, 2002, unpaginated second page). Link explicitly uses the Earth Charter to show the link between social and ecological peace. His success in doing so is an example of the possibility raised in the thesis of this chapter. He has stated:

> The merging of social and economic justice efforts with environmental integrity advocacy is a home for peace. Peace and justice advocates usually overlook the violence/injustice between man and the biosphere. Similarly, environmental activists have too frequently been oblivious to the violence/injustice between humans. The Earth Charter has provided a bridge connecting all forms of violence and their interdependencies. It is that uniqueness, that wholeness, that inspired us to offer the Earth Charter as a framework for discussing a sustainable future.

Community Education and Activism.[6] In Kenya, the Earth Charter is used in community development and forest conservation programs. The objective of the grass roots civic education program of the Green Belt Movement is to enhance knowledge, attitudes, and values that support sustainable socioeconomic and ecological welfare. (See www.geocities.com/gbm0001/all_Frames.html). These educational initiatives are directed toward care for people and to hold the government accountable. The founder and coordinator of the Green Belt Movement and Earth Charter Commissioner, Wangari Maathai, has written, "there are enormous thought provoking words in this document and what we should do is instead of just reading through, reflect on what these words mean so that we can be moved to action." The Earth Charter serves as a values framework for the Green Belt Movement which is now in twelve African countries. This educational use of the Earth Charter can also serve as an important case study at the community level in developing countries.

The work of the Ngadjuri Earth Charter group in the Barrossa Valley in Australia illustrates how a single Earth Charter principle can be the basis for education and action—and of how seamlessly peace and environmental education can be integrated. Principle 12 calls upon us to "uphold the right of all, without discrimination, to a natural and social environment supportive of human dignity, bodily health, and spiritual well-being, with special attention to the rights of indigenous peoples and minorities." The local group is a collaboration between rural women and the Wirrigu, a local Aboriginal group. A long-term commitment has been made through a gift of land to the Wirrigu people to create a Ngaijuri sanctuary as a resource for activities related to principle 12. For example, according to the *Earth Charter in Action 2000*:

During one of their Earth Charter meetings, the group hosted a special guest-speaker, a 45-year-old Aboriginal Wirrigu woman who shared her experiences as a "stolen generation" child. She spoke about being placed in white foster homes and being systematically abused, her slide into self-destruction, but also her climb out of it. She now works with Aboriginal people in "Healing Circles" to help them transcend the sense of loss and grief caused by the many cruelties carried out historically and through certain current attitudes. Deeply impacted by her account, the *Ngadjuri* Earth Charter group offered their support to her future work, including cooking at the Healing Circles and helping to maintain the one-hectare *Ngadjuri* sanctuary, which has been placed in her hands. (Earth Charter International Secretariat, 2001, p. 13)

The group also meets regularly to discuss other single principles of the Earth Charter—and how to incorporate them into daily life. The group then uses their work to educate the broader community.

Municipal Education. In Brazil, the Earth Charter movement is under the intellectual leadership of Earth Charter Commissioner and theologian Leonardo Boff. He has presented the Earth Charter on many occasions and greatly raised public awareness of it. There have been several conferences on the Earth Charter and adoptions at the local level. For example, the Earth Charter Initiative works with the City of Sao Paulo with its huge population of over a million students. The system has 183 *nucleos de acao educativa* (nuclei of educative action) made up of five or so schools. The work of these groups is for an interdisciplinary, pedagogical examination of values, principles, and actions generated by the Earth Charter at the local community level.

Also in Brazil, the Paulo Freire Institute, which has contributed significantly to interpreting the Earth Charter, uses its principles as the basis for conscientization. According to the Director of the Institute, Moacier Gadotti, (n.d.), the Earth Charter's value lies in the contribution it makes to an ethic that will strive against the social injustice and inequality that currently prevail in the world. Gadotti has written: "In our book, *Pedagogy of Earth,* we defend the need for an Earth Charter associated with a peace process, a culture of peace. And, since the Earth Charter is an ethical document, it requires education to become better known." The Paulo Freire Institute has created an international network of educators in 24 countries who are involved in the implementation of Earth Charter principles. The Institute has undertaken research on Earth Charter pedagogy.

The municipality of San José, Costa Rica, with the advice of the Earth Council, developed a document and plan entitled, "The Municipal Community Enroute to Sustainable Development." At the heart of the effort was the formulation of the city's own vision of the Earth Charter "in order to integrate ethical principles and values into everyday activities." (www. earthcharterusa.org). Participants included over 80% of the city's work force of police officers, administrators, sanitation and health workers, and infrastructure employees. Awareness and personal commitment was raised for middle management through training directed at community awareness. According to the website description:

> Over the six-month duration of the project, fifteen training sessions were held, attended by the majority of municipal personnel, to define desirable strategies towards the implementation of sustainable development. In addition to the presentation of the initiative, an exercise was completed to ascertain the opinions of the participants regarding the moral attitudes which should be shared by the personnel of the city government on sustainable development. A code of ethical behavior based upon twenty-one desirable virtues was adopted by seminar participants in mid-1999. In early 2000, the Mayor of San José convened a public meeting to present the results of their Earth Charter process, the Municipality of San José's version of the Earth Charter, and their commitments to its implementation. A panel of the Earth Charter with its principles has been inaugurated at the entrance to the Municipality main public building.

These are among thousands of examples which demonstrate the Earth Charter's power to evoke values and to provide a way forward toward a culture of social and ecological peace in an integrative manner. (Also see Appendix 8.1 for a list of teaching resources.) Earth Charter education can move learners toward the compassionate and sustainable future which is the aim of peace and environmental education.

CONCLUSION

> The Earth Charter promotes a culture of tolerance and nonviolence, and recognizes that environmental protection, human rights, equitable human development and peace are interdependent and indivisible. . . . It also recognizes that any efforts to achieve these goals are doomed to fail if there is no common ethical framework which is shared by governments, business, civil society, and all walks of life. . . . The Earth Charter offers a way forward by adopting this integrated approach. It links the various stakeholders who have an impact on our future.
>
> —Ruud Lubbers, p. 2–3

From the 1972 Stockholm United Nations Conference on the Human Environment and especially from UNESCO's conference at Tbilisi, Georgia in 1977, a definition was proposed for a new synthesis of ideas from social education, conservation education, and nature study that came to be known as environmental education. It was defined in the light of daunting environmental challenges and a widespread demand for public participation in resolving environmental problems and for participatory education. Definitions of environmental education from this seminal era hold up remarkably well a quarter century later, because they include the social and cultural environment and the need for taking action consistent with knowledge and values. Indeed, the values dimension of environmental education invites an ethical framework, such as the Earth Charter, as it invites the concept of sustainability.

Similarly, peace education has moved from the disarmament and nuclear education of the 1960s and 1970s to the comprehensive peace education of the 1980s with its concern for social responsibility—which by that time was increasingly defined to include ecological responsibility. Peace education's embrace of development education, with its explicit concern for the impact of Western-style unsustainable economic development on the developing world, has brought it even closer to education for sustainable development.

According to Aline M. Stomfay-Stitz (2001):

Peace education has often been described as multifaceted and multidisciplinary with a myriad of dimensions. In addition to the building blocks or underlying foundation of nonviolence, included also are peace and social justice, economic well-being (providing for basic needs), political participation, conflict resolution and ecology. . . . This definition has been enriched by the research of Riane Eisler and Betty Reardon, among others, whose curriculum models have concern for peace and ecology as interwoven threads for education. (p. 1)

As both peace education and environmental education undergo a reorienting toward sustainability, they look increasingly overlapping in content, philosophy, and in the problems with which they are concerned. The Earth Charter, with its explicit and integrated concerns for respect and care for the community of life, ecological integrity, social and economic justice, and democracy, nonviolence, and peace, sees these principles as interdependent and integrated in defining sustainability. Thereby, it offers exciting possibilities as both fields continue to reconceive their work toward an ethic of ecological sustainability. Such a reconception is important to deal with both education problems, such as curriculum formulation, as well as societal problems, such as globalization. This is a critical time to

strengthen the capacity of education to respond to the challenge of building a culture of social and ecological peace. The Earth Charter can serve as an inspiration
and guide to the connectedness, interdependence, and, even, indivisibility of the
kindred fields of peace education and environmental education so much in need
of integration.

NOTES

1. Unattributed, often used expression to describe the response to the
Earth Charter at the United Nations Conference on Environment and Development—the Earth Summit.

2. For a detailed and thoughtful account, see Steven C. Rockefeller, "History of the Earth Charter" in *Earth Ethics*, pp. 16–20 (Washington, DC. Center
for Respect of Life and Environment, winter, 2000). I believe it is the only written account of this history. My writing depends heavily on this description and
on conversations with Steven C. Rockefeller, Mirian Vilela, Kamla Chowdhry,
Brendan Mackey, and Rick Clugston.

3. The Earth Charter Initiative is located at the University for Peace and
will soon be more directly supported by it.

4. As a way of identifying and explaining the sources of the ethical values in
each principle, an "Earth Charter Commentary" is being written by Steven C.
Rockefeller, Chair of the drafting committee and Johannah Bernstein, an international lawyer, who was involved throughout the drafting process. The explanation
of each principle includes its definition and meaning, its origin and, in some cases,
why a specific language was chosen. The Commentary includes a section on law
which relates the specific principle to an array of international declarations, treaties,
United Nations commission reports, and occasionally, to existing national laws.
The section on civil society included in the Commentary explains how the principle relates to the many nongovernmental organizations' declarations and reports on
ethics and sustainability. The commentary is a scholarly and sophisticated work of
meticulous detail. S. C. Rockefeller and J. Bernstein (2002) have published the commentary for part I. The commentaries on parts II, III, and IV are being developed
and will be published on the Earth Charter website as they are completed.

5. The Earth Charter Commissioners are, by region:

Africa and the Middle East
Amadou Toumani Toure (Co-chair)
Princess Basma Bint Talal of Jordan

Wangari Maathai, Kenya
Mohamed Sahnoun, Algeria

Asia and the Pacific
Kamla Chowdhry (Co-chair), India
A. T. Ariyaratne, Sri Lanka
Wakako Hironaka, Japan
Pauline Tangiora, Aotearoa/New Zealand
Erna Witoelar, Indonesia

Europe
Mikhail Gorbachev (Co-chair), Russia
Pierre Calame, France
Ruud Lubbers, the Netherlands
Federico Mayor, Spain
Henriette Rasmussen, Greenland
Awraham Soeterndorp, the Netherlands

North America
Maurice F. Strong (Co-chair), Canada
John Hoyt, United States
Elizabeth May, Canada
Steven C. Rockefeller, United States
Severn Cullis Suzuki, Canada

Latin America and the Caribbean
Mercedes Sosa (Co-chair), Argentina
Leonardo Boff, Brazil
Yolanda Kakabadse, Ecuador
Shridath Ramphal, Guyana

6. For one of the best uses of the Earth Charter in community education and activism, see chapter 3 for a description of Abelardo Brenes-Castro's "Integral Model of Peace Education."

REFERENCES

Clugston, R. M., Calder, W., & Corcoran, P. B. (2002). Teaching sustainable development with the Earth Charter. In W. L. Filho (Ed.), *Teaching for sustainability in higher education* (pp. 547–564). Frankfort au Main: Peter Lang Publishers.

Earth Charter Commission. (2000). *The Earth Charter*. San José, Costa Rica. Retrieved from: http://www.earthcharter.org.

Earth Charter Education Advisory Committee. (in press). *Synthesis: An educational philosophy for the Earth Charter*. San José, Costa Rica: Earth Charter Secretariat.

Earth Charter International Secretariat. (2001). *The Earth Charter in action 2000*. San José, Costa Rica.

Earth Charter International Secretariat. (2000a). *Earth Charter briefing book*. San José, Costa Rica.

Earth Charter International Secretariat. (2000b). *The Earth Charter initiative handbook*. San José, Costa Rica.

Earth Charter USA. (n.d.). *Earth Charter: A brief history*. Earth Charter Facilitator Resource Kit.

Gadotti, M. (n.d.). Pedagogia de la tierra y cultura de la sustentabilidad. Retrieved 8/19/02 from Paolo Freire Institute website http//www.paolofreire.org

Hassan, P. (2002, Winter). The Earth Charter: The journey from The Hague 2000. In *Earth Ethics*, 24–25. Washington, DC: Center for Respect of Life and Environment.

Link, T. (2002). *Earth Charter: Pathway to a sustainable future?* Retrieved from Michigan State University web site: http://www.ecofoot.msu.edu/new/earthcharterflyer.htm.

Lubbers, R. (2001, December 6). Untitled address to the Nobel Peace Prize centennial symposium. Oslo, Norway.

Mackey, B. (2001, December). Update on the Earth Charter education program. *Earth Charter Bulletin*. San José, Costa Rica: Earth Charter International Secretariat.

Rockefeller, S. C. (2002, Winter). History of the Earth Charter. In *Earth ethics*, 16–20. Washington, DC: Center for Respect of Life and Environment.

Rockefeller, S. C., & Bernstein, J. (2002, March). *Earth Charter commentary: Part I, respect and care for the community of life*. Draft published privately, not for publication or citation.

Rockefeller, S. C. (1996). Principles of environmental conservation and sustainable development: Summary and survey. Private publication.

Stomfay-Stitz, A. M. (2001). *Peace education and ecological sustainability: A blueprint for the future*. Paper presented at the annual meeting of the American Educational Research Association, Seattle, Washington.

World Commission on Environment and Development. (WCED). (1987). *Our common future.* Oxford, England: Oxford University Press.

APPENDIX 8.1

Earth Charter Teaching Resources

There is a limited number of resources available for teaching the Earth Charter. The Earth Charter International Secretariat is working to capture more of the many fine ways in which it is taught in various cultures and countries. The list includes academic commentary and analysis, and practical resources including courses and methods.

Brenes, A. (2001). Earthly dimensions of peace. *The Journal of Peace Psychology.* Retrieved 1/12/03 from: http://www.earthcharter.org/resources/speeches/culture_for_peace.doc.

Calder, W. (2000, October). Higher education and the Earth Charter initiative. *The Declaration* (4) 1. Washington, DC: University Leaders for a Sustainable Future.

Casey, H. M., & Morgante, A. (Eds.). (1998). *Human rights, environmental law, and the Earth Charter.* Boston: Boston Research Center for the 21st Century. Casey and Morgante (see below) provide disciplinary perspectives developed during the Earth Charter drafting process.

Casey, H. M., & Morgante, A. (Eds.). (1997). *Women's views on the Earth Charter.* Boston: Boston Research Center for the 21st Century.

Davis, C. (n.d.). Earth Charter: Vermont initiatives. Retrieved 1/12/03 from the University of Vermont's Vermont Studies Program web site, http://www.uvm.edu/~crvt/spring01.htm. This visual artist offered an elective course in anticipation of a September, 2001 event "For love of Earth, a celebration of the Earth Charter," at Shelburne Farms, Vermont.

Del Signore, G. (n.d.). Riflessioni sulla Carta della Terra. Federazione nazionale pro natura Contact: press@cartadellaterra.it.

The Earth Charter Initiative website: http://www.earthcharter.org/education/. The website includes a downloadable document of "stimulus material"—one page each for creative arts, language, mathematics, science, and technology curricula.

Earth Charter International Secretariat. (2000, April). The Earth Charter resource booklet for educators of children. San José, Costa Rica: Earth Charter Secretariat.

Earth Charter USA Campaign website: http://www.earthcharterusa.org/ec_inaction.htm.

Ferrero, E., & Holland, J. *The Earth Charter: A study book of reflection for action.* Retrieved 1/12/03 from the St. Thomas University website: www.ECreflection4action.org. This interpretive downloadable book traces the historical development of the Earth Charter and provides an extensive commentary on its principles.

Gadotti, M. (n.d.). Ecopedagogy program. Retrieved 1/12/03 from the Paolo Freire Institute website http://www.paulofreire.org/eco.htm. Paolo Freire Instititute is active in teaching the Earth Charter in Brazil.

Hessel, D. T. (2002, June). Sustainability as a religious and ethical concern. In John C. Dernbach (Ed.), *Sustainable development in the United States ten years after the Earth Summit: An assessment and recommendations.* Washington, DC: Environmental Law Institute. This chapter makes frequent reference to the Earth Charter in a religious and ethical context.

Miller, P., & Westra, L. (Eds.). (2002). *Just ecological integrity: The ethics of maintaining planetary life.* Lanham, Maryland: Rowman and Littlefield Publishers. The book includes academic analysis of Earth Charter ethical principles.

Morgante, A., Ed. (1997). *Buddhist perspectives on the Earth Charter.* Boston: Boston Research Center for the 21st Century.

UNESCO. Teaching and learning for a sustainable future, a multimedia professional development program prepared for UNESCO by J. Fien and others. Retrieved 1/12/03 from http://www.unesco.org/education/tlsf/. This broad resource includes specific sections on teaching the Earth Charter specifically.

Zint, M. (n.d.). Education and sustainability, an unpublished working bibliography. Available from zintmich@umich.edu. This broad resource includes many citations overarching peace education and environmental education.

Contributors

ABELARDO BRENES-CASTRO is Professor of Psychology at the University of Costa Rica and Professor of Peace Education at the University for Peace. He received his Ph.D. in Psychology from the University of Birmingham (England) in 1977. He has been involved both in activist and academic work in the areas of peace, human rights, and sustainable development since 1983. He was director of the Central American Program for the Promotion of Human Rights and Peace Education in 1992, and the Central American Program for a Culture of Peace and Democracy, from 1994 to 2001. In 1998, he joined the drafting team of *The Earth Charter* and is currently a senior advisor for this initiative.

PETER BLAZE CORCORAN is Professor of Environmental Studies and Environmental Education at Florida Gulf Coast University. He is a Senior Fellow in Education for Sustainability at University Leaders for a Sustainable Future in Washington, D.C. Corcoran is a Senior Advisor to the Earth Charter International Secretariat and is a member of the Earth Charter Education Advisory Committee. He is a past president of the North American Association for Environmental Education and is active in environmental education internationally. Corcoran is a founder of the Higher Education Network for Sustainability and the Environment and of the Global Higher Education for Sustainability Partnership.

IAN HARRIS is chair of the Department of Educational Policy and Community Studies at the University of Wisconsin-Milwaukee. He earned his undergraduate degree in 1967 at St. John's College in Annapolis, Maryland, an M.S. in Education at Temple University in 1969 and in 1976, completed a Ph.D. in Foundations of Education at Temple University. Dr. Harris's research interests include community development, alternative schools, school desegregation, male gender-identity development, and peace education. He is author of *Peace Education* and

Messages Men Hear: Constructing Masculinities, and over fifty articles on topics that range from accountability in education to the roots of male violence.

FANNY HEYMANN studied andragogy in Amsterdam and psychology in Sweden. She recently retired as Associate Professor in Communication and Innovation Studies within the Department of Social Sciences of the Wageningen University in the Netherlands. Her special interests lie in the promotion of intercultural communication. Her Ph.D. research focused on the development of a new extension methodology based on the articulation of information needs, motivation, and problem awareness.

PATRICIA M. MISCHE is the Lloyd Professor of Peace Studies and World Law at Antioch College. She earned her Ph.D. in Education at Teachers College (Columbia University). She is the author of more than 100 articles and several books, most recently *Ecological Security and the United Nations System: Past, Present, Future* (1998), and coeditor of *Toward a Global Civilization? The Contribution of World Religions* (2001). Her recent areas of research include the contributions of religions to a culture of peace and relationships between ecology and peace.

ISABEL ORELLANA is professor and member of the Canada Research Chair in Environmental Education at the faculty of education of the University of Québec at Montréal (UQAM). She holds a Ph.D. in Environmental Education, a masters in Environmental Sciences from UQAM and a masters in Agronomical Engineering and Sciences from the Superior Institute *Vassil Kolarov* (Bulgaria). Her principal research interests are the learning community and the social processes of knowledge construction and of emancipatory socioenvironmental change in environmental education.

LUCIE SAUVÉ is professor at the faculty of education of the University of Québec at Montréal (UQAM) and chairholder of the Canada Research Chair in Environmental Education. She is member of the Institute of Environmental Sciences, Director of the UQAM postgraduate program in environmental education and codirector of the international research journal *Éducation Relative à l'Environnement*. She has collaborated both on national and international research projects on the professional development of environmental educators, community education, and environmental health education.

FRANS C. VERHAGEN is an environmental sociologist with a background in divinity. He earned a masters degree in International Affairs and a Ph.D. in Applied Sociology from Columbia University. He is presently Director of Sustainability

Education and Research with Earth and Peace Education Associates International (EPE) in New York City <www.globalepe.org>. He taught Earth Science in New York City public schools for seventeen years, during which time he developed the Earth Community School model of secondary education. He has founded and chaired several environmental organizations and since 1989 has been producer and host of a monthly program for public access TV, which deals with the fundamentals of environmentalism and sustainable living.

ARJEN E. J. WALS is an Associate Professor within the Education and Competence Studies Group of the Department of Social Sciences of the Wageningen University in the Netherlands. He specializes in the area of environmental education and participation. His Ph.D., obtained from the University of Michigan in Ann Arbor (U.S.A.) under the guidance of Bill Stapp, focused on young adolescents' perceptions of nature and environmental issues and their implications for environmental education. He is the (co)author of over 100 publications on issues related to environmental education and serves on the editorial board of four research journals: the *Canadian Journal of Environmental Education, Environmental Education Research, The Southern African Journal of Environmental Education Ethics and Action,* and *Tópicos en Educación Ambiental.* Email: arjen.wals@wur.nl.

ANITA L. WENDEN is currently Director of Peace Education and Research for Earth and Peace Education Associates International (New York City) and is Professor Emerita of York College, City University of New York (1982–2004). She earned a master's in Applied Linguistics and a doctorate in Adult Learning from Teachers College, Columbia University in 1972. Dr. Wenden's educational specializations, her research interests, and her published writings are on the relationship between social and ecological peace, learner autonomy and learner beliefs, language and peace, critical language education, and cultural literacy. She is the founder and review editor of the Peace Education Commission's *Journal of Peace Education* published by Taylor and Francis.

Index